D0383838

A FalconGuide to Mount St. Helens

Help Us Keep This Guide Up to Date

Every effort has been made by the author and editors to make this guide as accurate and useful as possible. However, many things can change after a guide is published—trails are rerouted, regulations change, techniques evolve, facilities come under new management, etc.

We would love to hear from you concerning your experiences with this guide and how you feel it could be improved and kept up to date. While we may not be able to respond to all comments and suggestions, we'll take them to heart and we'll also make certain to share them with the author. Please send your comments and suggestions to the following address:

The Globe Pequot Press
Reader Response/Editorial Department
P.O. Box 480
Guilford, CT 06437

Or you may e-mail us at:

editorial@GlobePequot.com

Thanks for your input, and happy trails!

Barstad, Fred.
A Falcon guide to Mount
St. Helens : a guide to
2005.
33305212713121
la   08/31/07

Exploring Series

A FalconGuide to Mount St. Helens

A Guide to Exploring the Great Outdoors

Fred Barstad

FALCON®

GUILFORD, CONNECTICUT
HELENA, MONTANA

AN IMPRINT OF THE GLOBE PEQUOT PRESS

ΛFALCONGUIDE®

Copyright © 2005 by The Globe Pequot Press

All rights reserved. No part of this book may be reproduced or transmitted in any form by any means, electronic or mechanical, including photocopying and recording, or by any information storage and retrieval system, except as may be expressly permitted by the 1976 Copyright Act or by the publisher. Requests for permission should be made in writing to The Globe Pequot Press, P.O. Box 480, Guilford, Connecticut 06437.

Falcon and FalconGuide are registered trademarks of The Globe Pequot Press.

All photographs by the author except where otherwise noted.
Maps by XNR Productions Inc. © The Globe Pequot Press

Library of Congress Cataloging-in-Publication Data is available.

ISBN 0-7627-2871-X

Manufactured in the United States of America
First Edition/First Printing

The Globe Pequot Press assumes no liability for accidents happening to, or injuries sustained by, readers who engage in the activities described in this book.

Contents

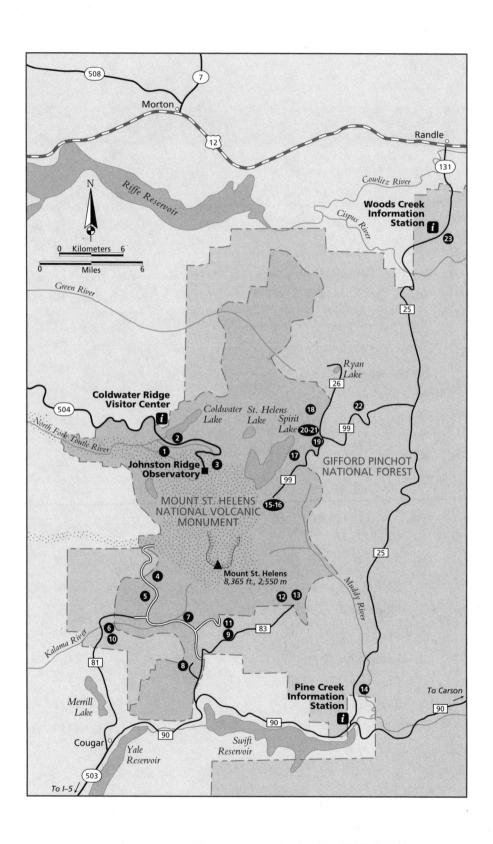

Acknowledgments

Thanks to all the people who helped me to prepare my earlier book *Hiking Mount St. Helens*. Information from that book and extra information obtained at the same time were of tremendous help when compiling data for this one.

I would also like to thank Bill Coffman, John Simac of Tacoma Mountain Rescue, and Jerry Walsh, Gifford Pinchot Park interpreter, for contributing valuable information; and Dave Kaufman, Karla Evans, and Donna Clarambeau for hiking with me on the trails and contributing their insight and impressions. Thanks also to Mike Barstad and Bob and Diana Leith for photographic help. Most of all thanks to my wife, Suzi Barstad, for hiking and camping with me and editing the raw text.

Introduction

In the spring of 1980, Mount St. Helens became the site of the most recent volcanic eruption in the forty-eight contiguous United States. This book was written to help familiarize you, the reader, with the volcano and its surrounding geographic, geologic, and historic features, as well as its flora and fauna. This information will enhance your tour whether you hike, ski, snowshoe, or ride. This book covers nearly all of the extensive trail system within Mount St. Helens National Volcanic Monument, as well as many points of interest along the roads to the trailheads. A few of the routes described are in areas that were largely unaffected by the 1980 eruption, allowing the visitor to see the flora and fauna that was here before the mountain blew. Other trails are close to the crater, in the heart of the area devastated by the lateral blast. The ancient and modern geological features are discussed to give the reader a background of the many events it took to form this spectacular topography.

In each trail description are explanations of the diverse flora, which is in many cases slowly but surely reclaiming its now altered domain. Mammals, birds, fish, and amphibians also survived in many locations and quickly started the process of recolonizing the rest. For some animals, notably the Roosevelt elk, the now more-open terrain has made living conditions much better, but other species are struggling to hold onto what was once theirs. Read on to find out what happened when the mountain blew its top and how the many diverse species are adapting and in many cases prospering in their now much changed environment.

Natural History

Not long ago Mount St. Helens' smooth sides, little scarred by erosion, made it one of the most beautiful mountains in the Cascades. Its modest glaciers had not dug deeply into its flanks as they had on other Cascade volcanoes. Pumice covered many of its slopes, and the timberline was much

Mount St. Helens from Spirit Lake before the eruption. PHOTO USDA FOREST SERVICE/JIM NEILAND

lower than on the peak's close neighbors. Layers of fine white soil were found close to the surface in many areas near the mountain. Early-day European settlers and Native Americans told stories of fire, smoke, and hot rocks being ejected from the heights. They also were in awe of Spirit Lake, where the rocks (pumice) floated and the wood (wet hemlock) sank.

The signs were all there. We should have known that Mount St. Helens was not the benevolent remains of a dead volcano that it appeared to be.

The low timberline was there because it takes trees several centuries to work their way back up a volcano's slopes after an eruption has removed them. The smooth pumice-covered slopes had not had time to become deeply eroded because it hadn't been many centuries since the volcano last erupted. The pumice rocks that floated in Spirit Lake confirmed the recent volcanic activity, and old-timers even spoke of seeing smoke and fire. Still, it was not until the middle of the twentieth century that scientists began to realize that Mount St. Helens was not an extinct volcano, but a very much alive mountain simply resting between eruptive cycles.

Even with this new information, most people thought that the mountain would retain its beautiful and benign character forever. Fun seekers flocked to the shores of Spirit Lake. Scouts rowed across the clear waters to their isolated campsites on the far side, and climbers ascended the ice-covered north slopes.

But the earth is an ever-changing place, with cycles of its own. Water evaporates into the atmosphere, condenses and forms clouds, falls back to the earth's surface as rain or snow, then flows to the ocean or into a basin, only to be evaporated again. Oxygen is breathed in by animals and combined with carbon to form carbon dioxide, which is exhaled back into the atmosphere. Plants absorb the carbon dioxide, separate it from the carbon, which they use, and release the oxygen back into the air.

Rock, too, goes through a cycle just as water and oxygen do. Volcanoes are a major part of this "cycle of rock." The big difference between the cycle of rock and those of water and oxygen is the time it takes—in rock's case millions or even billions of years.

A very simplified explanation of the cycle of rock goes like this. Igneous rock is expelled from the interior of the earth through volcanic action. Then water and wind erode it and carry it downhill, eventually reaching the seafloor. On the seafloor the sediment settles and compresses to become sedimentary rock. Further compressing and heating caused by the tremendous weight of the succeeding layers of sediment and the interior heat of the earth turn the material into metamorphic rock. This metamorphic rock is eventually melted by either being pushed deep enough into the earth or being moved on a tectonic plate into a subduction zone, where it is forced down and under another heavier plate. Once melted the rock, now igneous again, is eventually expelled back to the earth's surface through volcanic action, completing the cycle. Of course, this is a very simple explanation of a complicated process; parts of the cycle may happen several times before it is finally completed.

The concept of tectonic plates now accepted by most scientists holds that the earth's crust comprises about ten major and several minor plates.

These plates float and move on the earth's molten (or semimolten, because of the extreme pressure it's under) mantle. Generally speaking, there are two types of these plates: oceanic and continental.

In some cases these plates slide alongside each other, grinding along in a "steady by jerks" fashion. They catch on each other, then break loose and slip. When they catch, tremendous stresses build up; when they break loose and slip, this energy is released as an earthquake.

Sometimes the plates collide head-on. Two plates obviously can't occupy the same space, so something has to give. In some cases the plates buckle and form a mountain range, as is happening where the Indian subcontinent is currently colliding with Asia to form the Himalayas. In other cases one of the plates slides beneath the other in a process called subduction. The spot where one plate dives beneath the other is called a subduction zone.

The tremendous pressure of the subduction creates enough heat to melt the rock of the underlying plate and form a magma chamber. The magma in this chamber, being less dense than the overlying plate, seeks out a weak spot, forces its way to the surface, and becomes a volcano. This subduction process is currently going on in many places around the Pacific Rim. In fact, the circle of volcanoes around the Pacific Ocean—where two-thirds of the earth's active volcanoes are located—is often called the Pacific Ring of Fire.

The plates beneath the Pacific Ocean are called spreading plates: They spread out from a midocean ridge, a place where magma is extruded from cracks in the plate. The upwelling magma produces a ridge on the ocean floor and pushes plates apart, adding new ocean floor.

The relatively small Juan de Fuca Plate lies to the west of the Pacific Northwest Coast from southern British Columbia to northern California. This small spreading plate dives beneath the North American Plate, providing the necessary ingredients for Cascades volcanoes—including Mount St. Helens.

Mount St. Helens sits atop terrain composed mostly of faulted and folded ancient, igneous rock. Glaciers and streams eroded the landscape into nearly its present form long before the volcano itself began to form.

Some 40,000 years ago, the formation of Mount St. Helens began, with explosive eruptions similar to, but larger than, those of recent times. These

The bulge on the north side of the mountain. PHOTO USGS/PETER W. LIPMAN

eruptions of mainly dacite lava have continued intermittently until the present, with sometimes long periods of dormancy between events.

About 2,000 years ago, after a 300-year dormancy, the composition of the lava changed for a period. Now the volcano erupted basaltic lava alternately with dacite and andesite. The basalt, being of lower silica content, flowed more freely and is responsible for forming the lava tube caves on the southern slopes of the mountain. The upper parts of the mountain were formed during the last 2,000 years by continuing eruptions of mostly dacite and andesite.

The Big Event

Mount St. Helens has erupted several times in recorded history, notably in 1800 and from 1842 until 1857. After 1857 there was a 123-year period of dormancy, though the mountain still showed signs that it was not dead, but

The eruption May 18, 1980. PHOTO USGS/AUSTIN POST

only sleeping. Fumaroles released small amounts of gas from a low rock ridge, called the Boot, along a popular north-side climbing route. The Boot, which was swept away by the landslide that began the eruption on May 18, 1980, was almost directly above the present-day Lava Dome.

On March 20, 1980, the mountain began to awaken from its 123-year sleep, with an earthquake far beneath the surface. By the twenty-fourth of that month, many quakes were being recorded on seismographs. On March 27 a traffic reporter from a Portland, Oregon, radio station, flying above the low cloud deck close to the mountain, reported steam and ash spewing from a hole in the snow very close to the mountain's summit.

When the weather cleared enough to allow further overflights, it was discovered that a crater had opened on the top of the mountain and that cracks had developed east and west from the summit. The cracks were an indication that the north side of the mountain had started to slump. Washington's governor declared a 10-mile-wide Red Zone around the mountain in an attempt to keep sightseers and others out of danger. Roadblocks were set up and staffed; the Federal Aviation Administration also set up a restricted area around the peak. Even so, people circumvented the roadblocks, and many planes infringed on the restricted area.

On March 30 the enlarging crater produced more than ninety small ash and steam eruptions. By early April seismographs began to record harmonic tremors—small but nearly continuous earthquakes occurring beneath the mountain, indicating that magma was moving. The steam and ash eruptions continued intermittently. The north side of the mountain bulged, and by late April it was growing at a rate of 5 feet per day. Parts of the bulge were now more than 450 feet higher than they'd been a few weeks earlier. During the last week of April and the first week of May, the seismic activity decreased. Then, on May 8, an eruption threw ash and steam 13,000 feet into the air, and the harmonic tremors resumed. On May 12 an earthquake registering 5.0 on the Richter scale triggered a small landslide.

At a few seconds after 8:32 A.M. on May 18, a 5.1-magnitude earthquake shook the mountain. For a few seconds, the bulge quivered and rippled; then it broke loose, producing the largest landslide, called the Debris Avalanche, in recorded history. Less than thirty seconds after the slide began, a dark plume of ash appeared from near its point of origin. Within another thirty seconds the entire north slope of the mountain was engulfed in ash, obscuring it from view. Mount St. Helens was literally exploding. Instead of up, the blast was being directed toward the north.

As the Debris Avalanche slid from the side of the mountain, the tremendous pressure that had been building beneath was released. This release of pressure in turn caused a lateral blast to charge north at more than 500 miles per hour. Made up of hot gases, boulders, and ash, the blast traveled as far as 16 miles north of the mountain, flattening nearly all the vegetation in a 180-degree arc for about 12 miles from the crater. The eruption continued for nine hours.

Later in the day mudflows, often referred to by their Indonesian name *lahars*, rushed down many of the streams radiating from the peak. The largest and most destructive lahar followed the Toutle River Valley all the way to the Cowlitz and Columbia Rivers. The sediment choked the shipping channel in the Columbia, reducing its depth from nearly 40 feet to only 12 feet.

As a result of the North Fork Toutle River Lahar and other eruptive events on May 18, the Weyerhaeuser Company lost three logging camps, thirty log trucks, twenty-two crew buses, thirty-nine railcars, and 16 miles of railroad track along with 650 miles of roads and nineteen bridges. Besides the equipment and infrastructure losses, the company also lost 12 million board feet of timber.

Two new lakes and many ponds were formed when the Debris Avalanche dammed streams and made depressions between the hummocks that held water.

The 10-mile-wide Red Zone on the north side of the mountain was not nearly big enough. Fifty-seven people were killed in the eruption. In a few cases their bodies and even their cars were never found. Nearly all these people, most of them outside the Red Zone, died of asphyxiation from the ash and hot gases.

Close to the volcano was not the only area affected by the eruption. The skies were darkened over central Washington, to the point that the streetlights came on during the day in Yakima. The ash fell so thick that it closed Interstate 90, stranding motorists. When the ash fell on crops, they became unusable. The sharp ash particles stuck to fruit and were impossible to wash off. These same tiny particles were small enough to pass

A logging camp on the South Fork of the Toutle River after the eruption.
USGS/PHIL CARPENTER

through the air filters on cars and other equipment, causing the quick destruction of their engines.

There were four more smaller but still major eruptions, including ash clouds and pyroclastic flows, in the summer and fall of 1980. During one of these eruptions, the wind had temporarily shifted and was blowing from the northeast. This allowed the people of Portland, Oregon, and the northern Willamette Valley to experience the problems that their neighbors to the northeast were already all too familiar with.

Mount St. Helens erupted with decreasing frequency and intensity between 1980 and 1986. Since then its activity has been confined to small earthquakes and minor steam emissions from the Lava Dome in its crater. Lahars have originated from the mountain during this time. These mud-flows are not necessarily caused by volcanic heat, but rather by normal pre-cipitation saturating the loose volcanic soils.

Change and Recovery

It may seem to human eyes as if Mount St. Helens' eruptions destroyed everything in their path, but this is not really what happened or is happening. Nature doesn't waste anything; it only recycles. The time it takes nature to recycle may be beyond our comprehension, but it will happen. While the eruption destroyed much of the life close to it, it also covered the ground with nutrient-rich volcanic ash. The downed and buried logs are rotting and adding organic matter to the new soil.

Plants and animals quickly returned to the Blast Zone. Some of them, like the Roosevelt elk, have benefited from the loss of the dense forest. The open ground allows much more of their favorite foods to grow. The chances of seeing elk in spring—while they are still on their winter range—are excellent from Washington Route 504. The Lakes Trail and the Hummocks Trail have the best elk-viewing potential. By mid-June most of the elk have moved to higher ground.

Fish survived in many of the lakes that were still snow covered when the eruption came. They had a very difficult time living in the heavily silted water at first, but now they are doing very well in several lakes. The eruption and Debris Avalanche killed all the fish in Spirit Lake, but wild fish have now been found there again. It's thought that they may have come down from St. Helens Lake, a higher lake that was covered with snow at the time of the eruption. A stream connects the lakes, but there are waterfalls along its course. If they did come down the stream, it must have been an exciting ride! Many burrowing animals also survived the blast beneath the snow cover. The ones that survived quickly went to work repopulating the area.

Future Volcanic Events

Although Mount St. Helens is quiet now, that doesn't mean it has finished erupting—or even that the present eruptive cycle is over. It's still a very young volcano, and in all likelihood it will continue to erupt intermittently in the future. These eruptions could include relatively quiet lava flows, but considering the history of the volcano, they will probably be explosive, maybe more so than the 1980 eruption. Scientists are constantly monitoring the mountain; hopefully they will be able to predict an eruption far

Mount St. Helens from Spirit Lake after the eruption

enough in advance to prevent the loss of life that happened in 1980. The study of volcanoes is a young science, but more is being learned every day. Eventually the accurate prediction of volcanic events well in advance may be possible.

Cascades Climate

The ridgeline of the Cascade Range, rising a mile or more above the Pacific Ocean in most places, creates a barrier to moisture-laden storms coming from the west. Over the western slope of the range, the air is forced to rise and therefore cool. Cooler air can hold less moisture, so it precipitates out in the form of rain or snow; some parts of this area see up to 150 inches of rainfall per year. At times low clouds (sometimes called a marine deck) may fill the western canyons and valleys, while the higher ridges and peaks are basking in sunshine. Because of this wet climate, the western side of the

Cascades is covered with dense forest, except where logging or fires have disturbed it.

Over the higher peaks of the Cascades, clouds sometimes seem to get stuck and continue to drop precipitation even after the main storm has passed. Snowstorms and freezing temperatures can occur at any time of year. The higher peaks, notably Mount Adams, and to a lesser extent Mount St. Helens, at times make their own weather. Cloud caps can appear from an otherwise clear sky. In these caps heavy wind, fog, and rain or snow can combine to make hiking miserable, difficult, and dangerous, if not impossible.

As the air passes the crest and begins to drop, it warms by compression (sometimes called the Chinook effect). This warmer air is able to hold more water, so annual rainfall totals become much lower; in some cases the clouds just evaporate. Because of the drier climate, the forest gradually thins out.

The range is also a temperature barrier. On the western slopes the ocean moderates the climate. It's rarely very hot in summer; in winter the cold continental air from the interior only occasionally spills over the crest. East of the crest the winters are much colder and the summers, hotter.

Mount St. Helens is only 84 miles from the Pacific Ocean and in a direct line with the mouth of the Columbia River. These two factors influence the local climate around the mountain to some degree. The mountain is the first real barrier for ocean breezes coming up the Columbia River. When these winds are forced upward by the mountain's slope, cooled clouds often form. These clouds may also hang around longer than they do over Mount Adams only 30 miles farther inland to the east. Overall this causes the Mount St. Helens region to have a slightly wetter and milder climate than its close neighbor.

Large Animals

Black-tailed deer are the most commonly seen large animal in the southern Washington Cascades. In fact, some people see them too closely when they hit them with a car. Blacktails (*Odocoileus hemionus columbianus*), a slightly smaller and darker subspecies of mule deer (*O. h. hemionus*), inhabit the damp western slopes of the Cascades as well as the Coast Range. Typical of

Roosevelt elk

a forest-loving animal, the antlers of a blacktail are much smaller than those of a mule deer. The eponymous tail is wider than that of a mule deer and completely black on its upper side. When alarmed, a blacktail will generally run with its tail carried horizontally, but they occasionally flag (hold their tail straight up).

The wetter western slope is the home of the Roosevelt elk (*Cervus elaphus roosevelti*). Roosevelt bulls, which may weigh more than 1,000 pounds, are the largest animals to inhabit the Cascades. Roosevelts are common and may be expected almost anywhere on the west slopes of the mountains. Probably the best time and place to see these magnificent animals is along Washington Route 504 in May and early June, between Hoffstadt Visitor Center and Johnston Ridge Observatory.

Black bears (*Ursus americanus*) are found throughout the Cascade Range. These bears are generally shy and not often seen, but hikers and backpackers should be aware of the possibility of an encounter. For more information about hiking and camping in bear country, pick up a copy of the pocket-size *Bear Aware* by Bill Schneider, another FalconGuide.

Cougars (*Felis concolor*), also known as mountain lions, though seldom seen by hikers, are also found throughout the region.

Human History

People have lived in the lower valleys around Mount St. Helens for well over 6,000 years, and possibly as long as 12,000. Sites that were occupied about 5,000 years ago have been found in the upper Lewis River Valley south and southeast of the mountain. Aboriginal peoples from the lowlands made trips into the mountains to hunt, pick berries, and gather plant material for a variety of uses. As you will see in the hike descriptions that follow, many of these plants were used for medicinal purposes.

Explorers

The first recorded sighting of Mount St. Helens by European explorers was on May 19, 1792, when Captain George Vancouver (or more likely one of his men) spotted it from aboard ship while in the lower Columbia River. A few months later, after the peak's exact location was plotted, it was named for the British ambassador, Baron St. Helens.

The journals of the Lewis and Clark Expedition (1805–1806) tell of a very high, dome-shaped peak visible from the lower Columbia River, near its mouth. The expedition did not note any volcanic activity at that time, but there is good evidence of a major eruption in 1800. By the early 1820s Fort Vancouver was established as a post for the British-owned Hudson's Bay Company. From then on written records document the volcanic activity of Mount St. Helens.

In 1853 Washington's first governor, Isaac Stevens, appointed George McClellan to look for passes through the Cascade Range. In July of that year, the McClellan Expedition left Fort Vancouver and ascended the Lewis River Valley, close to the southern slopes of Mount St. Helens. The expedition, after considerable rough traveling, made it to the Trout Lake Valley.

Settlers, Loggers, Miners, and Recreationists

The town of Toutle, southwest of the peak, was established in 1876, when logging of the area began. In the 1890s prospectors began their exploration of the region, and in 1901 a wagon road was built to Spirit Lake. This allowed for youth camps, public campgrounds, and resorts to be built at the lake. In 1946 the road to Spirit Lake was paved.

Harry Truman

Probably the most widely known and celebrated resident of the Toutle River Valley was Harry Truman, born October 30, 1896, in West Virginia. He moved west with his family in 1907 to Chehalis, Washington. Harry enlisted at the beginning of World War I and was sent to Europe. On the way there his ship was torpedoed and sunk; he was rescued. Soon he became a master airplane mechanic and often made test flights of the aircraft he was working on. On one of these flights, his plane was attacked by a German fighter. His plane was hit but made it back in one piece. After the war it is said—probably truthfully, at least in part—that Harry made his living for a time bootlegging and rum-running.

Before long Harry opened a garage in Chehalis. Master mechanic that he was, this profession suited him well, but the mountain country around Spirit Lake intrigued him. In 1928 Harry bought a half interest in a lodge at Spirit Lake. Later that year he bought the other half interest in the lodge, where he would live until his death.

Many improvements were made on the lodge, and outbuildings were built. After he'd lived there for nearly fifty-two years, it's easy to understand why a now much older Harry Truman would not leave the place when evacuation was ordered in spring 1980. Harry was last seen on the evening of May 17, 1980, at his lodge. When the mountain blew the next morning, it took with it both Harry Truman and all he had worked more than half a century to build. It's probably just as well that Harry died that day; he would not have wanted to live anywhere else.

Climbing the Mountain

While Native Americans hunted and gathered plants and berries in the country around Mount St. Helens, it's unlikely that they made the climb to its summit. They could easily have done so, but they really didn't have a reason to. Their spiritual beliefs—and fears, in many cases—kept them from the terrain near the tops of volcanoes.

On August 27, 1853, Thomas Dryer, the founder of the *Oregonian* (a Portland, Oregon, newspaper), and four other climbers claim to have reached the summit. Although there is controversy about some of Dryer's other mountaineering claims, it seems likely that this party was indeed the first to reach the summit of Mount St. Helens. The route that is believed to have been used by the Dryer party was somewhat west of the popular Monitor Ridge Route. The second group of climbers to reach the summit was a party of five gold prospectors on September 28, 1860; it was fourteen years before another ascent was recorded. The first woman reached the top in 1883.

The first climb on the north side of Mount St. Helens took place in 1893, and before long that became the most popular route for climbing the mountain. This of course all changed in 1980 when Mount St. Helens reawakened from 123 years of dormancy. Presently most climbers try for the summit via the Monitor Ridge Route.

Safety and Hazards

Livestock and Bikes

Meeting stock traffic is fairly common on the southwest side of Mount St. Helens National Volcanic Monument, as well as along and north of the Green River Trail. It's a good idea to know how to pass livestock with the least possible disturbance or danger. If you meet parties with stock, try to get as far off the trail as possible. Equestrians prefer that you stand on the downhill side of the trail, but there is some question whether this is the safest place for a hiker. If possible, I like to get well off the trail on the uphill side. It's often a good idea to talk quietly to the horses and their riders; this seems to calm many horses. If you have the family dog with you, be sure to keep it restrained and quiet. Dogs cause many horse wrecks.

Bike riders may be encountered along many of the trails. It is the bicyclist's obligation to watch out for hikers and horses, but it is a good idea to watch for them, too. Bikes are fast and quiet, so pay close attention when you are on trails that are open to their use.

With a little common sense and consideration, all types of trail users can have a safe and pleasant experience.

Being Prepared

There are a few simple things you can do that will improve your chances of staying healthy while you are out in the monument.

One of the most important things to do is be careful about your drinking water supply. There are only a few places in the monument where you can get water from a tap. All surface water should be filtered, chemically treated, or boiled before drinking, washing utensils, or brushing your teeth with it. The water may look clean and pure, and it may be, but you can never be sure. In many cases there is no water along the trail, so you need to take along all that you will need. If you use a filter, be sure it has a fairly new cartridge or has been recently cleaned before you leave on your hike. The lightly silted water in many streams at Mount St. Helens clogs filters quickly.

Check the weather report before heading into the mountains. Stormy weather with wind, rain, and even snow is possible at any time of year. Cool weather with fog in the mornings is common through much of summer. Hypothermia is one of the most common problems in this damp climate. Be sure to have rain and wind gear along and dry clothes to put on when you stop.

The opposite is also the case at times. Warm sunny weather on the exposed slopes or on the pumice plain can cause quick dehydration. At these times light-colored, loose-fitting clothes and lots of sunscreen are what you need. Keep well fed and drink plenty of liquids.

If you are planning a long or difficult excursion, be sure to get into shape ahead of time. This will make your trip much more pleasant as well as safer. Because of the relatively low elevation of most of the trails in this area, altitude-related problems are generally minimal. The summit climbs described in Trails 9 and 11 may be an exception to this for a few people.

Volcanic hazards are always present on this active volcano. There is the chance of an unexpected eruption at any time. It is, however, very unlikely that the scientists monitoring the mountain will not be able to predict an eruption in advance. Almost any information about volcanic activity or potential volcanic activity at Mount St. Helens is broadcast over the local

TV stations. If there is any question about possible volcanic activity, check with the Forest Service at Monument Headquarters or one of the visitor centers before you begin your hike.

Read the complete description for the trail you have decided to take before you begin. This will help you avoid trails that may be difficult for any member of your party. Most important is to think about what you are doing while you are out. Use your head to stay out of dangerous situations and to get out of them if they happen. Your thoughts, knowledge, and physical conditioning are the most important things you can take along on your trip.

Zero Impact

Making campfires and cutting switchbacks have probably caused more negative impact to the environment than any other hiker activities. As traditional and nice as campfires are, their use should be limited. Small fires at low elevations may be okay if regulations permit, but building fires in alpine meadows or any alpine area is not a good practice. It takes years for the fragile alpine environment to recover from even a small campfire. Take along a backpack stove; it's easier to use anyway. If you must build a fire, be sure you extinguish it completely. Campfires are prohibited within the Blast Zone.

Cutting switchbacks is extremely hard on trails and hillsides. This practice causes much erosion and destroys plant life. It's always best to stay on the trail and not take shortcuts. It also usually takes less energy to follow the trail. Where the trail is braided, try to stay on the main route. Do not dismantle rock cairns; they may be the only thing marking the route in some areas.

Campsite selection is very important in maintaining a healthy environment. Make camp in the timber and avoid camping in meadows. Be careful not to trample vegetation. Camp well away from lakes and at least some distance from streams. Camping is prohibited in the Restricted Zone and permitted only at designated sites within the Mount Margaret Backcountry. Check Forest Service regulations about campsite selection. When leaving, pack out all your trash and any other trash you find. We all need to do our part to keep our wild areas beautiful and clean forever.

Mount St. Helens from near Windy Ridge Trailhead

Administration and Special Regulations

The USDA Forest Service—Gifford Pinchot National Forest administers Mount St. Helens National Volcanic Monument. This is different from most national monuments in the country, which are administered by U.S. Department of the Interior—National Park Service. The difference in administration makes for much different regulations than you'll find at most national parks and monuments. This area's regulations were implemented to protect the unique environment, facilitate scientific study, and allow for many user groups to be accommodated.

Mountain bike use is allowed on many trails within the monument. Horses (and other stock) are prohibited in much of the Blast Zone to prevent the introduction of nonindigenous plants, which would invalidate much of the scientific research. There are still many trails open to horses, however, and special accommodations are made for them in places. Off-trail travel and camping are prohibited within the Restricted Zone.

All in all these regulations seem to be working very well. As I hiked the trails to gather information for this book, I had no unpleasant encounters with other trail users. Everyone, and especially the backcountry rangers, was friendly, courteous, and helpful.

Passes and Permits

As of summer 2003, a Monument Pass is required to visit most sites along Washington Route 504, which leads to the Coldwater Ridge Visitor Center and Johnston Ridge Observatory. Elsewhere in the monument a Northwest Forest Pass is required at many sites. These pass requirements seem to change frequently. Contact Monument Headquarters or one of the visitor centers for current information about which pass may be needed for a particular site. The permit requirements stated near the beginning of each hike description are as of summer 2003; these can change at any time.

Backcountry permits are required for the Mount Margaret Backcountry. These permits may be obtained through Monument Headquarters. Contact the headquarters or one of the visitor centers for more information.

Climbing permits are required for each person climbing higher than 4,800 feet elevation on the south side of Mount St. Helens. (The rest of the mountain is within the Restricted Zone, so no off-trail travel is permitted.) There is a limit on the number of permits available between May 15 and October 15. Permits for dates between May 15 and October 15 can be reserved through Monument Headquarters. Call the climbing hotline at (360) 247–3961, then send your application to:

Climbing Coordinator
Mount St. Helens NVM
42218 NE Yale Bridge Road
Amboy, WA 98601

Do not send money with your application. If the requested date is available, you will receive a confirmation in the mail. If not, you will be sent a list of available dates. Climbers with permit reservations must purchase their permits before 5:30 P.M. the day before the climb at Jack's Restaurant (5 miles west of Cougar on Washington Route 503). The cost of the permits is $15 per person.

A number of unreserved permits are available at Jack's Restaurant. These permits are made available through a lottery. Sign up for the lottery at 5:30 P.M. the day before you want to climb; the permits will be awarded at 6:00 P.M.

The rest of the year, between October 15 and May 15, you can pick up your free permit at Jack's without getting a reservation or going through the lottery.

How to Use This Guide

I have personally hiked all the trails described in this book, many of them in both directions. The mileage was very difficult to gauge exactly. Mileage totals from Forest Service signs and maps were taken into account whenever possible. I also kept track of my times while hiking, and used these to calculate mileage. The final mileage figures were derived by combining these means, and in some cases by pacing off the distance.

Global Positioning System

GPS coordinates for the trailheads, most major trail junctions, and key points are given near the beginning of each trail description. If you are proficient in the use of a GPS receiver, these can be very helpful, but remember that the government used to scramble GPS signals, but says that practice has been discontinued. Who knows? Be aware that this may cause the readings to be a little off. Usually the reading you will get on your receiver will be within 30 yards of your actual location, but it could be much farther off.

Difficulty Ratings

The trails in this book are rated easy, moderate, or strenuous based on the roughness of the trail, the elevation change, and the difficulty of following the route; trail length and time involved were not taken into account. Some trails in the monument seem to have gotten less maintenance than is needed to keep them in good shape. Be aware of this when you are preparing for your outing, and be sure to allow enough time to safely negotiate sections of trail that may be in poor condition.

The trails that are rated easy generally have gentle grades and are easy to follow; there may, however, be short sections that are rocky or eroded. Anyone in reasonable condition can explore easy trails given enough time.

Trails rated moderate will climb or descend more steeply than easy trails. They may climb 500 or 600 feet per mile and have fairly long sections that are rough or eroded. Some route-finding skills may be required to follow these trails. If route finding is required for a particular trail, the description will note this. A person in good physical condition can negotiate these trails with no problem. However, people in poor condition and small children may find them grueling.

Trails rated strenuous are best left to expert backpackers and mountaineers. These trails may climb or descend 1,000 feet or more per mile and be very rough. Sections of these trails may be very vague or nonexistent; excellent route-finding skills are a requirement for safe travel.

Maps

If you want one map for this whole area, the USDA Forest Service Mount St. Helens National Volcanic Monument map, with the waterfall on the cover, is the one to get. This topo map (aka the Brown Map) covers the entire area. Most but not all of the trails are shown. The scale of 1:63,360 is a bit small, and the tiny printing can be difficult for some people to read, but this map is adequate for most trails in the monument.

Many of the monument's trails are fairly new, and some of the United States Geological Survey (USGS) quad maps have not yet been updated to show them. In each of this book's trail descriptions, the names of the quad maps that cover the area are included; whether they depict the trails or not is also noted.

Access

The descriptions in this book are arranged by the access routes that you will take to reach them. The west-side trails are reached from Washington Route 504. On the south side of the monument, the trailheads are accessed from forest roads off Washington Route 503 Spur. The east-side routes are reached from Forest Roads 25, 99, and 26. Each description includes its own driving directions.

The driving directions for each trail (see the Finding the Trailhead section) assume that you are coming from Portland or Seattle. The south-, east-, and north-side trails can also be reached from Interstate 84 at Hood River. If you are coming from the east on I–84, leave the freeway at Hood River. Cross the bridge over the Columbia River and turn west onto Washington Route 14. Follow WA 14 west for 15 miles, then turn north and drive 1 mile to Carson. Head north from Carson for 26.5 miles. Then turn left (northwest) onto Curly Creek Road and drive 5.1 miles to the junction with Forest Road 90. Turn left (west) onto FR 90 and follow it 4.2 miles to the junction with FR 25. This junction is 24.3 miles south of the junction of FR 25 and FR 99, or 18.6 miles east of Cougar. To reach the west-side trails, it is necessary to come in from Interstate 5.

The south- and east-side trails can also be reached from exit 110 off Interstate 90 at Ellensburg. From exit 110, take Interstate 82 south for 31 miles to exit 31 at Yakima. Then turn west onto U.S. Route 12 and follow it for 89 miles to Randle. Pick up the driving directions from Randle in the Finding the Trailhead section of many of the descriptions.

Route maps

These are your primary guides. They show the accessible roads and trails, points of interest, water, towns, landmarks, and geographical features. They also distinguish trails from roads, and paved roads from unpaved roads. Selected routes are highlighted, and directional arrows point the way.

Elevation profiles

This book uses elevation profiles to provide an idea of the length and elevation of hills you will encounter along each route. In each of the profiles, the vertical axes of the graphs show the distance climbed in feet. In contrast, the horizontal axes show the distance traveled in miles. It is important to understand that the vertical (feet) and horizontal (miles) scales can differ between trails. Read each profile carefully making sure you read both the height and distance shown. This will help you interpret what you see in each profile. Some elevation profiles may show gradual hills to be steep or steep hills to be gradual. Elevation profiles are not provided for trails with little or no elevation gain.

Map Legend

══⟨12⟩══	U.S. highway
──⟨7⟩──	State highway
──[81]──	Forest road
───────	Other paved road
═══════	Gravel road
▪▪▪▪▪▪▪	Featured trail
---------	Other trail
▶▪▪▪▪▪▪	Cave trail
‒ ‒ ‒ ‒	Snow trail
─ ─ ─ ─	Park boundary
⊔⊔⊔⊔⊔⊔⊔	Crater
⨝	Bridge
⛺	Campground
•—•	Gate
⸫	Lava or lahar
◨	Overlook/viewpoint
℗	Parking
)(	Pass/saddle
▲	Peak/elevation
■	Point of interest
▮	Ranger/guard station
⌕	Spring
START ⫯🥾	Trailhead
ℹ	Visitor information
∬	Waterfall

Western Region

Access via Washington Highway 504

The twisting ribbon of asphalt that was once Washington Route 504, up the Toutle River Valley from Interstate 5, was used for decades as the main access route to Spirit Lake and the slopes of Mount St. Helens. The 1980 eruption and subsequent Debris Avalanche, lahar, and flood wiped out much of this scenic old route. The route endures today, though its character and location are much changed.

As you approach the mountain on the new Spirit Lake Highway, you leave the valley floor. By the time you reach the Coldwater Ridge Visitor Center, 43 miles from I–5, you are high above the debris-filled Toutle River Valley and well into the Blast Zone of the May 18, 1980, eruption of Mount St. Helens.

After passing Coldwater Ridge the highway descends to the foot of Coldwater Lake and Lakes Trailhead. Shortly you reach the trailheads for Trail 1, Hummocks Loop, and Trail 2, Coldwater Loop. The highway then follows South Fork Coldwater Creek for a couple of miles before climbing to Johnston Ridge Observatory and the trailhead for Trail 3, Coldwater Peak.

Western Region

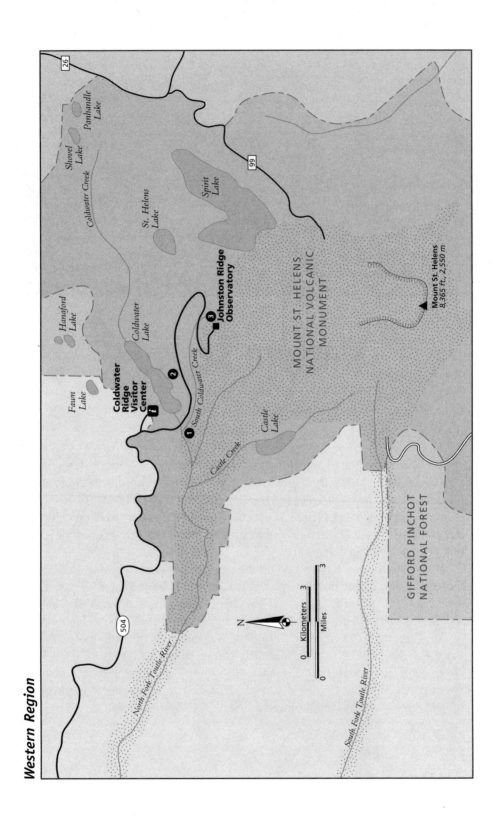

HIGHLIGHTS: This is a relatively short and easy hike through the remains of the 1980 Debris Avalanche. You should have plenty of time to stop at the points of interest before reaching the trailhead or (better) on the way back.

START: Hummocks Trailhead.

DISTANCE: 2.3-mile loop day hike.

DIFFICULTY: Easy to moderate.

SEASON: April through October.

TOTAL CLIMBING: 300 feet.

TRAILHEAD ELEVATION: 2,500 feet.

PERMITS: None at the Hummocks Trailhead. A Mount St. Helens National Volcanic Monument Visitor Pass is required at Coldwater Lake Recreation Area where Birth of a Lake Trailhead is located.

MAPS: Mount St. Helens National Volcanic Monument, aka Brown Map. Elk Rock USGS quad covers the area but does not show this trail.

SPECIAL CONSIDERATIONS: A few short sections of the trail are quite steep and have relatively poor footing, so good hiking shoes or boots are recommended.

PARKING AND TRAILHEAD FACILITIES: There is parking for several cars but no other facilities at the trailhead.

FINDING THE TRAILHEAD: Hummocks Trailhead is located 2.4 miles southeast of Coldwater Ridge Visitor Center on Washington Route 504. To reach it from Portland or Seattle, take exit 49 off Interstate 5 (49 miles north of the Columbia River Bridge or 120 miles south of Seattle) and drive east on WA 504.

There are several points of interest along the route to Hummocks Trailhead. The first is the Mount St. Helens National Volcanic Monument Visitor Center located 5.3 miles from I–5, on the south (left) side of WA 504. If you haven't already purchased your Monument Pass, you can buy it here. The pass is required at Coldwater Ridge Visitor Center, Johnston Ridge Observatory, and Coldwater Lake Recreation Area. The visitor center is operated by Washington State Parks and is open June 15 through September 1, 9:00 A.M. to 6:00 P.M., with shortened hours during the off-season.

Twenty-one miles from I–5, the Sediment Retention Structure Viewpoint and Trailhead are a short distance to the right (south) on a paved road. There is a sign marking the turnoff. At the end of the road are a parking area, souvenir

Hummocks Loop (Trail 229)

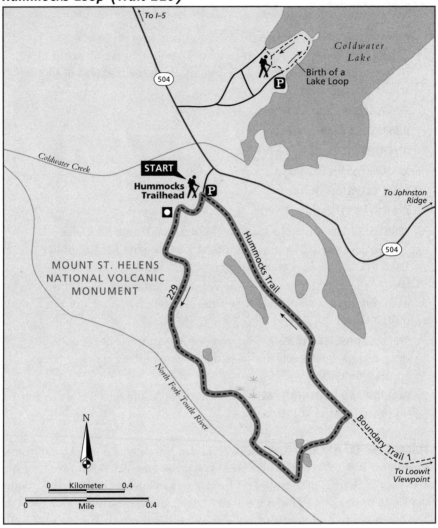

shop, and restrooms. From the south end of the parking area, a well-maintained gravel trail leads a short distance to a viewpoint where the Sediment Retention Structure is in full view. Watch for Roosevelt elk from the viewpoint. They are commonly seen across the river to the north. Before you reach the viewpoint, there will be a path to the right. This path leads to the southwest end of the structure; from there, you can walk out on the structure itself.

During the summer and fall of 1980, debris dams were hastily built on both the North and South Forks of the Toutle River several miles upstream from the

Hummocks

spot where the Sediment Retention Structure is located, at a cost of $21 million. The dam on the North Fork was 43 feet high and more than a mile long. On Christmas Day of that year, the first really heavy rains of the winter season spawned a mudflow, which quickly overwhelmed the North Fork Debris Dam and washed tremendous amounts of silt and debris on down the Toutle River. The smaller, 600-foot-long dam on the South Fork was maintained until September 1981 but then removed to allow for fish passage.

The Army Corps of Engineers decided that a much larger dam was needed to contain the sediment. The present site for the Sediment Retention Structure, 17 miles downstream from the crater, was picked, and the massive project, costing $60 million, was completed in November 1989. The structure is a mile long and 125 feet high and designed to contain mudflows as large as or possibly even larger than the devastating 1980 event. Even without major mudflow events, the sediment basin behind the structure is expected to be filled by 2035.

Twenty-six miles from I–5 is Hoffstadt Bluff Visitor Center, managed jointly by Cowlitz County and the Washington Department of Transportation.

Food service, a gift shop, and restrooms are available here, and helicopter flights over the mountain can sometimes also be arranged.

Thirty miles from the freeway is the Hoffstadt Creek Bridge and Viewpoint. The viewpoint is on the north (left) side of the highway at the west end of the bridge, at the edge of the Blast Zone. The Hoffstadt Creek Bridge is one of fourteen bridges built during the construction of the new WA 504 after the 1980 eruption and resulting lahar removed and buried much of the old Spirit Lake Highway. The bridge is 2,340 feet long and 370 feet above the creekbed at its highest point. Reader boards at the viewpoint explain many interesting facts about the destruction that occurred.

The Forest Learning Center, a joint venture of Weyerhaeuser Company, Washington State, and the Rocky Mountain Elk Foundation, is located 33 miles from I–5. Exhibits here cover forest ecosystems and forest management.

Coldwater Ridge Visitor Center, 43.5 miles from I–5, has many exhibits pertaining to the plants and animals that now thrive in the Blast Zone of Mount St. Helens. There is also a restaurant, bookstore, gift shop, and huge windows that offer a panoramic view of the mountain. This visitor center is open May 1 to late October from 10:00 A.M. to 6:00 P.M. The visitor center may be open at a reduced schedule during the off-season; check with Monument Headquarters if you are planning a trip between November and April.

Forty-five and a half miles from I–5, turn right onto the Hummocks Trailhead access road. There is a sign marking the trailhead. There are really two trailheads for this loop trail. They are about 50 yards apart, one at each end of the parking area.

KEY POINTS:

0.0 Hummocks Trailhead (GPS 46 17.176 N 122 16.306 W).

0.2 Viewpoint of Coldwater Creek Canyon. Continue straight (south).

0.7 Marsh. Continue straight (southeast).

1.6 Junction with Boundary Trail. Go left (northwest).

2.3 Hummocks Trailhead (GPS 46 17.176 N 122 16.306 W).

THE HIKE: The entire Hummocks Loop wanders through the jumbled, mounded, and chaotic (hummocky) landscape of the remains of the Debris Avalanche deposited by the May 18, 1980, eruption of Mount St. Helens. The huge landslide swept the upper 1,300 feet of the peak into the valley of the North Fork Toutle River. Some of the rocks and other volcanic debris you see along the route may have been at 9,000-feet-plus elevation near the summit of this once much higher, symmetrical mountain.

Roosevelt elk (*Cervus elaphus roosevelti*) are very common along this trail in spring; I saw more than a hundred of them when I hiked this trail in April. Coyotes (*Canis latrans*) can often be seen or at least heard, especially if you're on an early-morning hike.

To hike the loop in a counterclockwise direction, as described here, leave the Hummocks Trailhead parking area at its west end. At first the trail climbs a few feet; shortly it bears right to head northwest and begins to descend. A couple of hundred yards from the parking area, you make a switchback to the left in a thick grove of young red alders (*Alnus rubra*). Note the damage to the young trees caused by elk rubbing their antlers and chewing on them.

Ideally suited to this environment of recently disturbed mineral soil with little humus content, the red alder has been quick to colonize many places on Debris Avalanche deposits and along the Toutle River. Red alder is a fast-growing but short-lived (old at fifty, with a maximum age of about a hundred years) deciduous tree. It may reach heights of up to 100 feet but is usually somewhat shorter. The tree's smooth, gray bark often has patches of white lichen and/or moss clinging to it. The red alder's 2- to 4.5-inch long catkins appear in spring well before the leaves. The catkins have a red tinge, giving dense stands of these trees an overall rusty look from a distance at this time of year. The small brown cones, up to 1 inch long, hang on the branches in clusters through winter.

Red alder is easily distinguished from the mountain alder (*Alnus incana*), which is also common around Mount St. Helens, by its size and erect shape; the mountain alder is a many-branched shrub. The leaves of the red alder are blunt toothed whereas the mountain alder's leaves are sharply saw-toothed.

Like all alders, the red alder is a nitrogen-fixing species, which means it has the ability to extract nitrogen from the atmosphere and "fix" or deposit what it doesn't use in the soil. This is accomplished with the help of bacteria on the alder's root, which combines oxygen from the air with the nitrogen before depositing it in the soil. The leaves of alders also have a high nitrogen content. When they fall to the ground and decay, the nitrogen-rich compost adds even more nutrients to the soil. Nitrogen in the soil is essential for the growth of most plants, so the alders here are paving the way for future plant communities.

Native Americans considered the wood of the red alder to be the best fuel for smoking salmon. The easily worked wood was and still is used for making bowls and many other items, and the bark was used to make an orange or red dye. The wood of the red alder is often used for firewood; it splits very easily when green. When cut, the wood turns to a rusty red color.

A short distance farther along, look to your right for a view of the new canyon dug by Coldwater Creek through the Debris Avalanche deposit. There is a short path to the right here, but regulations require that hikers stay on the main trail. The route descends a short distance on a moss-covered slope, then flattens before descending slightly to a pond. The tread passes the pond 0.3 mile past the viewpoint and soon comes alongside a marsh filled with cattails (*Typha latifolia*), where there is a good chance of spotting waterfowl.

After passing the marsh you cross a stream and the North Fork Toutle River comes into view, 150 yards to the right. Dwarf mountain lupine (*Lupinus lyallii*), a tiny lupine with slightly hairy leaves, makes its appearance here on the drier slopes. The dwarf mountain lupine, like members of the pea family, is a nitrogen-fixing plant. This pioneer plant, even though it is very small, is adding nutrients to the mineral soil, making it suitable for the plants that will follow. The North Fork Toutle River has also cut deeply into the Debris Avalanche deposit in places. The trail is now heading southeast, so Mount St. Helens is in view ahead.

The trail follows the riverbed bank, well away from the river, for 0.2 mile. Along the banks of the river, several subspecies of lupines (*Lupinus* spp.) bloom in early June. The route then bears left (northeast) and climbs, passing a couple of ponds where you can often see Barrow's goldeneye (*Bucephala islandica*) as well as other types of ducks. Roosevelt elk are commonly seen near these ponds. A small wooden bridge, which may be flooded in spring, eases the stream crossing between the ponds. Both red and mountain alders, willows (*Salix* spp.), and other scrubs form a thick growth near the ponds. Common horsetails (*Equisetum arvense*) sprout in places next to the trail. The trail climbs gently after passing the ponds. It passes another pond and at 1.6 miles (0.3 mile from the bridge) comes to a junction with the Boundary Trail 1, at 2,520 feet elevation.

The Boundary Trail turns to the right (southeast) at the junction to climb 3 miles to Loowit Viewpoint and Trailhead, next to WA 504. It then continues another 0.6 mile to a trailhead close to the Johnston Ridge Observatory. This section of the Boundary Trail traverses the lower slopes of Johnston Ridge for most of its 1,680-foot climb. Along the way are views of both Coldwater and Castle Lakes, which were formed by the eruption and Debris Avalanche.

Part of the Boundary Trail is marked with posts, as it can be a little hard to follow on the pumice-covered ground. Pumice is usually light in color and, being full of tiny bubbles, is light enough to float on water. A solidified form of highly gas-charged lava, pumice, like obsidian, is high in silica content. Pumice could be defined as gas-charged obsidian.

To continue on the Hummocks Loop, turn left at the junction and head northwest. Both the Hummocks and Boundary Trails follow the same route from the junction back to the parking area 0.7 mile away. On the way back the tread passes a couple more ponds before reaching the parking area at its southeast corner.

Viewpoint of Coldwater Lake on Birth of a Lake Loop

OPTIONS: A short (only 0.5-mile-long) barrier-free interpretive loop along the shore of and out over Coldwater Lake, the Birth of a Lake Trail makes an interesting add-on to the Hummocks Loop. To reach Birth of a Lake Trailhead, drive 0.2 mile northwest on WA 504, then turn northeast and drive a short distance to the parking area and trailhead.

The paved trail leaves the parking area at its north end, next to a signboard with a map of the area. As you work your way along the lakeshore for the 250 yards to the junction with the boardwalk, you will see several interpretive signs. Along the trail grow Cardwell's penstemon (*Penstemon cardwellii*) and lupine.

As is explained on the signs, Coldwater Lake was formed when the Debris Avalanche blocked Coldwater Creek at the beginning of the May 18, 1980, eruption of Mount St. Helens. Coldwater Lake is 3.5 miles long and 0.5 mile wide and has a maximum depth of 200 feet. The basin that drains into it covers 19 square miles.

Turn right (north) at the junction, and follow the boardwalk out over the shallow waters of the lake to points of interest out there. When the lake was formed, the waters were a soupy mix of soil and fragments of the shattered forest. Oxygen-using bacteria—brought in by wind, by flowing water, and on the feet and feathers of waterfowl—consumed the organic matter in the water and quickly depleted the oxygen. This provided ideal conditions for bacteria that don't need oxygen to grow. These non-oxygen-using bacteria multiplied to the point that there were as many as fifty million of them in a drop of lake water and continued to consume the organic matter and chemicals in the lake. Winter rains and wind stirred the waters enough that it was somewhat reoxygenated, and the oxygen-using bacteria reappeared. This back-and-forth process continued, and in about three years the microorganisms had cleaned the lake enough that the water was nearly clear.

Life now abounds in the shallow waters around the lake's shoreline. Water boatmen (*Corixida* spp.) and water striders (Gerridae family), aka water skippers, move across the surface, buoyed by the water's surface tension. Great diving beetles of the Dytiscidae family swim and dive, while northwestern salamanders (*Ambystoma gracile*), Pacific tree frogs (*Hyla regilla*), and red-legged frogs (*Rana aurora*) make their homes among the shoreline vegetation.

Rainbow trout (*Salmo gairdneri*) have been planted in the lake and now provide opportunities for anglers. Barrow's goldeneye and several other species of waterfowl, including Canada geese (*Branta canadensis*), cruise across the surface and fly overhead. The chewed-off trunks of alders and willows attest to the fact that beavers (*Castor canadensis*) have moved in.

Back on the main trail, continue on, passing a viewpoint and the path to the boat launch area to the south end of the parking area where you started. You will climb over a small rise between the path to the boat launch and the parking area. This is a great hike for well-supervised children.

HIGHLIGHTS: This entire hike is within the Blast Zone of the May 18, 1980, eruption, and features elk and blacktails.

START: South Coldwater Trailhead.

DISTANCE: 10.8-mile loop day hike (9.7 miles with a car shuttle).

DIFFICULTY: Moderate.

SEASON: June through October. The section of this trail along Coldwater Lake is usually snow-free by April.

TOTAL CLIMBING: 1,380 feet.

TRAILHEAD ELEVATION: 2,520 feet.

PERMITS: None at South Coldwater Trailhead. A Mount St. Helens National Volcanic Monument Visitors Pass is required at the Coldwater Lake Recreation Area (Lakes Trailhead).

MAPS: Mount St. Helens National Volcanic Monument, aka Brown Map. Elk Rock and Spirit Lake West USGS quads cover the area but don't show these trails.

SPECIAL CONSIDERATIONS: The entire length of the South Coldwater Trail 230A is within the Restricted Zone. This means that hikers are required to stay on the trail, even though cross-country hiking would be easy in this fairly open area. As you descend along the Coldwater Trail 230, the Restricted Zone is to the left (the trail is the boundary). Along the Lakes Trail 211, the Restricted Zone is again on both sides of the trail. The only places where you can legally leave the trail to get access to Coldwater Lake are marked.

The grade of the trail is moderate all the way around the loop. However, the 1.9-mile section of the loop on the Coldwater Trail 230—this descends from the junction with the South Coldwater Trail to the junction with the Lakes Trail—may be obscured by dense brush

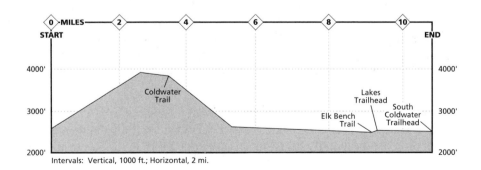

Intervals: Vertical, 1000 ft.; Horizontal, 2 mi.

Coldwater Loop (Trails 230A, 230, 211)

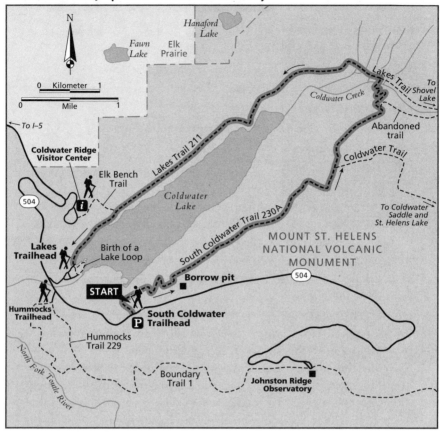

and hard to follow. Be sure your route-finding skills are up to finding a faint trail before you try this loop. Contact any visitor center or Monument Headquarters for current trail conditions.

The South Coldwater Trail is open to hikers and mountain bikers; no stock or dogs are allowed. The Lakes Trail along Coldwater Lake is open to hikers only.

PARKING AND TRAILHEAD FACILITIES: There is parking for several cars but no other facilities at the South Coldwater Trailhead. The Lakes Trailhead has restrooms and picnic tables.

FINDING THE TRAILHEAD: To reach South Coldwater Trailhead from Portland or Seattle, take exit 49 off Interstate 5 (49 miles north of the Columbia River Bridge or 120 miles south of Seattle). Drive east on Washington Route 504 for

46 miles to the trailhead, which is on the left side of the highway. The trailhead is 3.3 miles east of Coldwater Ridge Visitors Center. If you have two cars available, you may want to park one at the Lakes Trailhead and avoid the 1.1-mile hike along the access road and WA 504.

KEY POINTS:

0.0 South Coldwater Trailhead (GPS 46 17.144 N 122 15.239 W).

3.4 Junction with Coldwater Trail. Bear left (north-northeast).

5.3 Junction with Lakes Trail. Turn left (west).

9.0 Junction with Elk Bench Trail. Continue straight (southwest).

9.7 Lakes Trailhead (GPS 46 17.481 N 122 16.018 W). Hike southwest on access road, then turn left (southeast) onto WA 504.

10.8 South Coldwater Trailhead (GPS 46 17.144 N 122 15.239 W).

THE HIKE: This hike leads you up a ridge from South Coldwater Trailhead on the South Coldwater Trail, passing demolished logging equipment. You'll then descend into Coldwater Canyon on the Coldwater Trail. Once you reach the canyon bottom, you'll hike along Coldwater Lake on the Lakes Trail to Lakes Trailhead. Early in the season (April and May) elk are very common along the Coldwater Lake section of this route, which can be accessed at that time from Lakes Trailhead, but the higher elevations of the loop will probably still be snow covered. Black-tailed deer (*Odocoileus hemionus columbianus*) are common along the lake in all seasons.

The South Coldwater Trail 230A leaves from the southwest corner of the parking area. At first you climb gently through scattered willows (*Salix* spp.), black cottonwood (*Populus trichocarpa*), red alder (*Alnus rubra*), and mountain alder (*Alnus incana*).

The stumps between the trees, the shrubs, and the lack of downed logs all reveal that this area was logged before the 1980 eruption. Notice that many of the stumps were chewed and rounded off at the top by the blast and "stone wind." Shortly, as you round a poorly defined ridge, the Coldwater Ridge Visitors Center comes into view to the northwest, high above Coldwater Lake.

If you hike this section of trail in late spring, you will probably see Roosevelt elk. Two subspecies of elk (aka wapiti), the Rocky Mountain and the Roosevelt, roam the Cascade Range. The Mount St. Helens area on the wetter western slopes of the mountains is the home of the slightly larger and darker Roosevelt elk (*Cervus elaphus roosevelti*). Roosevelt bulls, which may weigh more than half a ton, are the largest animals to inhabit the Cascades. Roosevelts are common and may be expected almost anywhere on the west slopes of the mountains. The lower, semi-open slopes and valley bottoms of the

Smashed logging equipment

Blast Zone are a winter range for the large animals. By June most of them have left for the higher country to the northeast.

The route, which is marked with posts, crosses an abandoned roadbed 0.5 mile from the trailhead. This roadbed, like all the abandoned roads on this hill, is badly drifted in with pumice from the 1980 eruption. The path makes a switchback to the right, then crosses the rounded ridgeline. On the ridgeline you make a wide switchback to the left as you cross another roadbed. Wood groundsel (*Senecio sylvaticus*) is a common flower along this section of the route. The weedy annual with many yellow flowers grows to 2 feet tall or slightly higher.

As you climb along the ridge, you will pass much evidence of pre-eruption logging in the form of roads and skid trails. An abandoned borrow pit is passed 1.3 miles from the trailhead. This pit, at 3,150 feet elevation, was dug to furnish rock for the construction of the logging roads; it's shown on the quad map. A logging operation was in progress in this area at the time of the eruption. You'll pass the remains of a portable spar pole 0.8 mile after the borrow pit. This broken and twisted equipment shows the tremendous force of the 1980 eruption. It is easy to pick out the sections that were not yet logged at the time of the blast by the thousands of logs that now lie on the ground. A short distance past the portable spar pole is a half-buried Caterpillar tractor. These were far from the only losses of logging equipment suffered in the eruption and subsequent mudflow and flood. In all Weyerhaeuser lost three logging camps, twenty-two crew buses, thirty log trucks, and thirty-nine railcars along with 650 miles of roads, nineteen bridges, and 16 miles of railroad track. Besides the equipment and infrastructure, the company also lost 12 million board feet of timber.

The route generally follows another abandoned roadbed for the next mile as you traverse along the left side of the ridgeline to the junction with the Coldwater Trail 230. This junction, at 3,830 feet elevation and 3.4 miles from South Coldwater Trailhead, is the end of the South Coldwater Trail. You'll find a campsite 0.3 mile up the Coldwater Trail. Camping at this site or any of the others in the Mount Margaret Backcountry requires a backcountry permit, which may be obtained at Monument Headquarters or the Coldwater Ridge Visitor Center. From the campsite the Coldwater Trail continues another 1.8 miles southeast to St. Helens Saddle and the junction with the Boundary Trail.

To continue on the Coldwater Loop, bear left (almost straight ahead) and follow the Coldwater Trail heading north-northeast. The next 1.9 miles of trail descends a north-facing slope that is covered with brush. If not recently maintained, the trail may be brushed in here and sometimes difficult to follow. Take your time heading down and try to stay on the trail. You will first descend along the slope of Coldwater Canyon, then make several switchbacks as you drop down to Coldwater Creek. Partway down the switchbacks, a path turns off to your right. This is a now abandoned section of the Coldwater Trail. Bear left, staying on the main trail, and descend to the bridge over Coldwater Creek. A short distance after crossing the bridge, you will come to the junction with the Lakes Trail 211. You are now 5.3 miles from South Coldwater Trailhead and back down to 2,600 feet elevation. If you were to turn right at this junction, you'd have a strenuous 12.4-mile hike to Norway Pass Trailhead. Turn left and head west on the Lakes Trail to continue this loop.

Common ravens (*Corvus corax*) frequently cruise over the lake and the surrounding hills. These large black birds boast a length of about 2 feet and a wingspan of up to 4.5 feet. They are often mistaken for crows, but ravens are much larger.

In 0.6 mile the route reaches the head of Coldwater Lake. The lake was formed when the Debris Avalanche from the 1980 eruption blocked the mouth of Coldwater Creek Canyon. Coldwater Lake is within the Restricted Zone, so you must stay on the trail. There is, however, an access point (marked with a sign) to the lake at its head. If you want to approach the lakeshore, it's okay to do so at the access point.

The trail parallels the lakeshore as it heads southwest. As you pass through the red alder thickets, look for trees that are scarred by elk, which like to rub their antlers and chew on the bark. When I hiked this section of trail in April, I had elk in sight all the way from the head of the lake to Lakes Trailhead. After hiking 1.9 miles along the lake, you will cross a stream with a waterfall that drops in stages from the ridge above. As is often true in the Blast Zone, this stream may be dry by midsummer.

Most of the drier spots along the slope above the northwest shore of Coldwater Lake have good populations of dull Oregon grape plants. The dull Oregon grape (*Mahonia nervosa*) is a short evergreen shrub with hollylike leaves. It produces blue berries in clusters that resemble small grapes. Aboriginal people ate the tart berries in small quantities, and a yellow dye was made from the bark.

Salal is another common plant here. The berries of the salal were often mixed with those of the dull Oregon grape to sweeten it. Salal (*Gaultheria shallon*) is one of the most common understory shrubs in the Mount St. Helens area; it often nearly covers the forest floor on drier sites. Salal is an evergreen broadleaf shrub that can grow up to 15 feet tall, but it usually is less than shoulder height. Its 2- to 4-inch-long leaves are leathery and oval shaped. The small pinkish white flowers are urn shaped, much like those of the huckleberry, while the fruits range from reddish blue to dark purple. Salal berries were an important food for Native Americans. They were eaten raw or dried for storage.

Another 0.8 mile brings you to another lake access point, also marked with signs; there is a restroom to the right of the trail. Fireweed (*Epilobium angustifolium*) has colonized many sites in this volcanically disturbed area. The Blast and Singe Zones caused by the 1980 eruption have provided excellent habitat for this member of the primrose family. Fireweed can attain a height of 9 feet under perfect conditions, but is usually 3 to 5 feet tall. The deep pink flowers grow from the upper part of the stem, forming a spire-shaped cluster.

The junction with the Elk Bench Trail 211D is reached 0.3 mile past the access point and 9 miles from South Coldwater Trailhead. The Elk Bench Trail turns to the right and climbs west, gaining 530 feet of elevation in 0.7 mile, to the Coldwater Ridge Visitors Center. To continue this hike stay on the Lakes Trail.

In many places along the lakeshore and scattered on the slope above, black cottonwood trees have quickly outpaced the surrounding vegetation. The black cottonwood is a fast-growing tree that can reach a height of 150 feet or more; it generally lives at low to medium elevations, on moist sites. Its large leaves, 3 to 5 inches long, are a dark, shiny green on top and silvery beneath. The leaves, which are broad and sharp pointed, have conspicuous veins and fine teeth on their margins, and are suspended on a slender, round stem. The bark of the black cottonwood is ashy gray and on older trees becomes deeply furrowed.

Hairy catkins appear early in spring on the twigs, well before the leaves have emerged. Small, round, green capsules form on the catkins. Inside each capsule are the tiny cottony seeds that give the tree its name. The terminal buds of the cottonwood are very sticky with sweet-smelling resin.

Very popular with Native Americans, the sweet inner bark and cambium tissues were eaten in spring and early summer. These parts had to be eaten quickly after harvest because if left too long, they would ferment. The resinous buds had many medical uses, from curing baldness and sore throats to treating rheumatism. Gum from the resin was used as glue to hold feathers to arrow shafts. The fibers of the inner bark were used to reinforce other plant fibers in cloth making. Cottonwood trunks were sometimes used to make dugout canoes, and the wood was used as fuel for smoking fish.

The wood of the black cottonwood is straight grained, light, and moderately strong, but not very durable. It works easily and takes a good finish. Present uses of the wood are lumber, plywood, veneer, and box making. Bees collect the resin and use it in their hives to cover and seal off invaders that have been killed there, such as mice. This sealing prevents decay and protects the hive from the organisms that would inhabit the decaying body and cause danger of infection to the rest of the hive.

Young conifers, mostly Douglas fir (*Pseudotsuga menziesii*), are also scattered across the slopes above the trail. If Mount St. Helens remains quiet and there isn't a forest fire, these conifers will eventually grow tall and thick, shading out the cottonwoods and shrubs, and regrowing the forest as it was before the 1980 eruption.

In early May, before most of the plants and shrubs along the lake have put out their leaves, one shrub stands out on the slopes: the red-flowering currant (*Ribes sanguineum*). This shrub stands 3 to 8 feet tall and is covered with small, rose-colored flowers. The black berries of the currant were occasionally eaten by the members of several tribes of Native Americans, but were not highly regarded as food.

Still on the Lakes Trail, continue southwest for another 0.7 mile to Lakes Trailhead at the foot of Coldwater Lake. Vine maple is a common shrub along this part of the trail. The vine maple (*Acer circinatum*) is a small tree or large deciduous shrub. It usually grows up to about 20 feet tall, but on occasion may reach 40. The foliage is often thinly dispersed, giving the shrub a scraggly appearance. Vine maple's leaves have seven to nine pointed lobes and are 2 to 5 inches across. As with other maples (*Acer* spp.), its winged seeds normally grow in pairs. Vine maple grows as an understory shrub in much of the Cascades' low- to midelevation forest, provided the canopy is thin enough to allow in at least some direct sunlight. It also quickly colonizes areas that have been

Ocean-spray

logged or disturbed—as in this case by the volcanic eruption—allowing plenty of sunlight to reach ground level. An interesting characteristic of vine maple is the color that its leaves turn in autumn. If they have grown in good sunlight, they turn a bright red, but in a mostly shaded spot they will be golden yellow. The wood of the vine maple is hard and dense. It is quite flexible when first cut and was once bent and used in the construction of snowshoe frames. Some aboriginal peoples used the young shoots for weaving baskets and constructing fish traps.

In the damper draws ocean-spray (*Holodiscus discolor*) makes its appearance. The small, creamy white flowers of the ocean-spray form dense pyramid-shaped clusters at the ends of the woody stems. This shrub can grow more than 12 feet tall under the right conditions—and the right conditions prevail in some places along this route. Native Americans used the wood for making spears and arrow shafts, as wells as barbecue sticks and halibut hooks. Before the advent of nails, pegs made of ocean-spray wood were used as construction fasteners.

Steeplebush (*Spiraea douglasii*), a close relative of subalpine spirea (*S. densiflora*), is found in a few spots along the lakeshore. This deciduous, many-branched shrub grows up to 6 feet tall. At the top of the bush, tiny, pink- to deep-rose-colored flowers form slender spire-shaped clusters in July.

As you approach the trailhead, foxglove and oxeye daises become common along the trail. The oxeye daisy (*Chrysanthemum leucanthemum*) is a prolific perennial that was introduced from Europe and has become very well established in the northwestern United States. When you are hiking, you will generally only find it close to roads and along well-used trails. It often outcompetes native plants, especially on disturbed sites. The tiny seeds are easily transported by vehicles and lug-soled boots; try not to take them with you as you hike. The white flowers with yellow centers bloom at the top of slender stems up to 2 feet tall. While this flower may look good in some settings, it should not be transplanted into areas where it isn't present. Foxglove (*Digitalis purpurea*) is another imported plant; while very pretty when in bloom, it is poisonous.

As you can see from the wide variety of plants along the route, nature is quickly revegetating the landscape devastated by the volcano. In the absence of future volcanic eruptions, this process will continue so that in 400 or 500 years the place will look much like it did before May 1980.

From Lakes Trailhead hike southwest along the access road to WA 504, then turn left onto the highway and hike 1 mile to South Coldwater Trailhead, passing Hummocks Trailhead along the way.

OPTIONS: A much shorter and easier option to the Coldwater Loop is to descend the 0.7-mile-long Elk Bench Trail 211D from the Coldwater Ridge Visitor Center to a junction with the Lakes Trail along the shoreline of Coldwater Lake. Then hike the last 0.7 mile of the Coldwater Loop to Lakes Trailhead.

The nearby Birth of a Lake Trail can easily be hiked as part of the return trip from Lakes Trailhead to South Coldwater Trailhead. The nearby Hummocks Trail is a fairly easy hike through the deposits left by the May 18, 1980, Debris Avalanche that could be completed if you still have enough ambition after hiking the Coldwater Loop or descending along the Elk Bench Trail.

HIGHLIGHTS: This hike takes you northeast from Johnston Ridge, passing above St. Helens Lake. You'll then climb the open flower-covered slopes to the summit of Coldwater Peak, where a fire lookout once stood.

START: Johnston Ridge Observatory and Trailhead.

DISTANCE: 13.6-mile out-and-back day hike.

DIFFICULTY: Moderate to strenuous.

SEASON: July through September.

TOTAL CLIMBING: Approximately 2,100 feet.

TRAILHEAD ELEVATION: 4,200 feet.

PERMITS: Mount St. Helens National Volcanic Monument Visitors Pass.

MAPS: Mount St. Helens National Volcanic Monument, aka Brown Map. Spirit Lake West USGS quad covers the area but doesn't show the trail.

SPECIAL CONSIDERATIONS: This route is open only to hikers. The open ridgetop that the route follows nearly all the way is at times susceptible to inclement weather; check the forecast and take along rain and wind gear. Being in the open, as well as the light coloring and reflective qualities of this area's pumice soil, makes it likely that hikers along this route will get sunburned if they are not protected. Be sure to take along your sunscreen.

PARKING AND TRAILHEAD FACILITIES: There are restrooms, water, and more-than-adequate parking close to the trailhead. Be sure to allow enough time to visit the observatory, look at all the exhibits, and watch the eruption movie.

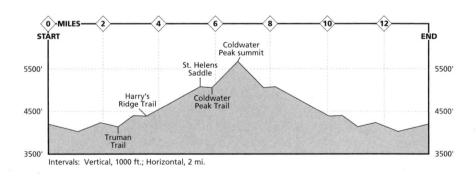

Coldwater Peak (Trails 1, 1G)

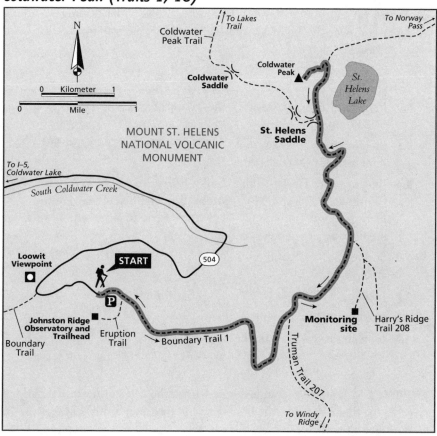

FINDING THE TRAILHEAD: To reach the starting point of this hike at Johnston Ridge Observatory, take Interstate 5 to exit 49 (49 miles north of the Columbia River Bridge or 120 miles south of Seattle). Then drive east on Washington Route 504 for 52 miles to the highway's end at the observatory.

Where the road crosses South Coldwater Creek a couple of miles before the Johnston Ridge Observatory, you cross the outlet of the tunnel that maintains the level of Spirit Lake. The difficult-to-see outlet is very close to and below the highway to your right. Notice the small amount of water flowing in the creek to your left and the much larger flow below the road to the right. It was feared that the rubble of the Debris Avalanche, which dammed the outlet to Spirit Lake, would fail, causing another catastrophic mudflow, much larger than the one that rushed down the Toutle River shortly after the 1980 eruption. In 1982 a pumping system was set up to maintain the lake at a safe level.

The pumps worked twenty-four hours a day for three years. In July 1984 work was begun on the tunnel through Coldwater Ridge. The drilling was done from the end near the highway, and by May 1985 the waters of Spirit Lake began to rush through it.

KEY POINTS:

0.0 Johnston Ridge Observatory and Trailhead (GPS 46 16.505 N 122 13.040 W).

2.5 Junction with Truman Trail (GPS 46 16.458 N 122 11.014 W). Continue straight (northeast).

3.6 Junction with Harry's Ridge Trail (GPS 46 16.900 N 122 10.370 W). Continue straight (north). **Option:** Turn right (southeast) onto Harry's Ridge Trail for a 0.8-mile round-trip to either an old volcanic monitoring site or a viewpoint.

5.5 St. Helens Saddle (GPS 46 17.752 N 122 10.755 W). Continue straight (north).

5.8 Junction with Coldwater Peak Trail. Turn left (west).

6.8 Coldwater Peak Summit (GPS 46 17.990 N 122 10.915 W).

13.6 Johnston Ridge Observatory and Trailhead (GPS 46 16.505 N 122 13.040 W).

THE HIKE: The Boundary Trail heads east from the east corner of the parking area; for the first 250 yards, the Boundary and Eruption Trails follow the same paved route. (See the options below for a description of the Eruption Loop.) Young noble fir (*Abies procera*) trees dot the slope along the trail as you traverse this north-facing slope, and in locations where there is enough moisture, mountain alder (*Alnus incana*) forms dense brushy areas. Mountain alder is easily distinguished from the red alder (*Alnus rubra*)—another tree common around Mount St. Helens—by its size and shape. The mountain alder is a many-branched shrub. The leaves of the red alder are blunt toothed whereas the mountain alder's leaves are sharply saw-toothed. Like all alders, the mountain alder adds nitrogen to the soil from its roots and by depositing its leaves on the ground.

To stay on the Boundary Trail heading for Coldwater Peak, bear left off the Eruption Trail at a switchback and continue southeast. Here Mount St. Helens and the Pumice Plain come into full view to the south. Both Cardwell's penstemon (*Penstemon cardwellii*) and small-flowered penstemon (*P. procerus*) bloom beside the path in early July. As the name implies, the small-flowered penstemon has much smaller flowers than do most penstemons. The flowers

Eruption-blasted stump

are a blue-purple color, considerably darker than those of the Cardwell's. The small-flowered penstemon is a perennial that sprouts each year from a woody base.

The Boundary Trail descends gently along the flower-covered ridge for a short distance. Besides the penstemons, pearly everlasting (*Anaphalis margaritacea*) is common here. The pearly everlasting is a perennial herb that grows from rhizomes. Its greenish gray leaves have white hairs on the bottom, giving the plant a slightly dusty appearance. The flowers are small, white with yellow centers, and clustered at the top of the stems. Not blooming until midsummer, the flowers often remain until the snow starts to fall.

After losing about 150 feet in elevation, the path flattens out and even climbs in a few spots. You will generally follow the ridgeline for the next 0.8 mile. The route then makes a right turn to head south across a steep hillside. Hang on to your children here, if you have them along: This traverse crosses a very steep and loose slope. A slip off the right side of the route could have disastrous results. The traverse lasts for 0.3 mile, then the tread turns left to cross a spur ridge.

As it crosses the spur ridge, the route turns to the northeast. You now traverse a gentler slope for 0.5 mile to the junction with the Truman Trail. Mount Adams and Spirit Lake are in view to the right along this traverse. The junction, at 4,150 feet elevation, is 2.5 miles from Johnston Ridge Observatory. Truman Trail crosses the Pumice Plain to Windy Ridge Viewpoint 5.9 miles away.

Continue on the Boundary Trail, which climbs to the northeast, reaching the ridgeline at the Spillover Saddle. This is where the Debris Avalanche immediately preceding the May 18, 1980, eruption crossed over the top of Johnston Ridge to descend into South Coldwater Canyon. The hummocks on both sides of the trail were part of the pre-1980 Mount St. Helens.

The route crosses the Spillover Saddle then traverses around the head of a basin to a junction with the Harry's Ridge Trail. This junction is 3.6 miles from Johnston Ridge Observatory at 4,380 feet elevation. From here it's a short hike to an abandoned volcano monitoring site on top of Harry's Ridge and a slightly longer hike to a viewpoint overlooking Spirit Lake.

To make the short but worthwhile side trip, turn right (southeast) onto the Harry's Ridge Trail. For the first 0.2 mile, the cairn-marked trail winds up a hillside covered with blasted-off stumps and flowers. Here you have a choice to make. You can follow the post-lined path across the ridgeline, then traverse the east-facing slope for 0.4 mile to a viewpoint; or you can bear slightly right (south) to follow the ridgeline path to its highest point, at an abandoned volcano monitoring site 0.4 mile away.

In either case Mount Adams is in view to the east. From either viewpoint the panoramic view is spectacular in all directions. To the south is the crater of Mount St. Helens, with the nearly black Lava Dome bulging in its center. To the east are Spirit Lake and Windy Ridge. The rugged peaks of the Mount Margaret Backcountry are to the north, and to the west is devastated, but now recovering, land along the Toutle River. It's interesting to note that just before you reach the viewpoint on Harry's Ridge, you cross directly over and 1,200 feet above the tunnel that was dug through the ridge to maintain the level of Spirit Lake. You also passed over the tunnel on the Boundary Trail a short distance south of the junction with the Harry's Ridge Trail. This trail, by the way, was named for Harry Truman, the lodge owner at the south end of Spirit Lake who died in the 1980 eruption. The spot where the lodge once sat is about 1 mile southeast of the viewpoints, far beneath the waters of Spirit Lake.

To continue on toward Coldwater Peak, continue north on the Boundary Trail. You will cross a saddle leaving the junction. Soon the route begins to climb. The path makes five switchbacks in the next 0.7 mile, gaining 600 feet in elevation as it climbs the ridge. As you climb higher, Mount Hood comes into view to the south. The now rough route continues to wind along the

The Boundary Trail below Coldwater Peak

ridgeline. The path passes through a window in the rock wall ridgeline, 1.8 miles beyond the junction with the Harry's Ridge Trail. Along the ridge Mount Rainier and St. Helens Lake come into view. After going through the window, another 0.25 mile of hiking brings you to St. Helens Saddle and the junction with the Coldwater Trail.

From the saddle at 5,080 feet elevation and 5.5 miles from Johnston Ridge Observatory, you can look down on sparkling St. Helens Lake with its many floating logs. St. Helens Lake was snow covered when the mountain blew, so its trout managed to survive the eruption. It's believed that some of these trout made their way down the lake's outlet stream, descending 1,100 vertical feet down the steep creekbed and over the waterfalls to Spirit Lake, where they reestablished a population. These fish must have had one heck of a water-slide ride.

After taking in the view from the saddle, hike another 0.3 mile north on the Boundary Trail to the junction with the Coldwater Peak Trail 1G, at 5,060 feet elevation. To head for Coldwater Peak, turn left (west) at the junction and follow the Coldwater Peak Trail. The route first climbs to the northwest. The lightly used trail quickly makes a switchback to the left and continues to climb the grassy slope. A couple more switchbacks bring you to the base of a cliff. As you climb through the lupine (*Lupinus* spp.) and red columbine (*Aquilegia formosa*), watch for less common subalpine spirea and the rather unique western pasqueflower (*Anemone occidentalis*), sometimes called western anemone.

Quick to grow and bloom after the winter's snow melts, the western pasqueflower's large white flowers open to brighten the subalpine meadows and slopes early each summer. This stout perennial is normally about a foot tall when flowering, but may reach twice that when it matures. At maturity the flower turns into a white hairy ball at the end of the now elongated stem—a configuration responsible for the common name "mouse on a stick." Other common names include tow-headed baby, mop-top, and old man of the mountains. This plant, like many members of the buttercup family, is poisonous.

Subalpine spirea (*Spiraea densiflora*) is a small deciduous shrub, generally growing to only about 2 feet tall. It inhabits mid- and upper elevations in the Cascades, growing under a wide variety of conditions from moist streambanks to rocky slopes. The small pink flowers of the subalpine spirea form flat or dome-shaped clusters at the ends of the stems.

The trail makes eight more switchbacks as it climbs to the summit of Coldwater Peak. A lookout was constructed on the peak in 1936 and was staffed for many years. At present there are some antennas, used for monitoring Mount St. Helens, near the summit. At 5,727 feet above sea level, Coldwater Peak is the fifth highest in the backcountry north of Spirit Lake. Like the entire ridgeline the peak sits on, it is part of the glacially eroded remains of the Spirit Lake

Pluton. The pluton is a large mass of intrusive rock that pushed up here some twenty million years ago. Considering that Mount St. Helens itself is only about 40,000 years old, these peaks and ridges sat here for a very long time before their now higher neighbor even began to build.

The open summit offers a fantastic 360-degree view, reaching from sharp-pointed Mount Hood in Oregon to the south to the nearly ice-covered dome of Mount Rainier to the northeast. Far below to the west, Coldwater Lake fills the canyon that before 1980 only had a creek flowing through it. In the distance to the southwest, Castle, another eruption-formed lake, sits at the base of Castle Ridge. To the southeast are Spirit and St. Helens Lakes; farther to the east is Mount Adams. Far in the distance Goat Rocks, the jagged, ice-eroded remnants of a volcano that has not erupted since the last major ice ages, form the northeastern skyline.

While you are on the summit taking in the view, watch and listen for the hoary marmots (*Marmota caligata*). These large rodents, also called whistle pigs, often make a very loud, shrill whistle to show their annoyance at your approach. Whistle pigs are cute and often very chubby looking. They need every bit of fat that they can put on to survive the long snowy winters hibernating. The marmots here on Coldwater Peak evidently survived in their burrows beneath the soil and snow when the mountain blew.

Return the way you came.

OPTIONS: Starting close by and ending at the same trailhead from which the Boundary Trail leaves the parking area, the Eruption Trail is a short but interesting loop hike. It starts at the east edge of the paved outdoor plaza next to Johnston Ridge Observatory. The tread first climbs gently, making three switchbacks, then winds up to an interpretive sign about stumps. Half-buried logs, penstemon, and fireweed (*Epilobium angustifolium*) line the route. Shortly you will come to another interpretive sign, this one about the Debris Avalanche. There is a paved cul-de-sac to the left of the trail 0.2 mile from the trailhead; a sign discusses new magma. This is the highest point on this trail, at 4,310 feet.

On the morning of May 18, 1980, David Johnston (along with his trailer and jeep) was camped at a volcano monitoring site near where you are now standing. The mountain erupted, causing a lateral blast of rocks, pumice, and extremely hot volcanic gases to sweep over this ridge at an estimated speed of more than 600 miles per hour—nearly supersonic. The blast was so powerful that all the trees on the slope facing the mountain were completely blown away. Even the soil covering this slope was not safe; the seething cloud also removed much of it. Johnston just had time to radio the volcano monitoring headquarters in Vancouver and get out one sentence before the blast hit him.

Needless to say, he was one of the eruption victims. His body was never found; nor were the remains of his trailer or jeep.

The trail descends from the cul-de-sac, passing another interpretive sign. Pearly everlasting crowds this part of the trail in August. After you make a switchback to the right, Coldwater Peak looms ahead. The Spillover, where the Debris Avalanche crossed over the top of Johnston Ridge, can be seen to the east. Beyond the Spillover is Harry's Ridge.

The trail makes a switchback to the left at its junction with the Boundary Trail, 0.3 mile from the trailhead. From here to the parking area 0.1 mile ahead, the Boundary and Eruption Trails are concurrent. The exit of the tunnel that now drains Spirit Lake can be seen below next to the highway. Once you have reached the parking area, turn left to get back to the observatory.

Another option for the more dedicated long-distance hiker is to continue another 9.7 miles along the Boundary Trail from the junction with the Coldwater Peak Trail to Norway Pass Trailhead. Making this one-way hike, however, requires a fairly long car shuttle.

Southern Region

Access from Washington Route 503–Forest Road 90

This side of Mount St. Helens was the least changed by the 1980 eruption. Old-growth and second-growth forest covers most of this region, much as it did before the big blast. Volcanic features are not lacking here, however. Lava flows from previous eruptions are exposed in several locations, and lahars flowed down many of the creekbeds during the 1980 eruption. Some of these lava flows were particularly fluid and formed lava tube caves. Trail 8, Upper and Lower Ape Cave, takes you into the longest of these caves. Trail 4, Sheep Canyon–Crescent Ridge Loop; Trail 12, Ape Canyon; and Trail 13, Lava Canyon, explore the lahars.

This is the only side of Mount St. Helens that is open to climbers. Trail 11, Ptarmigan Trail–Monitor Ridge, describes the route to the summit.

This side of the monument offers the best opportunities for winter recreation, with three roads to snoparks that are kept open through the snow season. Although they can also be hiked, Trail 9, Marble Mountain Snopark, and Trail 10, Kalama Ski Trail, are written with the cross-country skier and snowshoe hiker in mind. Trail 9 also includes the route to the summit of Mount St. Helens that is normally used in the winter season.

Southern Region

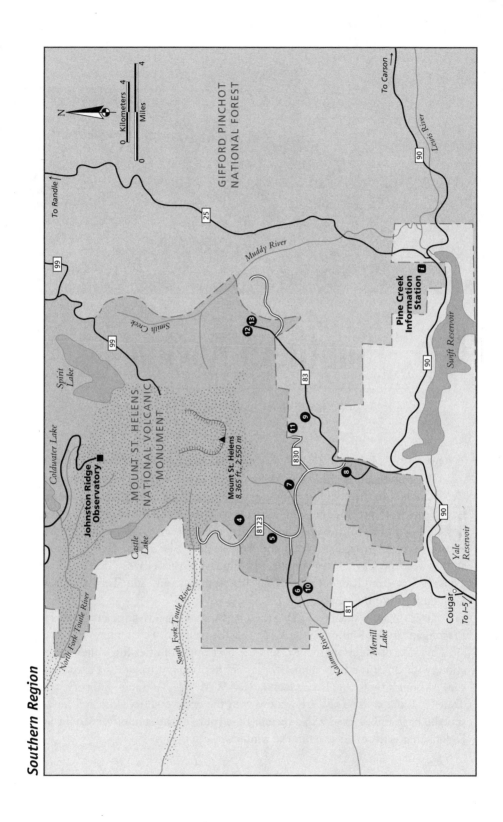

4 Sheep Canyon–Crescent Ridge Loop (Trails 238, 240, and 216)

HIGHLIGHTS: Starting in large old-growth forest, this hike climbs to near timberline. Then, as you descend Crescent Ridge, you can see the destructive power of a volcanic eruption in the form of blasted trees and lahars. Much of the more open terrain is covered with flowers through summer.

START: Blue Lake Trailhead.

DISTANCE: 11.5-mile loop day hike or two-day backpack.

DIFFICULTY: Moderate.

SEASON: Late June through September.

TOTAL CLIMBING: 2,270 feet.

TRAILHEAD ELEVATION: 3,210 feet.

PERMITS: Northwest Forest Pass.

MAPS: Mount St. Helens National Volcanic Monument, aka Brown Map. Goat Mountain and Mount St. Helens USGS quads cover the area but do not show these trails.

SPECIAL CONSIDERATIONS: Very close to the beginning of this hike, Coldspring Creek must be forded. Using wading sandals or other shoes to make this crossing is highly advised; hiking this entire trip with wet feet would not be pleasant. As of late summer 2003, at least one small section of the loop has slid away, making for a short but tricky passage. A small amount of trail maintenance would fix this problem.

PARKING AND TRAILHEAD FACILITIES: You'll find parking for several cars but no other facilities at the trailhead.

FINDING THE TRAILHEAD: From Portland or Seattle, take Interstate 5 to exit 21 (21 miles north of the Columbia River Bridge or 150 miles south of Seattle) at Woodland. Then drive east for 26.5 miles on Washington Route 503 (which becomes WA 503 Spur) to its junction with Forest Road 81. Turn left (north) and follow FR 81 for 11.3 miles to its junction with Forest Road 8123. Turn left onto FR 8123 and drive north for 1.7 miles to Blue Lake Trailhead.

Forest Road 8123 continues to Sheep Canyon Trailhead, but the washout at Coldspring Creek next to Blue Lake Trailhead prevents the use of the last 4.8 miles of the road, at least for the time being. The road may be reopened if and when the funds become available; it is presently on the Forest Service's road maintenance backlog. Starting from Sheep Canyon Trailhead would

Sheep Canyon–Crescent Ridge Loop (Trails 238, 240, and 216)

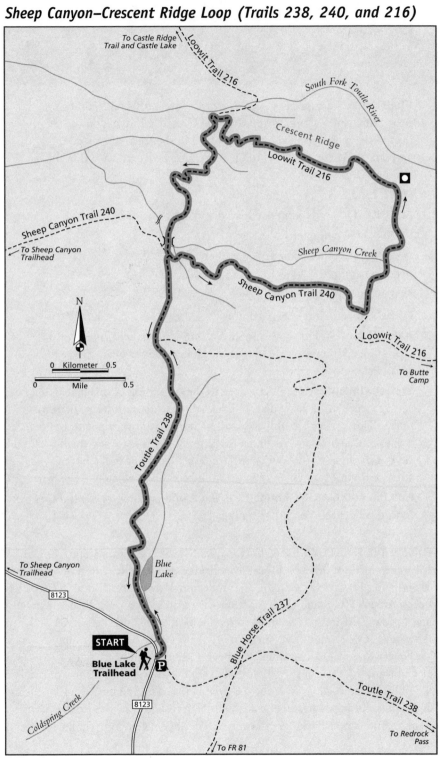

To Castle Ridge
Trail and Castle Lake

Loowit Trail 216

South Fork Toutle River

Crescent Ridge

Loowit Trail 216

Sheep Canyon Trail 240

To Sheep Canyon
Trailhead

Sheep Canyon Creek

Sheep Canyon Trail 240

N

Loowit Trail 216

To Butte
Camp

0   Kilometer   0.5

0   Mile   0.5

Toutle Trail 238

To Sheep Canyon
Trailhead

Blue
Lake

8123

Blue Horse Trail 237

START

Blue Lake
Trailhead

P

Toutle Trail 238

8123

To Redrock
Pass

Coldspring Creek

To FR 81

shorten this hike by 4 miles and reduce the elevation gain by more than 1,000 feet. Check with Monument Headquarters for the present status of FR 8123.

KEY POINTS:

- **0.0** Blue Lake Trailhead (GPS 46 10.114 N 122 15.678 W).
- **0.3** Blue Lake. Continue straight (north).
- **2.1** Junction with Blue Horse Trail. Continue straight (north).
- **2.8** Junction with Sheep Canyon Trail (GPS 46 12.001 N 122 15.586 W). Turn right (east).
- **4.5** Junction with Loowit Trail. Turn left (north).
- **7.1** Junction with Toutle Trail in South Fork Toutle River Canyon (GPS 46 12.607 N 122 15.179 W). Turn left (south).
- **8.6** Junction with Sheep Canyon Trail. Continue straight (south).
- **11.5** Blue Lake Trailhead (GPS 46 10.114 N 122 15.678 W).

THE HIKE: From the parking area at Blue Lake Trailhead, a broad path leads a few yards east to the Toutle Trail. Turn left (north) onto the Toutle Trail. In a short distance you will have to ford Coldspring Creek. The bridge that was once here was washed out at the same time as FR 8123. The tread then climbs gently along the west bank of Coldspring Creek for 0.3 mile to Blue Lake. As you climb, look to the right for a view of Mount St. Helens. There are two side paths leading down to the lake's shoreline.

Small but aptly named Blue Lake, like many of the lakes around the base of Mount St. Helens, was formed when a lahar deposit blocked the course of a stream. This particular lahar deposited its debris sometime between 1480 and 1800. During this period Mount St. Helens had at least two major eruptions that produced a larger volume of ejected material than did the 1980 eruption.

Beyond the lake the trail winds up through large timber. In many places vanilla leaf nearly covers the forest floor. The vanilla leaf plant (*Achlys triphylla*)

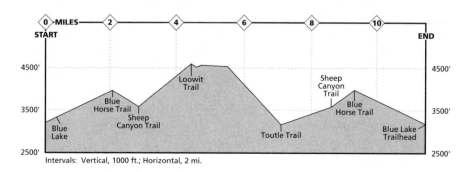

is a perennial that grows from rhizomes. It has three fan-shaped leaves that overlap at the base of the flower stalk. Its small white flowers cluster at the top of the stalk, forming a showy white spike. The leaves of the vanilla leaf plant were used by some groups of Native Americans as an insect repellent. Bunch-berry (*Cornus canadensis*), also called dwarf dogwood, is also common along this section of the route.

The path enters a more open area, with another view of the mountain, 1.1 miles above the lake. Broad-leaved penstemon (*Penstemon ovatus*) sprouts beside the tread, and thimbleberry (*Rubus parviflorus*) often grows in from the sides, brushing your legs as you hike along. At 0.7 mile farther along is the junction with the Blue Horse Trail, at 3,960 feet elevation. This junction, in Huckleberry Saddle, is 2.1 miles from Blue Lake Trailhead. The Blue Horse Trail leads 5 miles south to a trailhead on FR 81. There are several possible campsites in the timber next to the small meadows near the junction. Please don't camp in the meadows. The Toutle Trail goes straight ahead (north) at the junction.

Indian hellebore (*Veratrum viride*), which grows in and around this meadow, is one of the most poisonous plants you will encounter in the Cascades. Even so, it had a wide array of medicinal uses for Native Americans. Sometimes called corn lily, the Indian hellebore can grow to nearly 7 feet tall. It has large, pointed, prominently ribbed (almost pleated-looking) leaves. The false helle-bore (*V. californicum*) can be easily confused with the Indian hellebore at any time before the flowers come into bloom. When in flower it is easily distin-guished by its green blossoms; the blossoms of the false hellebore are white. In the southern Washington Cascades, Indian hellebore usually lives at middle to subalpine elevations.

As you continue north on the Toutle Trail through large timber that has escaped the mudflows for at least the last couple of centuries, you may notice a poor trail to the right. This trail follows a now abandoned route through Huck-leberry Saddle and should not be used. Leaving the broad saddle, the tread descends at a moderate grade. Half a mile after leaving the saddle, the trail makes a switchback to the right along the side of a semi-open canyon. A few yards past the switchback is the junction with the Sheep Canyon Trail, at 3,560 feet elevation. Turn right at this junction and cross a single-log bridge. A few yards after this crossing, there is a good campsite on the right side of the trail.

For the next 0.9 mile, the trail winds its way up the ridge on the south side of Sheep Canyon. When you are away from the edge of the canyon, you climb through old-growth forest and bear grass, but close to the rim the forest was stripped away by the mudflow from the 1980 eruption. Resembling a very large bunchgrass plant when it's not flowering, bear grass (*Xerophyllum tenax*) isn't even a member of the grass family but rather a type of lily. In the Mount St. Helens region, this evergreen perennial lives from middle elevations up to

Looking up Sheep Canyon

timberline, in both shaded and open areas. Where the trees shade them, individual bear grass plants may only bloom every five to seven years. In the open bear grass blooms more frequently, often nearly covering the slopes with a beautiful display. The small, creamy white bear grass flowers form an elongated oval, club-shaped cluster at the top of the up-to-4-foot-high central stem. Blooming occurs from June through August, depending on elevation. Native Americans wove the tough leaves of bear grass plants into baskets and hats. Elk and deer often feed on bear grass flowers, usually biting off the upper part of the stem along with the entire flower cluster.

The route bears to the right away from the canyon 3.8 miles from the trailhead. Now, at about 4,200 feet elevation, the composition of the forest begins to change. The trees are smaller and spaced farther apart. Black huckleberries (*Vaccinium membranaceum*) grow thickly, and if you are here in late August, you may want to take the time to enjoy their fruit. Between the trees and bushes, a few lupines (*Lupinus* spp.) sprout to add more color and to do their job of adding nitrogen to the nutrient-poor volcanic soil. At 0.2 mile after leaving the rim of Sheep Canyon, the trail crosses a gully. It then climbs out onto an old lava flow. From here the route winds its way up through thinning timber, mostly lodgepole pine, to the junction with the Loowit Trail near timberline, at 4,600 feet elevation, 4.5 miles from Blue Lake Trailhead.

This well-drained site on the western slope of the mountain, atop mostly loose volcanic debris, is an ideal site for the lodgepoles to grow. Lodgepole pine (*Pinus contorta*) is a two-needled pine, which means that the needles sprout from the twigs in groups of two—unlike the western white, which is a five-needled pine. The lodgepole is the only native two-needled pine in the area.

Turn left onto the Loowit Trail and head north. In a short distance the trail descends a little and crosses Sheep Canyon. Sheep Canyon Creek flows down the center of this mostly barren canyon, which is much broader here than it was down below.

The area you pass through just after Sheep Canyon was not heavily affected by the 1980 eruption; except for the ash fall, the vegetation is still much the same as it had been before the mountain blew. Leaving the canyon, the route climbs a slope covered with bear grass, Cardwell's penstemon (*Penstemon cardwellii*), and common red paintbrush (*Castilleja miniata*). Shortly beyond the canyon, the trail enters the Blast Zone. In contrast to the country only a short distance back, the trees that were standing here at the time of the eruption were broken off or blown to the ground. One mile from the junction with the Sheep Canyon Trail, a great viewpoint on the right side of the trail overlooks the South Fork Toutle Canyon, where you can see the effects of a large lahar.

The lahar that descended the South Fork Toutle River Canyon was what is known as a noncohesive lahar. These lahars generally begin when heavy rain,

Lodgepole pine cones

very quick snowmelt, or the sudden failure of a debris-dammed lake releases a large amount of water onto an easily eroded slope—as opposed to a cohesive lahar, which generally begins with a landslide.

In the case of the South Fork Toutle Lahar, hot pyroclastics from the eruption of Mount St. Helens at 8:32 A.M. on May 18, 1980, melted huge amounts of snow and ice on the slopes of the mountain. The water quickly picked up the easily eroded volcanic debris that made up the slopes. Much of this debris was in place before the eruption and not part of the material being ejected that morning by the volcano. The resulting lahar was the largest to flow from Mount St. Helens on eruption morning. The lahar, which looked like thin, brown concrete, surged down the South Fork Canyon. It continued along the South Fork Toutle River at a rate of about 20 miles per hour to the confluence with the North Fork Toutle River and beyond.

The South Fork Lahar preceded, by several hours, the much larger North Fork Toutle Lahar. The North Fork Lahar was a cohesive lahar that began when the north slope of Mount St. Helens collapsed and slid into the North Fork Canyon.

At the viewpoint the trail turns to the northwest and begins the long descent of Crescent Ridge. The route winds and switchbacks its way down, losing 1,400 feet of elevation in the next 1.6 miles. The descent route is along the edge of the Blast Zone. Sometimes you walk through blown-down timber, and at other times you are in old-growth forest made up mostly of large noble fir (*Abies procera*).

The route reaches another junction with the Toutle Trail 7.1 miles from the trailhead at the bottom of Crescent Ridge, at 3,180 feet elevation. At this junction near the South Fork Toutle River, the Loowit Trail turns to the right. See the options below for hikes to Castle Ridge and Castle Lake that leave from this junction.

Turn left at the junction and follow the Toutle Trail, climbing to the southwest on a brushy slope as you leave the South Fork Toutle River Canyon. Before long you will round a point, then cross a stream on a wooden bridge. Now the route follows close to the edge of the Blast Zone (aka Eruption Impact Zone). In one spot along this section, a small landslide has removed a short section of the trail. This area requires very careful stepping in the footprints of others, who have kicked steps into the unstable slope. Hopefully this section of trail will soon be maintained to alleviate the problem. This spot could be very difficult or even dangerous for the novice hiker.

Walk through large noble fir timber that was not blown down by the blast, interspersed with brush, much of which is mountain alder (*Alnus incana*) that has grown up since the eruption. Like the lupines mentioned above, the mountain alder is a nitrogen-fixing species, which means it can extract nitrogen from the atmosphere and "fix" or deposit what it doesn't use in the soil. The alder's leaves also are high in nitrogen. When they fall to the ground and decay, the nitrogen-rich compost adds even more nutrients to the soil. Essential for the growth of most plants, the nitrogen fixed by the alders here on these once denuded slopes is paving the way for other plants that will follow.

About 0.8 mile from the junction with the Loowit Trail, you leave the Blast Zone behind and hike through an old-growth forest of Douglas fir, western hemlock, and some of the largest noble fir trees you are likely to see. The route crosses a couple of draws then traverses into Sheep Creek Canyon. At the bottom of the canyon, you cross another wooden bridge over Sheep Creek. A few more yards of hiking brings you to the end of the loop, 1.5 miles from the junction with the Loowit Trail, at the junction with the Sheep Canyon Trail.

In the creekbed next to the bridge grow some beautiful stands of both Lewis (*Mimulus lewisii*) and yellow (*M. guttatus*) monkey flowers. At the end of the bridge (just as you step up on it) is a Rocky Mountain maple, a relatively uncommon shrub around Mount St. Helens. The Rocky Mountain maple (*Acer glabrum*) is easily confused with the vine maple (*A. circinatum*), but its leaves have only three to five pointed lobes rather than the seven to nine of the vine maple. It also grows in the western Cascades but is more common as you travel to the drier climates to the east.

If you have a little extra time and energy, turn right onto the Sheep Canyon Trail and descend a few yards to a side path, which will be on the right. This path leads a short distance to a viewpoint overlooking a waterfall in Sheep Creek. If you were to continue another 0.6 mile in this direction on the Sheep Canyon Trail, you would reach Sheep Canyon Trailhead at the end of the presently closed section of FR 8123.

After you have taken in the view of the falls, climb the few yards back to the junction of the Toutle and Sheep Canyon Trails. Then continue climbing southeast for 0.1 mile along the now combined Sheep Canyon and Toutle Trails to the junction where you first reached the Sheep Canyon Trail. Turn right at the junction and retrace your route for 2.8 miles to Blue Lake Trailhead.

OPTIONS: For an interesting side trip, head northeast on the Loowit Trail from the junction with the Toutle Trail in the South Fork Toutle Canyon. The route quickly crosses the South Fork Toutle River. There is no bridge, and the trail is vague at the crossing. After fording the river head upstream a short distance and find the trail again as it climbs the steep canyon slope to your left. For the next mile the tread switchbacks its way up through a dense stand of vine maple. In places the shrubs have overgrown the trail.

The vine maple is a small deciduous tree or large shrub. It usually grows to about 20 feet tall, but on occasion may reach 40. The foliage is often thinly dispersed, giving the shrub a scraggly appearance. Vine maple's leaves have seven to nine pointed lobes and are 2 to 5 inches across. As with other maples (*Acer* spp.), its winged seeds normally grow in pairs. An interesting characteristic of vine maple is the color that its leaves turn in autumn. If they have grown in good sunlight, they turn a bright red, but in a mostly shaded spot they will be golden yellow. As bright as the sunlight is on this south-facing slope, the leaves should almost all turn red.

Leaving the vine maple thicket, the route continues to climb along an open, mostly pumice slope. The trail is narrow and somewhat unstable here. You will reach the junction with the Castle Ridge Trail 216G, at 3,840 feet elevation, 1.4 miles after leaving the junction with the Toutle Trail. The Castle Ridge Trail is signed FAIRVIEW TRAIL at the junction and leaves Loowit Trail just below the rim of the South Fork Toutle River Canyon. The route heads west from the junction, climbing at a moderate rate. Shortly you will make a switchback as you climb to the rounded ridgeline. Along the ridge the path leads northwest through snags and downed timber. Flowers grow between the downed logs, creating beautiful gardens in this devastated area. If you happen to reach this ridge in the fog, don't be disappointed; certain light conditions caused by the fog seem to enhance this area rather than detract from it. The flowers are at their peak in early July.

The route reaches a small saddle 0.7 mile after leaving the Loowit Trail. Here the path turns to the northwest to traverse a slope for 0.1 mile to a junction with the Castle Lake Trail 221, at 3,980 feet elevation. Continuing to the northwest, the path climbs to its end at the junction with Weyerhaeuser Road 3000 in about 0.7 mile. End your hike at the junction or bear right (north) and descend the 4 more miles to Castle Lake.

As you leave the junction with the Castle Ridge Trail, the route traverses north across an open slope. You will reach an abandoned roadbed 0.2 mile from the Castle Ridge Trail. Turn right onto the roadbed and continue north. The route along the roadbed is marked with posts. The path reaches a saddle 0.2 mile farther along. Walk a few feet west in the saddle for a view of Castle Lake. Take the time to admire the view and watch for Roosevelt elk (*Cervus elaphus roosevelti*), the largest animals in the Cascades, which are common here.

From the saddle the wide, well-maintained path begins its descent to Castle Creek. Following an abandoned roadbed, the route descends at a moderate grade for a couple of miles. It then levels out and heads northwest to the foot of Castle Lake, at 2,510 feet elevation, 4 miles from the junction with the Castle Ridge Trail.

The Debris Avalanche, part of the May 18, 1980, eruption of Mount St. Helens—the same one that blocked Coldwater Creek to form Coldwater Lake—dammed South Fork Castle Creek to form Castle Lake. As at Spirit and Coldwater Lakes, it was determined that the relatively weak and erodable debris damming the lake could wash out, causing a catastrophic mudflow. To prevent this from happening, an outflow trench was constructed, thus stabilizing the lake at a safe level.

5 Goat Marsh (Trail 237A)

HIGHLIGHTS: This hike through the forest takes you to two lakes that were formed sometime between 1480 and 1780, when mudflow debris caused by Mount St. Helens volcanic activity blocked and altered the drainage pattern of a stream. A beaver-dammed stream flows between the lakes.

START: Kalama Ski Trailhead on Forest Road 8123.

DISTANCE: 2.8-mile out-and-back day hike.

DIFFICULTY: Easy.

SEASON: May through October.

TOTAL CLIMBING: Minimal.

TRAILHEAD ELEVATION: 2,880 feet.

PERMITS: None.

MAPS: Goat Mountain USGS quad.

SPECIAL CONSIDERATIONS: Mosquitoes can be very thick through mid-summer. Goat Marsh is a research area, so please tread lightly, leaving the flora and fauna as you found them.

PARKING AND TRAILHEAD FACILITIES: There is parking for one or two cars at the trailhead but no other facilities.

FINDING THE TRAILHEAD: From exit 21 (approximately 150 miles south of Seattle or 21 miles north of the Columbia River Bridge) off Interstate 5, at Woodland, drive east on Washington Route 503 (which becomes WA 503 Spur). Turn left (north) off this road 26.5 miles from I–5 onto Forest Road 81.

Slightly over 6 miles from WA 503, there is an outcropping of approximately 2,000-year-old cave basalt on the right side of the road. This lava flow shows good examples of tumuli, or pressure ridges, which form when a lava tube becomes plugged. The pressure builds up in the tube behind the plug and bulges the surface upward. Vine maple (*Acer circinatum*) grows from the lava, and if you're here in May, trilliums (*Trillium ovatum*) may be growing in the cracks.

Follow FR 81 for 11.3 miles from WA 503 to its junction with FR 8123. Turn left onto FR 8123 and drive north for 0.6 mile to the point where the Kalama Ski Trail crosses the road. There is a small sign at the junction.

KEY POINTS:

0.0 Kalama Ski Trailhead (GPS 46 09.270 N 122 16.151 W).

0.2 Junction with Goat Marsh Trail (GPS 46 09.276 N 122 16.378 W). Turn right (northwest).

Goat Marsh (Trail 237A)

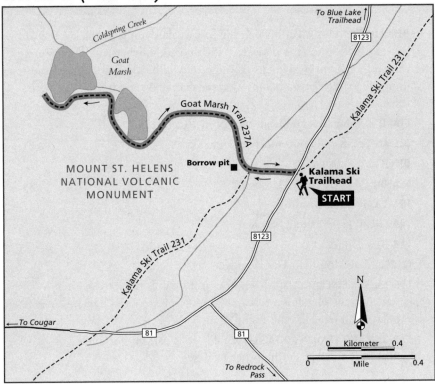

0.9 First lake. Continue straight.

1.4 End of trail next to second lake.

2.8 Kalama Ski Trailhead (GPS 46 09.270 N 122 16.151 W).

THE HIKE: Much of Goat Marsh Trail is really an abandoned roadbed that is reverting nicely to a trail. For the first 0.9 mile, the route is marked with blue-diamond cross-country ski trail markers. Hike west from the trailhead on the Kalama Ski Trail through the dense forest. Small to medium-sized lodgepole pines (*Pinus contorta*) are the most common trees as you cross this terraced lahar deposit, but there are scattered western hemlocks (*Tsuga heterophylla*), Douglas firs (*Pseudotsuga menziesii*), noble firs (*Abies procera*), Pacific silver firs (*Abies amabilis*), and western white pines (*Pinus monticola*). Kinnikinnick (*Arctostaphylos* spp.) covers much of the sandy ground between the trees.

In 0.2 mile you will reach the junction with the Goat Marsh Trail 237A. Turn right at the junction and head northwest, quickly leaving the lahar deposit and heading through the now larger western hemlock trees. The stately western hemlock, the state tree of Washington, grows best in cool, wet areas at

Pressure ridges in the lava along Forest Road 81

lower elevations; much of the country around Mount St. Helens provides nearly perfect habitat. Mature trees here can attain heights of 170 to 200 feet and live for more than 500 years if they are not disturbed by volcanic activities. The western hemlock is a very shade-tolerant species and prefers sites where the soil is high in humus content. Because of these preferences, western hemlocks are seldom pioneer trees.

The drooping central leader (at the very top of the tree) is the easiest way to identify a hemlock from a distance. There are two native hemlock species in the Mount St. Helens region, the western hemlock and the mountain hemlock. The western hemlock is the larger of the two and generally lives at lower elevations.

Western hemlock needles are short and uneven in length, varying from 0.5 to 0.75 inch long and yellow-green in color. The needles are irregularly spaced along the twigs. The cones are very small—0.75 to 1.25 inches long—and brown in color. After maturing and spreading their seeds, the cones drop to the ground intact. These cones may be thick on the forest floor beneath a mature tree. Western hemlock bark is rough, scaly, and brown. On old trees it becomes thick and furrowed. The bark is high in tannin and can be used for tanning purposes. Bark slivers from the western hemlock can be inflammatory and should be quickly removed.

Native Americans had a wide variety of uses for the western hemlock. There were several processes for making dye from its bark, one of which included steeping the bark in urine. The wood was carved into implements such as spoons, combs, and spear shafts. Certain curved pieces of hemlock were carved into fishhooks. The branches furnished a preferred material for sleeping on.

The wood of the western hemlock saws into top-grade lumber, and the fibers make some of the best paper. When cut, mature western hemlock trees are often hollow and in some cases nearly filled with water. Wet hemlock wood is so heavy that it may not even float on water.

The tread passes an abandoned borrow pit and soon comes to a wooden fence with a gate. The fence and gate are here to prevent motor vehicles from continuing to Goat Marsh. The route climbs very gently at first, then levels out.

Listen for the drumming of the male ruffed grouse (*Bonasa umbellus*) in this area if you are making this hike in spring, during their mating season. The drumming sound, which can be heard for up to 0.5 mile, is a slow and low *boom-boom-boom-boom*; it really doesn't sound as if a bird should make it. Ruffs, as ruffed grouse are often called, are gray-brown fowl with a prominent patch of black feathers on each side of their necks. These black feathers can be held erect, giving the ruffed appearance—hence the name. Female ruffs are experts at the broken-wing tactic, used to draw intruders away from their nests and chicks. The bird will scurry along the ground seemingly dragging a wing, causing a predator to follow, but staying just far enough ahead to be out of danger. When she feels that she is an adequate distance away from the nest or chicks, she takes flight, leaving her tormentor behind, wondering what happened. When the danger has passed, the female ruff returns to her business.

The forest floor beneath the larger trees is more open and covered with short huckleberry (*Vaccinium* spp.) bushes, bear grass (*Xerophyllum tenax*), and a variety of mosses. Where the trees offer shade, as they do here, individual bear grass plants may only bloom every five to seven years. In the open bear grass blooms more frequently. As you near the first lake, the hiking trail bears left off the marked ski trail.

A side path to your right here goes to a point overlooking the eastern end of the first lake. Along this short path prince's pine (*Chimaphila umbellata*)—a short, broadleaf, evergreen flower in the wintergreen family—grows in abundance. Red-winged blackbirds (*Agelaius phoeniceus*) call from their perches along the lakeshore, and ducks cruise the shallow waters. From the point there is a great view to the northeast of Mount St. Helens. The lower peak in front

Mount St. Helens and Butte Camp Dome over Goat Marsh

of the mountain is Butte Camp Dome, a volcanic plug dome much older than Mount St. Helens itself. To the northwest and close by is another plug dome, called Goat Mountain. This peak, which rises to 4,965 feet elevation just west of Goat Marsh, is a dacite plug dome that also far predates Mount St. Helens. A plug dome is a mound of lava that pushes up from a volcanic vent. The lava is too stiff to flow away, so it heaps up, around and over the vent.

Back on the main trail, the roadbed soon ends, as do the cross-country ski markers. The now poorly marked trail traverses around the south and west sides of the lake. Much of the forest floor on the hillside west of the lake is covered with salal (*Gaultheria shallon*). Among the most common understory shrubs in the Mount St. Helens area, salal often nearly covers the forest floor on drier sites. Salal is a broadleaf evergreen shrub that can grow up to 15 feet tall, but is usually less than shoulder height. Its leaves are leathery, 2 to 4 inches long, and oval shaped. The small urn-shaped flowers are pinkish white, and the fruits are reddish blue to dark purple. Salal berries were an important food for Native Americans. They were eaten raw or dried for storage.

As the trail leaves the first lake, it passes a beaver dam. Beavers (*Castor canadensis*) are the only members of the ancient rodent family Castoridae. In the rodent world the beaver is second in size only to the South American capybara. Growing through its entire life, the typical beaver reaches a weight of 40 to 60 pounds, though one huge specimen is known to have grown to 110. Beavers can be up to 4 feet long with about one-third of that length taken up by their broad paddle-shaped tails. At the base of a beaver's tail are two glands that secrete castoreum oil. By combing this oil through its fur, the beaver keeps itself slick and waterproof. With the aid of webbed hind feet, a beaver can swim up to 5 miles per hour, faster than a racing swimmer with fins. The inner two toenails on its feet are split to aid in grooming. Beavers have also been known to use these split nails to pick splinters from their teeth, a great idea for an animal that chews almost nothing but wood.

When alarmed, the beaver slaps its tail on the surface of the water. This slap is loud enough to awaken a person from a deep sleep. This happened to me once when I was spending the night sleeping on a boat in an area where a beaver clearly didn't want me to be. Even though this occurred on a large lake with no beaver lodge close by, the irate animal continued to slap the water and chatter at me until I left.

A pond is security for beavers. They try to stay close to the water as much as possible, venturing ashore only to collect bark and twigs for food, or to cut down trees for dam making and repair. To keep their ponds full, beavers spend lots of time working on their dams. As they build the dam higher, the pond becomes larger, often flooding the forest edge around it. This kills some trees and accounts for the standing dead snags in many beaver ponds.

Another project that takes up large amounts of the beaver's time is the construction and maintenance of its lodge, which looks like a large brush pile in the middle of the pond. Its entrance is located underwater, allowing for unrestricted access by the beaver but keeping out predators that are less qualified swimmers.

The path soon reaches the south side of another shallow lake. It works its way around to the southeast corner of this second lake and ends in the forest near the shore. Return the way you came.

Many Roosevelt elk (*Cervus elaphus roosevelti*) visit the lush, grassy openings of Goat Marsh. The largest and darkest subspecies of elk, Roosevelt bulls, which may weigh more than 1,000 pounds, are the largest animals to inhabit the Cascades. They are common and may be expected almost anywhere on the west slopes of the mountains. Watch for them in the open areas north of the lakes in the early morning and evening.

OPTIONS: The short hike to Kalama Springs is easily done on the same day that you make the hike to Goat Marsh. To reach Kalama Springs from Goat Marsh

Trailhead, drive southwest on FR 8123 for 0.6 mile to its junction with FR 81. Turn left (southeast) and follow FR 81 for 0.9 mile to an unmarked parking spot on the north side of the road (GPS 46 08.499 N 122 15.717 W). If you reach McBride Lake, you've gone a short distance too far.

The trail to Kalama Springs is a little vague in spots. It stays about 50 yards away from the river most of the way to the springs. First you will climb northwest over a couple of mounds of dirt that are there to block vehicle access. After walking a few yards through the red alders (*Alnus rubra*), the path enters a sandy area—a small lahar deposit from the 1980 eruption of Mount St. Helens.

Hike across the sand for a short distance and reenter the brush, which is now mostly mountain alders (*Alnus incana*), willows (*Salix* spp.), and huckleberries, before entering the coniferous timber. The still-sandy trail passes a couple of campsites as it continues to the northeast and becomes badly eroded for a short distance. The route soon makes a hard right turn, close to the base of a hill, 0.3 mile from the trailhead. It then goes a few yards east to Kalama Springs (GPS 46 08.663 N 122 15.423 W). At the wide springs the cold, clear waters of the Kalama River bubble out from beneath an old lava flow. A few large Douglas firs grow from the lava flow, attesting to its age. On the banks of the river, at least two species of willows form a thicket. Chew marks on the willows show that beavers are or at least once were here. Beavers must chew to keep their ever-growing incisors worn down; otherwise the teeth will eventually grow long enough to pierce the skull from the inside of the mouth.

6 Toutle Trail (Trail 238)

HIGHLIGHTS: The trail first follows the Kalama River with its moss-covered banks and splashing pools to McBride Lake. It then climbs along a forested slope, crosses a lava flow, and traverses through old-growth forest to a lahar. There are great views of Mount St. Helens from the lava flow and the lahar.

START: Kalama Horse Camp Trailhead.

DISTANCE: 8.7-mile shuttle.

DIFFICULTY: Easy to moderate.

SEASON: June through October.

TOTAL CLIMBING: 1,440 feet.

TRAILHEAD ELEVATION: 2,020 feet.

PERMITS: Northwest Forest Pass.

MAPS: Mount St. Helens National Volcanic Monument, aka Brown Map. Goat Mountain and Mount St. Helens USGS quads cover the area but don't show this trail.

SPECIAL CONSIDERATIONS: This route is heavily used by stock and receives some mountain bike traffic.

PARKING AND TRAILHEAD FACILITIES: There is a campground for equestrians at Kalama Horse Camp Trailhead, so there are restrooms and horse facilities. Parties without stock are asked to camp somewhere else, but it's okay to leave your car at the trailhead. At Blue Lake Trailhead there is parking for several cars but no other facilities.

FINDING THE TRAILHEAD: To reach Kalama Horse Camp, take exit 21 off Interstate 5 at Woodland (21 miles north of the Columbia River Bridge or approximately 150 miles south of Seattle), then drive east on Washington Route 503 (which becomes WA 503 Spur at a junction 23 miles from I–5) for 26.5 miles

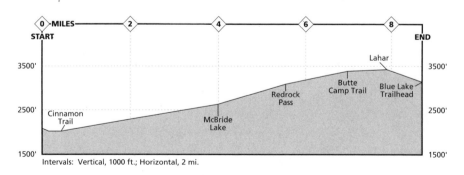

Toutle Trail (Trail 238)

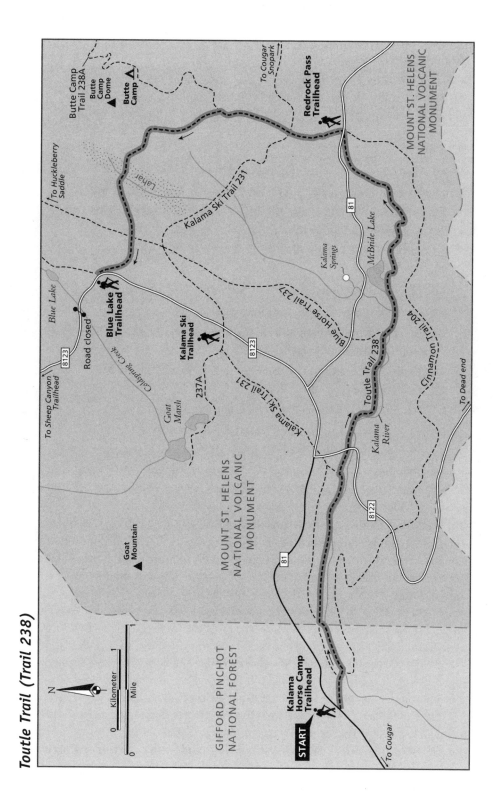

to the junction with Forest Road 81. Turn left (north) onto FR 81 and follow it for 8.6 miles to Kalama Horse Camp on the right.

To reach Blue Lake Trailhead where this hike ends, follow FR 81 for another 2.7 miles to its junction with Forest Road 8123. Turn left onto FR 8123 and drive north for 1.7 miles to Blue Lake Trailhead on the right.

KEY POINTS:

0.0 Kalama Horse Camp Trailhead (GPS 46 08.518 N 122 19.413 W).

0.2 Kalama Ski Trail and Toutle Trail separate. Bear right (southeast).

0.3 Junction with Cinnamon Trail (GPS 46 08.532 N 122 19.389 W). Continue straight (southeast).

2.3 FR 8122 (GPS 46 08.527 N 122 17.132 W). Continue straight (southeast).

3.6 Junction with Blue Horse Trail. Continue east on Toutle Trail.

4.0 McBride Lake. Continue straight (east).

5.5 Junction with Cinnamon Trail (GPS 46 08.593 N 122 14.179 W). Continue on Toutle Trail.

5.6 Redrock Pass and FR 81 (GPS 46 08.682 N 122 14.087 W). Continue on Toutle Trail.

6.1 Junction with Kalama Ski Trail. Continue straight (north).

6.8 Junction with Butte Camp Trail (GPS 46 09.409 N 122 13.971 W). Continue on Toutle Trail.

8.4 Junction with Blue Horse Trail. Continue straight (west).

8.7 Blue Lake Trailhead (GPS 46 10.114 N 122 15.678 W).

THE HIKE: The Toutle and the Kalama Ski Trails leave Kalama Horse Camp along the same route, heading east. The ski trail is marked with blue-diamond cross-country ski markers; in the places where the trails follow the same route, these markers will be visible well up in the trees. The path descends slightly through a mixed forest of conifers, with black huckleberry bushes (*Vaccinium membranaceum*) making up much of the understory, for a few yards to a wooden bridge over a small stream. A short distance past the bridge, the wide trail forks. The Kalama Ski Trail with its ski markers turns to the left (northeast). Bear right (southeast) at the junction and quickly reach the junction with the Cinnamon Trail 204, then cross another wooden bridge over a sometimes dry streambed. For information about the Cinnamon Trail, see the options below.

The trail then follows the Kalama River upstream. By keeping a close watch on the river, you may see an American dipper. Generally the thing you first notice about this bird is the unusual bobbing motion that it regularly makes with its body, often while standing on a streamside rock. The American dipper (*Cinclus mexicanus*) inhabits much of the mountainous regions of western North America, with a range that reaches from Alaska to southern California and Arizona, then south along the Sierra Madre Occidental through Mexico and into Central America. The dipper's plumage is a slate-gray color, often appearing black—especially when the bird is wet, which it is most of the time.

Dippers have the unique ability, much like that of a penguin, to fly underwater. Unlike the penguin, which is flightless, the dipper can exit the water directly into flight. Dippers can dive to depths in excess of 20 feet and, if the current isn't too strong, can walk on the bottom to feed. The dipper is always found very close to or in a stream. When it flies through the air, it is almost always directly over water and usually very low. Although it's not a migratory bird, the dipper does move to lower elevations in winter, always following a stream as it goes.

The dipper is sometimes called by its British name water ouzel. In the past this name was more commonly used than it is today.

The well-maintained tread makes a switchback to the left 0.7 mile from the trailhead then climbs out of the riverbed. After climbing for 0.1 mile, the path switches back to the right, well above the river, on the rim of the canyon. As it switches back, the Kalama Ski Trail rejoins the Toutle Trail.

Continuing to the east, the route generally follows the rim of the canyon for about 0.8 mile, then gets close to the river again. At the signed junction, 2 miles from the trailhead, the Kalama Ski Trail leaves this section of Toutle Trail for the last time. Here the blue-diamond-marked Kalama Ski Trail turns left, while the Toutle Trail goes straight ahead to the east-southeast.

As has been true much of the way along so far, the route is through a mixed, mostly coniferous forest. The species of trees include western white pine (*Pinus monticola*), lodgepole pine (*Pinus contorta*), western hemlock (*Tsuga heterophylla*), Douglas fir (*Pseudotsuga menziesii*), and a couple of varieties of true firs (*Abies* spp.): noble fir (*A. procera*) and Pacific silver fir (*A. amabilis*). Next to the sometimes log-choked river grows the shrubby mountain alder (*Alnus incana*). Prince's pine (*Chimaphila umbellata*), a small evergreen flowering plant, sprouts through the carpet of moss on the forest floor. A few large boulders protrude from the old terraced lahar deposit that you have been walking on all the way from Kalama Horse Camp Trailhead.

In another 0.3 mile you will cross FR 8122. Just to the left at this crossing is a nice campsite, which can be reached by car. The trail, which is well maintained and cleared wide for skiers in this section, climbs very gently on to the east after crossing the road. This part of the Toutle Trail is marked with blue diamonds. The tread follows the Kalama River upstream for another 1.3 miles to a junction with the Blue Horse Trail. The Blue Horse Trail, which is an abandoned road at this point, turns to the left and heads north.

Turn right at this junction and follow the abandoned road for a few yards, crossing the Kalama River. Just across the river, the Toutle Trail turns left off the road and heads on east. There is a path, which goes to another campsite to the left 0.1 mile after leaving the roadbed. Shortly after passing the campsite, look for a small waterfall on the right side of the trail. The trail passes beneath moss-covered cliffs for a short distance. Look for beaver dams in the river to the left. The tread crosses a couple of tiny steep streams and soon starts to climb above the south shore of McBride Lake. The lake, which is 4 miles from the trailhead, contains a good population of brook trout (*Salvelinus fontinalis*) and cutthroat trout (*Salmo clarki*). The access to the lake from the trail is difficult, but there is easy access from FR 81 on the north side.

The trail climbs away from the lake through old-growth forest. It follows a long-abandoned roadbed for a short distance 0.3 mile after leaving the lake. The path leaves the old-growth forest 4.6 miles from the trailhead. It then traverses slopes covered with huckleberry bushes and vine maple (*Acer circinatum*), crossing several tiny streams that may dry up in late summer. In this more open area, Roosevelt elk (*Cervus elaphus roosevelti*) are common. Watch for their almost round, cowlike tracks on the trail. Just before Redrock Pass, the trail reenters old-growth forest, with devil's club in some of the wetter spots.

If you ever somehow end up in a patch of devil's club, you will understand how it got its common name. Devil's club (*Oplopanax horridus*) can grow up to 15 feet tall but is usually less than 10. The 0.5-inch-long spines that cover the stems easily identify it. The stems don't branch heavily but are often crooked and tangled. Devil's club leaves resemble those of a maple on the top, but beneath they also have spines. The bright red, shiny berries are eaten with gusto by bears but are not considered edible for humans.

Devil's club was a plant of many uses to Native Americans. It was used medically to treat ailments from arthritis and rheumatism to ulcers. Charcoal from burning devil's club was used for making face paint and tattoos. The wood was carved into special fishing lures.

Reach a second junction with the Cinnamon Trail 5.5 miles from the trailhead. Just past this junction, notice the Smith's fairy-bells (*Disporum smithii*) growing on the right side of the trail. The Smith's fairy-bells is a perennial plant growing up to 3 feet tall from rhizomes. Its leaves are oval shaped with pointed ends. Creamy white, bell-shaped flowers sprout from the ends of the stems, usually in groups of two but occasionally singly or in groups of three. Soon after the snow melts, about June 1, trilliums (*Trillium ovatum*), avalanche lilies (*Erythronium montanum*), bleeding hearts (*Dicentra formosa*), and salmonberries (*Rubus spectabilis*) also brighten the trailside in this area.

Another 150 yards of walking brings you to Redrock Pass, at 3,110 feet elevation. The Toutle Trail crosses FR 81 at the pass, heads north making a

Devil's club

switchback, then climbs out on top of a 1,900-year-old flow of *aa* lava. (*Aa* is a Hawaiian term referring to lava with a rough, broken surface.) Vine maple grows from the surface. The tread crosses this chunky flow for 0.3 mile, then enters an older, smoothed-off flow covered with bear grass (*Xerophyllum tenax*) and small timber. The well-used path crosses an abandoned roadbed 0.4 mile from Redrock Pass Trailhead, and reaches one last junction with the Kalama Ski Trail 0.1 mile farther along.

The Toutle Trail crosses the Kalama Ski Trail at the signed junction and continues north, entering old-growth timber. The path crosses a dry wash 0.5 mile after crossing the ski trail. The junction with the Butte Camp Trail is reached 0.2 mile farther along. This junction is 1.2 miles from Redrock Pass at 3,340 feet elevation. The Butte Camp Trail connects with the Loowit Trail and is used by climbers doing routes on the southwest side of Mount St. Helens.

Leaving the junction with the Butte Camp Trail, the Toutle Trail turns to the northwest and circles the base of Butte Camp Dome for 0.7 mile to a small stream crossing. The stream flows from a spring a short distance above the trail. This may be the only source of water along this trail. Butte Camp Dome is a 4,856-foot-high volcanic plug dome—a mound of lava that pushes up from a volcanic vent. The lava is too stiff to flow away, so it heaps up, around and over the vent. The eruptions that built Butte Camp Dome far predate the relatively young Mount St. Helens volcano.

Past the stream, the trail climbs gently along the base of the dome, then heads west to cross a lahar deposit. The trail may disappear temporarily in the main wash of the lahar. If it does, look for a cairn on the far side to pick up the trail again. The Toutle Trail reaches its highest elevation, 3,480 feet, as it crosses this deposit.

Now head west through a smaller forest of mostly lodgepole and western white pines. The porous, sandy makeup of the lahar deposit makes the soil generally drier here than it is in close-by areas where organic soil has had more time to form. Thus these trees are generally more widely spaced and smaller. Drought-resistant trees such as the lodgepole pine often become the dominant species.

You will reach the junction with the Blue Horse Trail 0.5 mile after crossing the lahar. This signed junction is 2.8 miles from the trailhead at Redrock Pass. Another 0.3 mile northwest along the path brings you to Blue Lake Trailhead. A side trail leads a few yards west to the parking area at 3,210 feet elevation.

OPTIONS: For a shorter trip you can end or begin your hike at Redrock Pass. Use the Cinnamon Trail 204 as a return route from this pass for a 14.1-mile loop. While it's all at a moderate grade, this loop does add nearly 2,000 feet of climbing. To follow this option turn right onto the Cinnamon Trail 5.5 miles from Kalama Horse Camp.

The Cinnamon Trail generally follows the ridgeline south of FR 81 from its junction with the Toutle Trail near Redrock Pass to another junction with the Toutle Trail near Kalama Horse Camp, making it an excellent but more challenging return route for hikers and equestrians doing the Toutle Trail. Black huckleberries grow along most of the route, providing fruit for the hiker by late July or early August.

From the junction with the Toutle Trail 0.1 mile west of Redrock Pass, the Cinnamon Trail climbs to the south, making seven switchbacks and gaining 560 feet of elevation in the first mile to reach the ridgeline. Along the way it climbs through mature forest of Pacific silver fir, noble fir, and western hemlock (*Tsuga heterophylla*). Devil's club grows in the damper spots beneath the large old trees, while in the openings vine maple and mountain alder make a brushy mix. Pacific bleeding hearts and pearly everlasting (*Anaphalis margaritacea*) sprout wherever there's a little bit of ground not covered with trees and bushes.

Mount St. Helens from Cinnamon Trail

As you reach the ridgeline, there is a great view of the southern slopes of Mount St. Helens, which is close by to the north. To the east the 12,276-foot-high, ice-clad summit of Mount Adams rises above the hazy hills. The trail continues south along the ridge through now smaller timber. Occasionally lupine (*Lupinus* spp.) and bear grass grow from the sandy soil. Soon the tread swings around to the southwest, then to the west, staying close to the ridgeline. Watch below and to your right for a glimpse of McBride Lake. At 0.6 mile after reaching the ridgeline, there is a small marshy meadow on the right side of the path. The route makes a half circle around the southern side of the meadow, then continues on along the ridgeline. Steller's jays (*Cyanocitta stelleri*) abound in this second-growth forest; you may see them or at least hear their screeching calls, often mimicking those of the red-tailed hawk.

Along the ridge the trail goes through or traverses the edge of several relatively recent clear-cuts, which are growing up with young noble and Douglas firs. In these more open areas, there is enough direct sunlight reaching ground level for foxglove to grow and bloom. An import from Europe, foxglove (*Digitalis purpurea*) is a large, usually biennial herb, up to 6 feet tall, that has become well established in the Northwest. Its bell-shaped, pink-purple or sometimes white flowers bloom in profusion, from the upper portion of the stalk, in July. The foxglove is a highly poisonous plant.

The Cinnamon Trail descends to a saddle on the ridgeline 2.2 miles from the junction with the Toutle Trail. At this point you are back down to 3,270 feet elevation and have lost all but about 150 feet of the elevation you gained in the beginning. From the saddle the tread climbs again. As you regain elevation, the sharply pointed spire of 11,240-foot-high Mount Hood, 60 miles to the southeast across the Columbia River in Oregon, comes into view.

The grade soon moderates and the path continues to follow the ridgeline, heading generally west. In the sandy soil atop the ridge, running club moss attempts to invade the trail in several places. The stems of the running club moss (*Lycopodium clavatum*) creep along the ground, sometimes forming a loose, bright green mat up to several yards wide, rooting at intervals as it grows. Along these creeping stems the plant shoots up erect scaly stalks up to about 10 inches high, with cones where the seeds are produced. At least one Native American tribe believed that anyone who handled this plant would become lost.

At 4.7 miles from the junction with the Toutle Trail, elevation 3,750 feet, the Cinnamon Trail crosses a gravel road (GPS 46 07.780 N 122 16.910 W). After climbing slightly you will soon cross this same road again, then quickly cross yet another road before reaching the ridgeline and the highest point on the Cinnamon Trail at 3,930 feet elevation. As you reach the ridgeline, there will be a path that turns to the right to follow the ridge east. Don't take this; it's simply a game trail, even though at times it may look as well used as the Cinnamon Trail. Head northwest along the ridgeline and you will soon begin to descend.

As you begin your descent, mountain cat's ear lilies welcome you, with their light cream-colored blooms, in the forest openings. Also called subalpine mariposa, the mountain cat's ear (*Calochortus subalpinus*) is a perennial herb up to about a foot tall. The flowers are hairy, about 1.25 inches across, and have three petals. Oregon grape (*Mahonia nervosa*) and broad-leaved penstemon (*Penstemon ovatus*) also show up intermittently along the trailside, as does the leopard lily (*Lilium columbianum*), aka tiger lily and Columbia lily. Trilliums are also present but have usually finished blooming by the time hikers are likely to take this trail. As you descend, western red cedar (*Thuja plicata*) starts to show up in the mix of forest trees.

A mile after you started your descent, the route crosses another gravel road. By this time you are down to about 3,300 feet elevation. In a few yards you cross one more road. Close to the roads, the oxeye daisy (*Chrysanthemum leucanthemum*)—a non-native species—has invaded the disturbed soil. In another 0.3 mile the trail reaches yet another gravel road. Cross this and continue on a spur road, which is closed, blocked, and gradually reverting to a trail. The route follows this roadbed for a little more than 0.3 mile; then the road ends and the trail continues through the forest, descending the northwestern slope of Cinnamon Peak.

Where the trail has been cut into the slope, notice the light gray volcanic ash just below the forest duff. This ash is from the recent eruptions of Mount St. Helens. In many places the leaves and needles that constantly fall from the trees have had enough time only to cover it with an inch or two of duff.

The trail finally leaves the slopes it has been traversing 7.9 miles from the junction with the Toutle Trail. Now you hike across the old terraced lahar deposits close to the Kalama River. Both black (*Vaccinium membranaceum*) and red (*V. parvifolium*) huckleberries grow on these sandy deposits, as does salal (*Gaultheria shallon*). A quarter mile onto the relatively flat lahar deposits, there will be a trail junction. The trail to the left goes to Kalama Falls; you bear right (west-southwest). Soon the trail makes a switchback to the right and descends a short distance to the bridge over the Kalama River at 1,980 feet elevation. A short distance beyond, the route rejoins the Toutle Trail, 8.5 miles from the junction where the two trails separated.

HIGHLIGHTS: This hike takes you across lava beds and through forest from Redrock Pass Trailhead on the Toutle Trail to a junction with the Butte Camp Trail, then on to the Loowit Trail at timberline on the southern slope of Mount St. Helens.

START: Redrock Pass Trailhead.

DISTANCE: 7.6-mile out-and-back day hike or backpack.

DIFFICULTY: Moderate.

SEASON: July through September.

TOTAL CLIMBING: 1,640 feet.

TRAILHEAD ELEVATION: 3,110 feet.

PERMITS: Northwest Forest Pass.

MAPS: Mount St. Helens National Volcanic Monument, aka Brown Map. Mount St. Helens USGS quad covers the area, but this trail is not shown.

SPECIAL CONSIDERATIONS: After the snow melts there is no water along this route above Butte Camp. Mosquitoes are often bad on this side of the mountain until late summer.

PARKING AND TRAILHEAD FACILITIES: You'll find parking for several cars but no other facilities at the trailhead.

FINDING THE TRAILHEAD: Drive to exit 21 (21 miles north of the Columbia River Bridge or approximately 150 miles south of Seattle) off Interstate 5, at Woodland. Then drive 26.5 miles east on Washington Route 503 (which becomes WA 503 Spur), turning left (north) onto Forest Road 81. Follow FR 81 for 13.5 miles to Redrock Pass Trailhead.

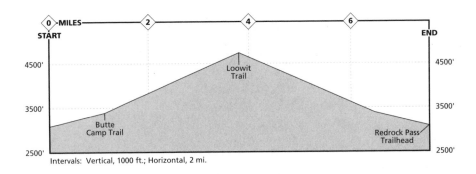

Butte Camp (Trails 238, 238A)

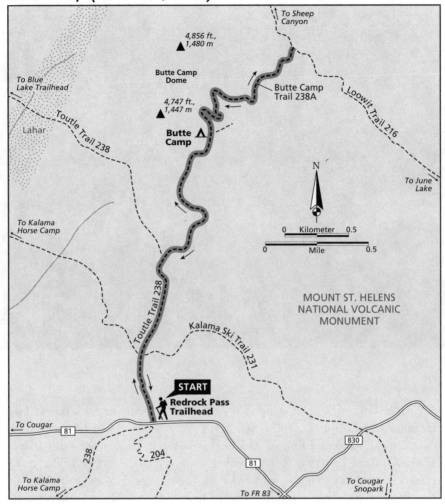

KEY POINTS:

0.0 Redrock Pass Trailhead (GPS 46 08.682 N 122 14.087 W).

0.5 Junction with Kalama Ski Trail. Continue straight (north).

1.2 Junction with Butte Camp Trail (GPS 46 09.409 N 122 13.971 W). Turn right (northeast).

2.4 Lower Butte Camp. Continue straight (northeast).

3.8 Junction with Loowit Trail (GPS 46 10.527 N 122 13.023 W).

7.6 Redrock Pass Trailhead (GPS 46 08.682 N 122 14.087 W).

False hellebore

THE HIKE: This route follows the Toutle Trail 238 for its first 1.2 miles. The tread leaves FR 81 at Redrock Pass, heads north (making a switchback), then climbs out on top of a flow of *aa* lava that is about 1,900 years old. (*Aa* is a Hawaiian term referring to lava with a rough, broken surface.) The tread crosses this chunky rough flow for 0.3 mile, then enters an older, smoothed-off flow covered with bear grass (*Xerophyllum tenax*), small noble fir (*Abies procera*), Pacific silver fir (*A. amabilis*), Douglas fir (*Pseudotsuga menziesii*), lodgepole pine (*Pinus contorta*), and western white pine (*Pinus monticola*) timber. A few clumps of subalpine spirea (*Spiraea densiflora*)—a shrub with beautiful pinkish red flower clusters—also grow on this old lava flow. The well-used path crosses an abandoned roadbed 0.4 mile from the trailhead, then reaches the junction with the Kalama Ski Trail 0.1 mile farther along. By the time you reach this junction, the timber has become larger. Cross the ski trail at the signed junction and continue north.

The tread now enters old-growth noble, Pacific silver, and Douglas fir timber, then crosses a dry wash 0.5 mile after crossing the ski trail. The junction with the Butte Camp Trail is reached 0.2 mile farther along, 1.2 miles from Redrock Pass, at 3,340 feet elevation.

Turn right at the marked junction onto the Butte Camp Trail 238A. The tread climbs to the northeast, through open forest on an old lava flow. Common red paintbrush (*Castilleja miniata*) and lupines (*Lupinus* spp.) dot the sides of the trail as you climb. Lupines are nitrogen-fixing plants that take nitrogen from the atmosphere and deposit or "fix" it into the soil, where it can be used by other plants. This characteristic makes the lupine a very important part of the vegetative reclamation of this volcanically altered region.

A little more than 1 mile from the junction, Mount St. Helens comes into view ahead. At 1.2 miles from the junction, the trail passes Butte Camp. The camp, elevation 3,990 feet, is on the left side of the trail, and has several good campsites. There is usually water in a small stream a few yards to the west. Monkey flowers (*Mimulus* spp.) and false hellebore brighten the meadows around the campsites.

Also called corn lily, the false hellebore (*Veratrum californicum*) stands up to 6 feet tall. Its wide, pointed, prominently veined leaves are up to 10 inches long. The small white flowers erupt from the main stem and short lateral stems at the top of the stalk forming a pyramid-shaped cluster. This is a poisonous plant, although aboriginal peoples had several medical uses for it. The false hellebore usually grows at middle elevations in the area around Mount St. Helens.

A close relative of the false hellebore that also lives in the Cascade Range is the Indian hellebore (*V. viride*). Indian hellebore can be easily confused with false hellebore at any time before the flowers come into bloom. When in flower, however, it is easily distinguished by its green blossoms. The Indian hellebore is even more poisonous than its cousin; it's one of the most poisonous plants in the Cascades. Nevertheless it had an even wider array of medical uses among Native Americans than did the false hellebore. In the southern Washington Cascades, Indian hellebore usually lives at middle to subalpine elevations.

A path turns to the right as you pass Butte Camp. This path is part of an older, now abandoned trail. There are really two Butte Camps, lower and upper. The one mentioned above is lower Butte Camp; the upper camp is now closed for research.

The two summits of Butte Camp Dome, a volcanic plug dome much older than Mount St. Helens itself, rise just to the west of Butte Camp. The higher is the northern peak, at 4,856 feet elevation. A plug dome is a mound of lava that pushes up from a volcanic vent. The lava is too stiff to flow away, so it heaps up, around and over the vent.

The trail makes a switchback to the right shortly after passing the camp. Here it enters an area where the lava is much older and has had more time to

Butte Camp Trail

develop a layer of soil; the trees are much larger. The Butte Camp Trail climbs at a steady grade for another 0.6 mile, then flattens out and soon comes to a viewpoint with a great vista to the south, Mount Hood in the distance. At this viewpoint, 2 miles from the Toutle Trail, the trail makes a hard left turn to head north and northeast, climbing gently through small lodgepole pines and subalpine firs.

The subalpine fir (*Abies lasiocarpa*), or alpine fir as it is commonly called, is typically an interior subalpine species. The smallest of the true fir species that inhabit the country around Mount St. Helens, its spire shape normally reaches 65 to 100 feet in height at maturity, but in some cases it can grow to 150 feet. The trunk diameter of the subalpine fir is usually less than 2 feet. The trees here high on the southern slope of Mount St. Helens are much smaller, however.

The 1- to 1.75-inch-long needles are bluish green in color and flat in cross section. They are attached all around the twig and tend to turn upward. The deep purple cones are 2 to 4 inches long, and—as with all true firs—they disintegrate on the tree.

Under certain conditions, usually at or near timberline, subalpine fir reproduces almost entirely by a process called layering: Heavy snows press the lower branches down to ground level; the branches take root and form a mat of low-growing trees. This process is the reason that you often see groups of small tightly spaced subalpine firs scattered over the slopes at or near timberline.

As the trees thin out at timberline, lupine and phlox (*Phlox diffusa*) almost cover the ground in spots. Phlox is a mat-forming perennial, usually less than 5 inches tall. The small flowers have five sepals and vary from nearly white to lavender in color. At the height of their bloom, the flowers may nearly cover the plant.

The trail climbs above timberline 0.5 mile past the viewpoint. After another 0.1 mile you'll reach the junction with the Loowit Trail, at 4,750 feet elevation. Return the way you came.

OPTIONS: You can make a 13.4-mile loop hike by turning left at the junction of the Butte Camp and Loowit Trails and following the Loowit Trail northwest to its junction with the Sheep Canyon Trail. Then turn left and descend northwesterly along the Sheep Canyon Trail to a junction with the Toutle Trail. Turn left again onto the Toutle Trail and follow it south and east, passing Blue Lake Trailhead, back to the junction where you started up the Butte Camp Trail. Then head south, staying on the Toutle Trail, to Redrock Pass, completing the loop.

Upper and Lower Ape Cave (Trails 239, 239A, 239B)

HIGHLIGHTS: The longest known lava tube cave in North America, Ape Cave offers a challenging scramble with a surface return trail along its upper portion, while Lower Ape Cave is an easier out-and-back underground hike.

START: Ape's Headquarters.

DISTANCE: 4.2-mile day hike with a 2.5-mile loop (upper section) and 1.7-mile out-and-back trail (lower section).

DIFFICULTY: When gauged by hiking standards, the upper cave is very strenuous and the lower is moderate.

SEASON: May through October.

TOTAL CLIMBING: Upper Ape Cave's exit is 360 feet higher than the main entrance, but you climb over several piles of boulders along the way for a total elevation gain of around 600 feet. You descend approximately 300 feet in the lower cave.

TRAILHEAD ELEVATION: 2,120 feet.

PERMITS: Northwest Forest Pass.

MAPS: Mount St. Helens National Volcanic Monument, aka Brown Map, and Mt. Mitchell USGS quad show the cave entrances but nothing else.

SPECIAL CONSIDERATIONS: There is no trail in Upper Ape Cave, and you must climb over and through several piles of boulders that have fallen from the sides and ceiling. The 8-foot-high vertical wall at Lava Falls must also be negotiated. There is no natural light in the cave, so each person should have at least two good sources of light along. Headlamps are best because in many places the use of both hands is necessary. Without light, getting through this cave is virtually impossible. The temperature of the cave is about 42 degrees year-round. Much of the time the cave drips almost everywhere, making the humidity nearly 100 percent, so dress for cool, damp conditions. If you wear glasses, be sure to put antifog on the lenses or they will be steamed up most of the time. Unless you have experience exploring unlit caves, don't attempt Upper Ape Cave alone or without a competent leader. Less ambitious cavers can explore the lower cave with few problems.

PARKING AND TRAILHEAD FACILITIES: You'll find ample parking and restrooms at the trailhead. Ape's Headquarters at the trailhead is an information station and a rental shop for the lanterns that many hikers use inside Ape Cave. Don't depend on getting your lighting equipment

Upper and Lower Ape Cave (Trails 239, 239A, 239B)

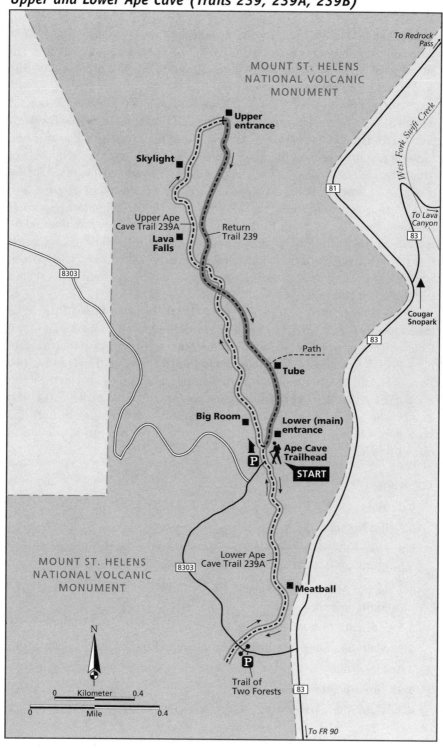

To Redrock Pass

MOUNT ST. HELENS
NATIONAL VOLCANIC
MONUMENT

West Fork Swift Creek

Upper entrance

Skylight

81

Upper Ape
Cave Trail 239A

To Lava
Canyon

83

Return
Trail 239

Lava
Falls

8303

Cougar
Snopark

83

Path

Tube

Big Room

Lower (main)
entrance

P

Ape Cave
Trailhead

START

MOUNT ST. HELENS
NATIONAL VOLCANIC
MONUMENT

Lower Ape
Cave Trail 239A

8303

Meatball

N

P

Trail of
Two Forests

83

0   Kilometer   0.4

0   Mile   0.4

To FR 90

here, however, unless you're sure the headquarters is open; call (360) 247–3900.

FINDING THE TRAILHEAD: Head north from Portland on Interstate 5 to exit 21 at Woodland, Washington; from Seattle, drive south on I–5 approximately 150 miles to exit 21. Then follow Washington Route 503 (which becomes WA 503 Spur) for 27.5 miles east to Cougar.

About 4 miles west of Cougar (1 mile east of Jack's Restaurant), the old Reese's Store is on the left side of the highway. The Reese family, the first people to reach the floor of Ape Cave, once ran this store, which is no longer in use. In times past the store was the place that climbers attempting the south side of Mount St. Helens registered. The climbing register box is still on the wall of the store. This historic building is on private property; please do not trespass.

Continue east from Cougar on WA 503 Spur. In 3.1 miles, just after passing the spillway for the Swift Reservoir Dam, you will notice a lava flow on the left side of the highway. This flow is representative of the flow of cave basalt that formed Ape Cave, as well as several other caves in the area. The spillway washed out in April 2002, possibly when some of its water found its way into and through a lava tube.

Continue east on WA 503 Spur, which shortly becomes Forest Road 90 at the Skamania County line, to its junction with Forest Road 83, 6.8 miles from Cougar. Turn left onto FR 83, continue for 2 miles, then turn left (north) again onto Forest Road 8303. Continue 1 mile north, passing the Trail of Two Forests parking area, to the entrance to the Ape Cave parking area on the right; it's marked with a sign. The trailhead is at the far end of the parking area, next to a building called Ape's Headquarters. From November through April the snow gate 0.8 mile from Ape Cave is generally closed and locked, adding an extra 1.6 miles to your hike.

KEY POINTS:

0.0 Main Ape Cave entrance (GPS 46 06.336 N 122 12.782 W).

0.2 Big Room.

0.8 Lava Falls.

1.0 Skylight.

1.2 Upper Ape Cave entrance (GPS 46 07.424 N 122 12.977 W). Head south on trail.

2.3 Side path to small lava tube. Continue straight (south).

2.5 Main Ape Cave entrance and entrance to Lower Cave.

3.0 Meatball.

3.35 Turnaround point.

4.2 Main Ape Cave entrance (GPS 46 06.336 N 122 12.782 W).

THE HIKE: Although other caves were known in the area as early as the 1890s, Ape Cave was not discovered until the mid-twentieth century. Probably in November or December 1951—the exact date has been lost to time—a logger by the name of Lawrence Johnson found the main entrance to Ape Cave. Johnson descended a short distance into it by climbing down a handy tree trunk. He then tossed rocks into the darkness and realized that he had found a much larger cave than could be seen from the surface. Johnson contacted the Reese family, who owned and operated a store a few miles west of the town of Cougar and were avid cavers. A few days later Leonard Reese was the first person to be lowered to the floor of Ape Cave.

Ape Cave was formed approximately 1,950 years ago by a lava flow that originated from Mount St. Helens. This flow's unique form of lava called cave basalt constructed the 12,810 feet of passages that make up the cave. Cave basalt is a form of *pahoehoe* (a Hawaiian word pronounced *pah-hoey-hoey*)—a low-silica-content lava. In the case of Ape Cave, this very fluid pahoehoe lava flow was deepened as it flowed down a preexisting streambed; the flow rate increased, and thus it stayed hotter than the surrounding lava flow. The lava along the sides of the streambed as well as a crust over the top cooled enough to solidify, encasing the lava stream inside. Then the remaining liquid lava flowed on out of the tube, leaving the longest lava tube cave known in North America.

At some time, possibly about 1480, a sandy lahar flowed into the cave's main entrance. This lahar filled portions of Lower Ape Cave, blocking it about 4,000 feet below (south of) the main entrance and leaving the sand and bits of light-colored pumice we see today.

From the parking area walk north between the restrooms and Ape's Headquarters. A short distance along the paved trail, you will reach the main entrance to Ape Cave. This is the lower entrance for Upper Ape Cave and the only entrance to Lower Ape Cave. Stop at the open-air shelter and read the informational signs inside before descending into the cave.

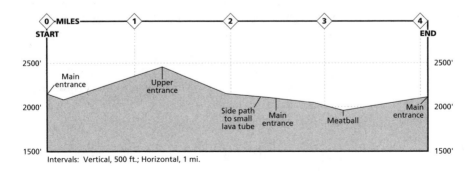

Intervals: Vertical, 500 ft.; Horizontal, 1 mi.

A hiker in Upper Ape Cave

Descend the two sets of stairs into the cave. It's a good idea to stop at the top of the second set of steps and let your eyes adjust to the lack of light before climbing on down to the cave floor. At the bottom of the second set of stairs is a sign pointing north to the upper cave, south to the lower. This is the point to stop and decide which section of the cave to do. If you are not sure of your caving skill, head into the lower cave described below.

If you're up for the challenging upper cave, the next 1.2 miles of this hike is through a lava tube cave with no trail. Turn on your headlamp and head north over the rough cave floor. About 400 feet up the upper cave is the Big Room, which is the largest open area in the cave and another turnaround point for the inexperienced. At the northwest corner of the Big Room, a short (about 160 feet long) side passage leaves the main cave. From here on you climb over, under, and through the boulder-strewn cave for about 0.6 mile to Lava Falls. In some locations the piles of boulders reach well over halfway to the roof of the cave.

On the right side of the cave, the thin veneer of basalt has crumbled off in places, exposing the redrock cinders that were part of the old streambed down which the lava flowed. The glaze on parts of the cave ceiling—in some cases rocks have fallen from the ceiling—is a product of the burning of superheated volcanic gasses. This happened as the flow diminished and no longer filled the cave completely. Some of this glaze flowed or dripped enough to form small stalagmites and stalactites.

In many parts of Ape Cave, you may notice that the walls and ceiling appear to sparkle in the light of your headlamp or flashlight. Tiny water droplets that are held in place by a phenomenon known as lava tube slime cause this sparkling. This odd slime forms in lava tube caves for reasons that are not yet well understood.

Lava Falls is a vertical 8-foot semicircular wall that you must climb to continue on up the cave. There are hand- and footholds, but they can be hard to find. A quarter mile farther up the twisting cave you will come to the Skylight, a place where the thin crust of lava covering the cave has collapsed, leaving an opening to the outside. The light from the outside, which descends through the opening in the cave ceiling, is a welcome sight for those not used to being in the absolute darkness of a cave. You are now 1 mile from the trailhead and have 0.2 mile to go before reaching the upper entrance, where you exit the cave. For now continue up the cave and plunge back into the darkness. More light is seen ahead in about another 300 yards, and soon you reach the Upper Ape Cave entrance at 2,480 feet elevation; this is not the end of the cave, but it is your exit point. (The cave continues north for about another 500 feet to the point where a lava seal blocks it.) Climb the two metal ladders and reenter the outside world.

Above the ladders climb the moss-covered lava for a few feet, then head south on the return trail. The path soon passes a small collapsed lava tube and enters a young forest of Douglas fir (*Pseudotsuga menziesii*), noble fir (*Abies procera*), western red cedar (*Thuja plicata*), western hemlock (*Tsuga heterophylla*), and vine maple (*Acer circinatum*), with a scattering of western white pine (*Pinus monticola*). The tread descends gently and follows an abandoned roadbed for a short distance, soon bearing right to enter a semi-open area that was logged long ago. The ground in the open area is nearly covered with bear grass (*Xerophyllum tenax*). In many places the trail crosses short sections of pahoehoe lava, whose surface looks like pieces of rope laid side by side usually in an arced position.

About a mile from the upper entrance, 2.2 miles from the starting point, the trail rounds the end of a lava flow. Soon you enter a flat sandy area. A couple of hundred yards in, a side path turns to the left (east). This path goes a few feet to the entrance of another small lava tube, then continues along the side of a lava flow for a short distance before ending. You continue south on the main trail, past the path and across the sand. The trail may be hard to see here, but there are usually human tracks on it.

The Skylight

Shortly the trail enters an area that was burned in a 1998 arson-caused fire. The tread crosses a couple of streambeds that are usually dry. A few more yards of hiking through the forest takes you to the main entrance of Ape Cave and parking area. The Upper Ape Cave Trail is maintained by the Oregon Grotto of the National Speleological Society.

If you are still up for more underground hiking, descend into the main cave entrance once again and turn left at the sign to enter the Lower Cave.

The lower section of Ape Cave is a far easier hike than is the upper section. This section of the cave is very popular, so traffic may be heavy. The main hazard in this part of the cave is the darkness. As with the upper section, two good sources of light are recommended for each person entering the lower cave. Because hiking this section requires little or no use of your hands, a lantern makes a good light source; I like to wear a headlamp as well. The cave floor is generally fairly smooth, but there are rocks lying on it that can be real shin busters; at one spot you must step down about 1.5 feet, and at another very tall hikers may have to duck for a low ceiling.

About 150 yards into the lower cave, if you are walking close to the left wall (most hikers do), comes the 1.5-foot step down. This is likely the only place in this section of the cave where you may want to use your hand for balance.

Much of the cave features horizontal "flow marks" on the walls. These flow marks indicate the levels at which lava flowed through the cave as the volcano's output diminished after the cave was originally formed.

Half a mile from the cave entrance, the Meatball comes into view overhead. This is the last and largest of several boulders that are stuck overhead. The round Meatball is a chunk of lava that was being rafted along while the molten lava was still flowing and became stuck in a narrow spot of the cave.

The cave divides into upper and lower passages 0.2 mile past the Meatball. Continue on a short distance in the lower passage. The passage quickly gets smaller and lower, as a sand deposit (which was washed into the cave by the lahar) fills it from the floor up. Soon you will be on your hands and knees. This is as far as most people go in the cave. If you crawl and slither any farther, be very careful not to go too far and get stuck. Don't crawl into the last section if you are alone. A person who gets stuck here could easily die from hypothermia. The upper passage is difficult to enter, and drop-offs in its floor make it very dangerous. When you are finished taking in the sights of the lower cave, turn around and retrace your route back to the main entrance.

Even though Ape Cave is plugged by sand at this point, it's believed that the tube extends on downslope for a considerable distance. Oly's Cave (about 2 miles to the south-southwest) is thought to be part of the same lava tube.

OPTIONS: After exploring either or both sections of Ape Cave to your satisfaction, you may want to make the short interpretive loop hike around the Trail of Two Forests. To reach the Trail of Two Forests parking area, drive south (back the way you came in) from the Ape Cave parking area for 0.8 mile on FR 8303. Then turn west (right) and enter the parking area.

Leaving the parking area, walk south for 45 yards on the paved trail to the junction and the beginning of the boardwalk. Bear left at the junction and go another 40 yards to a sign explaining the return of the forest after the eruption and lava flow 2,000 years ago. Soon another sign explains how moss breaks down lava so that other plants can take root.

A bit farther along, a paved path to the right leads 10 yards to the exit from the Crawl, which is a horizontal tree mold about 50 feet long and about 2.5 feet in diameter. It was formed when the hot lava surrounded a fallen tree. The tree burned and rotted away after the lava solidified, leaving a round hole through the rock. Read the signboards just ahead for more information.

The Crawl will probably be the high point of this hike if you have children along. The entrance for the Crawl is about 50 yards ahead on the trail. It can

Exiting the Crawl at Trail of Two Forests

easily be seen across the lava flow, to your left, from the end of the side path. If you have small children, it's best to leave an adult at the exit and send the children with another adult ahead to the entrance. This way you can talk the kids through the short cave. Lights are not necessary—the opening is straight and can be seen through. Be very careful at the entrance and exit, because it's possible to fall from the metal steps to the rocks below.

When you are finished with the Crawl, continue another 40 yards past the entrance to a sign explaining a lava log dam. One hundred yards beyond the log dam, a small lava tube cave is visible to your right out on the moss-covered lava flow. A short distance farther brings you to the junction where you got on the boardwalk. Turn left and walk the 45 yards back to the parking area on the paved trail.

Allow plenty of time to read the very informative signs along this trail. If you hike this path quietly, very early in the morning, you may see one or more of the many cottontail rabbits (*Sylvilagus* spp.) that inhabit the area.

9 Marble Mountain Snopark (Trails 245E, 216B, 245A)

HIGHLIGHTS: The trip to June Lake is one of the most popular ski tours from the Marble Mountain Snopark. If the snow is good, the skiing is easy. Other skiing and snowshoeing options are available, and the snopark also serves as a base for hiking and climbing trips.

START: Marble Mountain Snopark parking area.

DISTANCE: 4.4-mile out-and-back day ski.

DIFFICULTY: Moderate.

SEASON: Mid-December through mid-March.

TOTAL CLIMBING: About 500 feet.

TRAILHEAD ELEVATION: 2,670 feet.

PERMITS: A snopark permit is needed to leave your vehicle at Marble Mountain Snopark during the ski season. A Northwest Forest Pass is required to park at June Lake Trailhead. If you plan to make the winter climb from Marble Mountain Snopark to the summit of Mount St. Helens, a climbing permit is also required.

MAPS: Green Trails Mount St. Helens NW, Wash NO 364 S, is the only map I have found that shows all of the ski trails at Marble Mountain.

SPECIAL CONSIDERATIONS: Be prepared for wet conditions. The Pine Marten, June Lake, and Marble Loop Trails are closed to motorized traffic, but snowmobile traffic is allowed on Forest Road 83 east of the snow gate and on several other trails in the area. If you are a snowshoer rather than a skier, please don't walk in the ski tracks and mess them up for skiers. It's easy to walk a foot or two to the side, stepping across the tracks if need be—in fact, it's fun to break your own snowshoe trail.

PARKING AND TRAILHEAD FACILITIES: There are two large parking areas at Marble Mountain Snopark, one on each side of FR 83. The main parking area and the trailhead for the Pine Marten Trail is to the left (north) at the snow gate that blocks FR 83 east of the snopark to wheeled vehicles in winter. There are restrooms and a warming cabin at this parking area.

The parking area on the right (south) side of FR 83 has adequate parking but no other facilities and is the trailhead for Marble Loop.

Marble Mountain Snopark (Trails 245E, 216B, 245A)

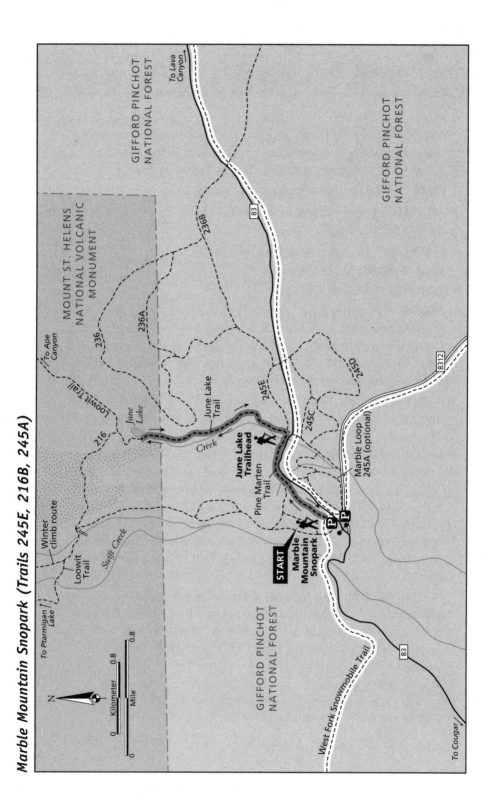

FINDING THE SNOPARK: From Seattle, drive south on Interstate 5 for approximately 150 miles to Woodland; from Portland, take I–5 north to Woodland. Then take exit 21 and drive east on Washington Route 503 (which becomes WA 503 Spur) through Cougar. WA 503 Spur becomes Forest Road 90 east of Cougar at the Skamania County line. Turn left off FR 90, 34.8 miles east of I–5 (6.8 miles east of Cougar), onto FR 83. Follow FR 83 for 4.6 miles to Marble Mountain Snopark.

KEY POINTS:

0.0 Marble Mountain Snopark parking area (GPS 46 07.879 N 122 10.223 W).

0.6 Junction with Rock Pit Ski Trail (GPS 46 08.173 N 122 09.888 W). Continue straight (northeast).

1.1 Junction with June Lake Trail (GPS 46 08.136 N 122 09.437 W). Turn left (north).

2.2 June Lake.

4.4 Marble Mountain Snopark parking area (GPS 46 07.879 N 122 10.223 W).

THE SKI: Marble Mountain Snopark is the hub for snowmobilers, cross-country skiers, and snowshoers on the southern slopes of Mount St. Helens. Because of its relatively low elevation, it has a fairly short season: Adequate snow cover for skiing can usually be found from December through March most years. The snow at the snopark is seldom very dry and often changeable, so it's generally best to be riding on no-wax skis. Most days are skiable here if you're prepared for the conditions, but some days are definitely better than others.

To most of us snow is simply water that is frozen when it falls from the clouds. In fact there is much more to snow, and all of it affects the quality of skiing you will experience at any given time.

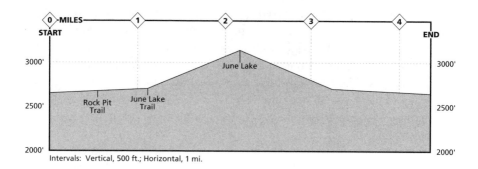

Intervals: Vertical, 500 ft.; Horizontal, 1 mi.

Like raindrops, snow crystals form around tiny particles of foreign matter, such as dust particles in the atmosphere. Snow is formed when water vapor precipitates from the atmosphere and sticks to these particles. Even though nearly all these crystals have a hexagonal (six-sided) shape, snow falls in many shapes and sizes. Snowflakes may fall as grains that feel almost like sand, as feathery crystals 0.5 inch across, or almost anything in between. Often these crystals cling together to form large compound snowflakes.

The density of new-fallen snow (how dry and light or wet and heavy it is) depends on the weather conditions. The lowest-density snow falls under moderately cold and very calm conditions. Under very cold conditions, snow will fall fine and granular with a slightly higher density. In general, however, the higher the temperature, the wetter and denser the new-fallen snow.

As soon as the snow reaches the ground, it begins to change. Both the temperature and the pressure from the snow stacked above affect the rate of this change. When the temperature is near freezing, the change is rapid; lower temperatures slow the process. In fact, when the temperature reaches about forty degrees below zero, the process nearly stops. First the crystals settle and break under the weight of the snow above them. Under warm conditions (at or near freezing), the points of the crystals may be quickly dulled, causing them to become much more rounded and shrink in size in less than a day. These conditions will make it necessary to rewax with a softer wax if you are on waxable skis, but they are no problem for waxless skis.

As they thaw and refreeze, the crystals that began as snowflakes are eventually re-formed into larger but still-rounded crystals of corn or spring snow. Skiing on corn snow requires very soft ski wax or even klister (a very soft wax that comes in a tube, like toothpaste) to make any progress at all with waxable skis.

Surface hoar, another form of ice crystal, is sometimes deposited on the surface of the snow on clear, cold nights. These feathery crystals sparkle brightly in the sunlight or in the beam of a headlamp. The crystals are sharp pointed and offer good traction for waxable skis. On top of a stable snowpack, they make for excellent, fast skiing.

When water vapor is transferred from one part of the snowpack to another, another type of metamorphosis takes place. The vapor is deposited in a form that is different from the original snow—as faceted ice crystals. If this process continues for long enough, the crystals may grow to considerable size and form into cup shapes. These crystals form a very weak structure. They become very soft when wet and lose all strength when crushed. Called depth hoar, this condition causes the snowpack to be very unstable and often leads to very high avalanche danger.

Marble Mountain itself, by the way, is a shield volcano composed of three scoria cones, rising to 3,537 feet elevation, approximately 1 mile southwest of

Marble Mountain Snopark warming hut

the snopark. The peaks are part of an ancient chain of volcanoes that extends south from Mount St. Helens to the Columbia River. Marble Mountain last erupted about 160,000 years ago.

The Pine Marten Ski Trail leaves from the northeast corner of the Marble Mountain Snopark parking area. In a short distance you'll cross the West Fork Snowmobile Trail as you head northeast through the second-growth forest. This area was logged some years ago, and many of the stumps remain. The young forest is predominantly Douglas fir (*Pseudotsuga menziesii*), but there are quite a few western hemlocks (*Tsuga heterophylla*) with their droopy tops mixed in. Noble firs (*Abies procera*) make up a small but significant part of the thick new growth, and an occasional western white pine (*Pinus monticola*) can be found as well.

The route is not completely flat, but rather undulates, never gaining or losing more than a few feet at a time. At 0.6 mile from the trailhead, you reach the junction with the Rock Pit Ski Trail, which turns left (west) to eventually join the Swift Creek Trail; you stay straight on the Pine Marten Trail. This junction is next to FR 83, which is a groomed snowmobile route in winter. For the next 0.4 mile, the Pine Marten Trail parallels FR 83 but stays out of sight of the road. One mile from the trailhead, the trail joins the road for a few yards to cross one of the forks of Swift Creek. Then you cut back into the young timber again for about 0.1 mile to the junction with the June Lake Trail. Turn left (north) onto the June Lake Trail and follow it north for a short distance to the June Lake Trailhead parking area. The ski trail follows the access road to June Lake Trailhead.

From here on you gain elevation steadily but gently. Leaving the trailhead, the trail heads north a few yards to the right of a creek. As you ascend gently through the second-growth forest of noble fir, Pacific silver fir (*Abies amabilis*), Douglas fir, and western hemlock, glimpses of the smooth, snow-covered south slopes of Mount St. Helens appear ahead. The path winds up through the woods, sometimes close to the creek and at other times some distance away.

A rough, relatively young, *aa* lava flow comes into view, to the left across the creek, 0.8 mile from June Lake Trailhead. (*Aa* is a Hawaiian term referring to lava with a rough, broken surface.) Here the view of the mountain really opens up. Soon you will climb over a small rise, before descending a few feet to a small flat. Beyond the flat area the trail climbs a few yards to a bridge over the outlet of June Lake. The lake is in view to the right only a few yards away.

Steep hills and cliffs surround June Lake, elevation 3,130 feet, on three sides. The hills next to the lake have never been logged, so a beautiful old-growth forest of Douglas fir, Pacific silver fir, noble fir, and western hemlock remains around about two-thirds of the shoreline. A waterfall plunges into the lake on the northeast side. Smaller falls enter the lake in a couple of other spots. June Lake is the destination of most of the people on this trail and is your turn-around point, although the trail continues to climb on the west side of the lake, winding its way up another 0.3 mile and 270 feet in elevation to a junction with the Loowit Trail.

OPTIONS: The Marble Loop is a short easy ski tour from the south parking area (GPS 46 07.762 N 122 10.188 W; elevation 2,610 feet) at Marble Mountain Snopark. The route undulates slightly but is nearly level. This is an excellent beginner trip if the snow conditions are good.

Like the Pine Marten Trail, the whole length of the Marble Loop is through second-growth forest. The route leads northeast from the parking area, passing the junction with the return route in just a few yards. You reach a junction with the Willow Trail 0.4 mile from the trailhead; a left at this junction would take you about 0.2 mile to FR 83, which is a groomed snowmobile trail in winter. Instead turn right and ski south on the combined Willow and Marble Loop Trails for 0.1 mile to another junction. The Willow Trail turns left (east) to join several other short, easy loop trails. Continue south from the junction on the Marble Loop, leaving the Willow Trail.

June Lake

The route follows a small stream for a short distance. If you turn around and look north here, the upper part of Mount St. Helens is in view. Soon the trail turns to the southwest and quickly reaches a junction with the Snomo Trail, which leads a short distance southwest to Forest Road 8312—another snowmobile route. Bear right at the junction and ski another 0.3 mile back to the parking area.

HIKING THE AREA: If you don't make it up to Marble Mountain in winter, all is not lost. You can continue east for 1.1 miles along FR 83 from the snopark to June Lake Trailhead, which is on the left side of the road. From there you can hike the easy trail to June Lake, as described above, and maybe on up to the junction with the Loowit Trail. In summer the June Lake Trail offers a wide variety of flowers. Common red paintbrush (*Castilleja miniata*) and lupines (*Lupinus* spp.) are the most common, but there is also the leopard lily (*Lilium columbianum*), aka tiger lily and Columbia lily. This beautiful perennial grows 3 or more feet tall. The flowers are bright orange in color with red to purple spots and petals that turn backward.

If you walk the Marble Loop in summer, you stand a good chance of encountering Roosevelt elk (*Cervus elaphus roosevelti*). These large animals are hard to spot in the dense brush that covers much of the area, but by walking slowly and quietly your chances improve. Sunrise offers the best opportunity for finding elk. Along the poorly defined paths, huckleberries often offer a tasty treat by late July. In the moist areas near the creek or a spring, look for musk flowers (*Mimulus moschatus*). These perennial relatives of the monkey flower offer up their bright yellow blooms in July. In a few spots white bog orchids (*Habenaria dilatata*) show up in the same type of setting.

During winter and early spring, when the road to Climbers Bivouac is closed and blocked by snow, Marble Mountain Snopark is the usual starting point for climbs to the summit of Mount St. Helens. This is a much longer route to the summit with an elevation gain of 5,755 feet. The route generally follows Trail 244 from the snopark north to the Loowit Trail. Then it heads west along the Loowit Trail, crossing Swift Creek above Chocolate Falls. From there it climbs north-northwest to join the Monitor Ridge route at about 7,500 feet elevation. Although this route is not technical by mountaineering standards, any winter climb is a serious undertaking. Take along all the equipment, food, and water that you will need to spend one or more nights here should you be stranded by the weather or an accident. Don't take this climb lightly; it can be fairly easy, but if the weather turns bad you could be in a struggle for your life. At times there is considerable avalanche danger along this route.

HIGHLIGHTS: A popular ski trail that sees some horse use, the Kalama Ski Trail is used as an access trail or combined with other trails to make loops. The trail is almost always in the woods and atop lahar deposits.

START: Kalama Horse Camp Trailhead.

DISTANCE: 10.9-mile shuttle day hike or backpack, with loop option.

DIFFICULTY: Moderate.

SEASON: June through October for hiking; December through March for skiing.

TOTAL CLIMBING: 1,240 feet.

TRAILHEAD ELEVATION: 2,020 feet.

PERMITS: Northwest Forest Pass or snopark permit, depending on the time of year.

MAPS: Goat Mountain and Mount St. Helens USGS quads cover the area, but this trail is not shown.

SPECIAL CONSIDERATIONS: Be prepared for wet conditions. If you are a snowshoer rather than a skier, please don't walk in the ski tracks. Instead walk a foot or two to the side, stepping across the tracks if you need to.

PARKING AND TRAILHEAD FACILITIES: You'll find water for horses, restrooms, and adequate parking at the trailhead. Parties without livestock are asked not to camp at the Kalama Horse Camp Campground.

FINDING THE TRAILHEAD: To reach Kalama Horse Camp, take exit 21 off Interstate 5 at Woodland (21 miles north of the Columbia River Bridge or approximately 150 miles south of Seattle). Then drive east on Washington Route 503 (which becomes WA 503 Spur at a junction 23 miles from I–5) for 26.5 miles

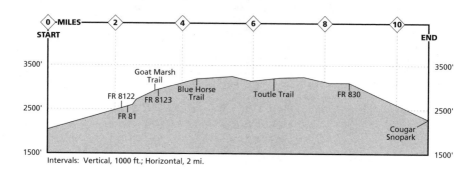

Kalama Ski Trail (Trail 231)

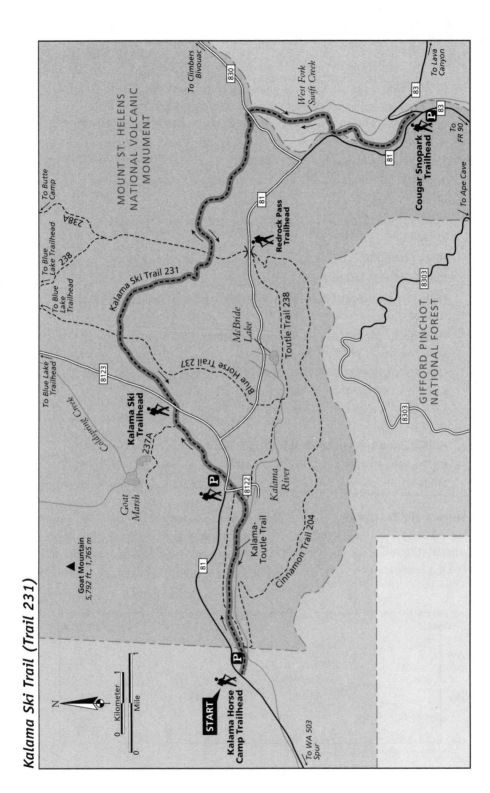

to the junction with Forest Road 81. Turn left (north) onto FR 81 and follow it for 8.6 miles to Kalama Horse Camp on the right; a sign marks the entrance.

KEY POINTS:

- **0.0** Kalama Horse Camp Trailhead (GPS 46 08.518 N 122 19.413 W).
- **0.2** Bear left (northeast) on Kalama Ski Trail, leaving Toutle Trail.
- **0.8** Rejoin Toutle Trail.
- **2.0** Bear left (northeast) on Kalama Ski Trail, again leaving Toutle Trail.
- **2.2** Cross FR 8122.
- **2.3** Cross FR 81.
- **3.1** Junction with Goat Marsh Trail (GPS 46 09.276 N 122 16.378 W). Bear right (east) on Kalama Ski Trail.
- **3.3** Cross FR 8123 (GPS 46 09.295 N 122 16.115 W).
- **4.3** Junction with Blue Horse Trail. Continue straight (east).
- **6.3** Junction with Toutle Trail (GPS 46 08.993 W 122 14.116 W). Continue straight (east).
- **8.5** Cross FR 830 (Climbers Bivouac Road).
- **10.9** Cougar Snopark (GPS 46 07.126 W 122 12.382 W).

THE HIKE: Most of the Kalama Ski Trail runs atop lahar deposits of varying ages, which were laid down during historic eruptions of Mount St. Helens. Note the spacing, type, and size of the trees as you hike and see if you can tell the relative age of the particular deposit you that are crossing. Recent deposits feature few trees, and those that exist are widely spaced. They may also show scars of the lahar. When the deposit has aged a century or so, lodgepole pine usually becomes the dominant species, although the trees will not be very large. After several centuries the soil will have gained enough organic matter to support a mature forest of Douglas and true firs, and finally the shade-tolerant hemlock will join in to create a climax forest.

Leaving Kalama Horse Camp Trailhead, the wide, well-marked Kalama Ski Trail and the Toutle Trail follow the same route eastward, descending a few feet through the forest. In about 0.2 mile and after crossing a wooden bridge, the trail forks. Your route, the Kalama Ski Trail, bears left (northeast) and climbs gently, while the Toutle Trail follows the Kalama River. For the next 0.6 mile, the trails parallel each other. The ski trail, which is marked with blue-diamond cross-country ski markers, climbs a gentle rounded ridge away from the river.

Just before rejoining the Toutle Trail, a path bears left off the ski trail. This path is easy to follow and rejoins the Kalama Ski Trail a couple of miles farther east, close to FR 8122. The unmarked path makes an excellent return route for hikers wishing to make 5.6-mile loop. To continue on the route, rejoin the Toutle Trail at 0.8 mile.

This dense fir and pine forest is the habitat of the Steller's jay. Common in the coniferous forests of western North America, the Steller's jay (*Cyanocitta stelleri*) is slightly larger than its eastern cousin the blue jay—up to 11 inches long, including the tail. Its general color is a dark blue, but the shoulders, neck, and head are black. Steller's jays are nonmigratory and the only crested jays that live in the Northwest.

The call of the Steller's jay is loud and varied. They are experts at imitating the call of a red-tailed hawk, which they often do. Many times I have looked for a red-tailed hawk after hearing its call, only to learn that the call was made by a Steller's jay. A true opportunist, the jay can be an aggressive thief. I have seen them steal sandwiches from small children when the parents were only a few yards away.

For the next 1.2 miles, both the Kalama Ski Trail and the Toutle Trail follow the bank of the Kalama River. At first the route is well above the river, but by the time the trails split again, the route is only a few feet above river level. At the well-marked junction 2.0 miles from Kalama Horse Camp Trailhead, the Kalama Ski Trail turns to the left again off the Toutle Trail. Follow the trail marked with blue diamonds to the northeast. In about 0.25 mile you will come to the unmarked junction with the path noted earlier. Bear right if you wish to continue on the Kalama Ski Trail; if you're going to make the 5.6-mile loop mentioned above, turn left (west).

A couple of hundred yards farther along the ski trail, you will cross Forest Road 8122, at 2,540 feet elevation. Continue a short distance northeast after crossing the road to cross FR 81. The ski trail then follows Forest Road 590 for a few yards northeast to a large parking area. At the northeast edge of the parking area, piles of dirt and stumps block FR 590.

Notice the oxeye daisies in and close to the parking area. The oxeye daisy (*Chrysanthemum leucanthemum*) is a non-native plant in our region. When you are hiking you will generally only find it close to roads. The tiny seeds are easily transported by vehicles and lug-soled boots; try not to take them with you as you hike. This prolific perennial was introduced from Europe and has become very well established in the northwestern United States. It often outcompetes native plants, especially on disturbed sites such as roadsides. The white flowers with yellow centers bloom at the top of slender stems up to 2 feet tall. While this flower may look good in some settings, it should not be transplanted into areas where it is not present.

The ski trail continues around the obstacles and follows the old roadbed, which is reverting to a trail. The old roadbed here is cut into a deposit of poorly

Oxeye daisy

sorted volcanic debris, put in place here by an ancient lahar. You will climb gently for the next 0.8 mile to the junction with the Goat Marsh Trail. Bear right (east) here on the Kalama Ski Trail.

You're hiking through a mixed-conifer forest of lodgepole pine (*Pinus contorta*), Douglas fir (*Pseudotsuga menziesii*), noble fir (*Abies procera*), and Pacific silver fir. The Latin name for the Pacific silver fir—*Abies amabilis*, which means "lovely fir"—fits this beautiful tree perfectly. It's a straight conifer with a relativity slender trunk for its height. Under the excellent growing conditions found in the Mount St. Helens region, silver firs normally reach 150 to 180 feet tall when mature.

The silver fir's needles are from 0.75 to 1.25 inches long, flat in cross section, and shiny green on their top sides. The lower side of each needle has two thin white bands, giving the tree its silvery appearance. The needles grow from all the way around the stem but turn upward and appear to be bunched on top.

Pacific silver fir cones are dark purple in color and from 3.5 to 5 inches long. Like all true firs, they stand erect from the branch and disintegrate there before falling to the ground, unless the squirrels prematurely clip them off.

Continuing east on the Kalama Ski Trail, reach Forest Road 8123 in 0.2 mile. The route crosses FR 8123, then climbs gently to the northeast through semi-open lodgepole pine forest.

The lodgepole pine is the most common pine in the Mount St. Helens area. The only other tree that can be easily confused with the lodgepole here is the western white pine (*Pinus monticola*). Unlike the western white, which is a five-needled pine, the lodgepole has needles that come out of the twigs in bundles of only two. The lodgepole is the only native two-needled pine in the area. Around Mount St. Helens, lodgepoles usually grow on well-drained sites, such as old lava flows and sandy lahar deposits.

The bark of a lodgepole is usually gray, scaly, and thin. Lodgepole cones are small, usually less than 2 inches long; they may remain on the tree and hold their seeds for several years after maturing. Many of these cones, even though they are mature, won't release their seeds unless a forest fire heats them. A few days after the fire has passed, the cones open, dispersing the seeds into the burned-over area. For this reason lodgepoles are often the first trees to regrow after a forest fire. It's a good thing that lodgepoles are able to do this, because their thin bark allows them to be easily killed by fire.

Along the coastlines of Oregon and Washington, *Pinus contorta* takes on a short, contorted shape—hence the Latin name. Here the tree is called shore pine. In inland areas such as around Mount St. Helens, it is nearly always straight trunked and may reach a height of 100 feet.

One mile farther along the Kalama Ski Trail, you will reach the junction with the Blue Horse Trail. To the left it's 3 miles along the Blue Horse Trail to a junction with the Toutle Trail in Huckleberry Saddle north of Blue Lake. To the right the Blue Horse Trail leads to FR 81 in 2 miles. The Kalama Ski Trail crosses the Blue Horse Trail and follows the blue diamonds heading east.

Past this junction the route is not well maintained for hiking, but it is easy to follow. There is another path to the left 0.3 mile past the junction with the horse trail. Don't take this path; instead follow the route marked with diamonds, heading southeast.

In another 0.3 mile you will come to an open area caused by a 1980 lahar. There may be no trail across the lahar deposit, so head southeast; the route will show up again as you enter the timber. The trail continues through large timber and semi-open areas for another 1.4 miles to the junction with the Toutle Trail. The route may be hard to spot in the open areas; watch for the blue diamonds.

At the junction, elevation 3,210 feet, the Toutle Trail crosses the Kalama Ski Trail for the last time. If you turned right onto the Toutle Trail, Redrock Pass Trailhead would be about 0.5 mile to the south. To continue on the Kalama Ski Trail, head east at the junction, through the young forest of noble, Pacific silver, and Douglas firs, along with some western hemlock (*Tsuga heterophylla*).

Foxglove

The drooping central leader (at the very top of the tree) is the easiest way to identify a hemlock from a distance. The state tree of Washington, the western hemlock grows best at lower elevations in wet, cool areas. Around Mount St. Helens, much of the countryside provides this nearly perfect habitat. Mature trees here can attain heights of 170 to 200 feet and live for more than 500 years if they are not disturbed by volcanic activities. The western hemlock is a very shade-tolerant species and prefers sites where the soil is heavy in humus content; it is thus seldom a pioneer tree. Western hemlock wood is very heavy when wet and may not even float on water.

A quarter mile from the junction, the route bears left (northeast) along the side of an area of dead trees that were killed by a 1980 lahar. Cardwell's penstemon (*Penstemon cardwellii*) is common along the trail in this area. Soon the trail heads east again, then gradually bends around to the southeast as it descends gently, crossing an old lava flow.

At 1.5 miles from the last junction with the Toutle Trail, the route enters an area that was logged many years ago. The old skid roads in this area can be confusing. The ski trail follows sections of these old roads as it winds its way through this semi-open area. If it weren't for the blue diamonds, it would be easy to lose the route here. The smooth south slopes of Mount St. Helens loom above to the north. Leaving the logged area, the ski trail follows an abandoned roadbed to Forest Road 830, which leads to the Climbers Bivouac. From here to the Cougar Snopark, the route receives less stock traffic and may be a little overgrown in spots.

The Kalama Ski Trail crosses FR 830, at 3,150 feet elevation, and soon descends to the south. The route crosses another road in about 0.25 mile, then drops gently along a logged section. From here on the ski trail follows an abandoned road all the way down to Cougar Snopark. Along the way you will pass three marked ski trails that turn to the right and lead to FR 81. Shortly before reaching the snopark, the trail narrows along a ridge; the roadbed has washed away at this point. Cougar Snopark, elevation 2,300 feet, is reached 2.4 miles after crossing FR 830.

Just before reaching the snopark, the route passes through a patch of foxglove. A large, usually biennial herb up to 6 feet tall, foxglove (*Digitalis purpurea*) is an import from Europe that has been introduced into the Northwest. Its pink-purple (sometimes white), bell-shaped flowers bloom from the upper portion of the stalk in July.

OPTIONS: The loop mentioned makes a good return for the lower section of the Kalama Ski Trail. Another loop option is to return on the Toutle Trail from the junction 6.3 miles from Kalama Horse Camp. By turning south on the Toutle Trail and following it back, your return trip will be 0.2 mile shorter.

11 Ptarmigan Trail–Monitor Ridge (Trail 216A, 216H)

HIGHLIGHTS: This hike takes you through dense forest and across an open slope with a great view. You'll then make the nontechnical but strenuous climb up the south side of Mount St. Helens to its summit on the rim of the 1980 eruption crater.

START: Climbers Bivouac Trailhead.

DISTANCE: 9.2-mile out-and-back mountain climb.

DIFFICULTY: Strenuous by hiking standards, but easy when considered a mountain climb.

SEASON: June through September.

TOTAL CLIMBING: 4,615 feet.

TRAILHEAD ELEVATION: 3,750 feet.

PERMITS: A Northwest Forest Pass is required to park at the Climbers Bivouac Trailhead; a climbing permit is required if you go above 4,800 feet elevation. The climbing permit also covers the parking.

MAPS: Mount St. Helens National Volcanic Monument, aka Brown Map, Mount St. Helens USGS, or Green Trails Mount St. Helens NW, Wash NO 364 S. All these maps show the Ptarmigan Trail, but none of them has the route marked above 4,800 feet elevation.

SPECIAL CONSIDERATIONS: Some years the road to the Climbers Bivouac may be blocked by snow until mid-June. Check with the Mount St. Helens National Volcanic Monument Headquarters if you are planning an early-season trip. The road may be plowed only one lane wide, so be very cautious while driving. During winter and spring when this road is closed, the usual route to the summit of Mount St. Helens starts at the Marble Mountain Snopark.

While the climb up Monitor Ridge to the summit of Mount St. Helens is not technical, it is a rough scramble much of the way. The weather above timberline is very changeable. It may be warm, clear, and sunny when you leave the trailhead, only to change into a dust storm or even a blizzard by the time you reach the summit. Rain and snow are normal before late June and possible all summer. During sunny weather these south-facing slopes can be very warm and dry. There is no water along this route after the snow melts. Under these conditions take plenty of water with you. Three quarts is not too much. When the route is snow covered, long slides are possible, so take your ice ax and know how to use it. It is often windy on the summit. The wind picks

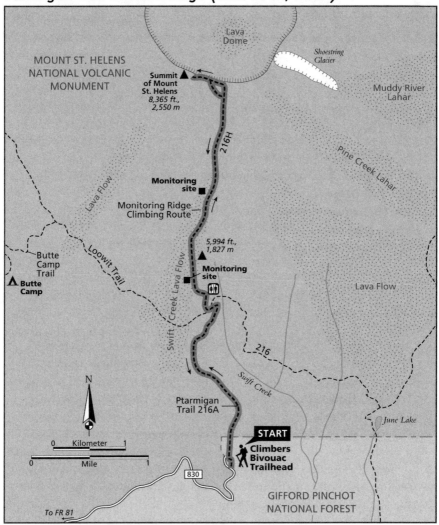

up the fine particles of pumice dust and at times creates minor dust storms. Goggles are almost a necessity under these conditions. Remember to protect your camera from the dust.

PARKING AND TRAILHEAD FACILITIES: There are restrooms and adequate parking at the trailhead. Camping is allowed at Climbers Bivouac.

FINDING THE TRAILHEAD: Head north from Portland or south from Seattle on Interstate 5 to exit 21 at Woodland, Washington (21 miles from the Columbia

River Bridge or about 150 miles from Seattle). Then drive east on Washington Route 503 (which becomes WA 503 Spur, then Forest Road 90) for 34.3 miles, passing Cougar, to the junction with Forest Road 83. Turn left onto FR 83 and follow it for 3.1 miles north to its junction with Forest Road 81. Turn left onto FR 81 and drive northwest for 1.6 miles to the junction with Forest Road 830. Turn right and head northeast on FR 830 for 2.6 miles to Climbers Bivouac Trailhead.

KEY POINTS:

0.0 Climbers Bivouac Trailhead (GPS 46 08.799 N 122 10.991 W).

2.1 Junction with Loowit Trail (GPS 46 09.865 N 122 11.433 W). Continue straight (north).

2.3 Trail ends; climbing route begins.

4.4 Crater rim.

4.6 Summit of Mount St. Helens (GPS 46 11.470 N 122 11.655 W).

9.2 Climbers Bivouac Trailhead (GPS 46 08.799 N 122 10.991 W).

THE HIKE: This route climbs through three of the four life zones encountered in Mount St. Helens National Volcanic Monument. The only place on the mountain where these zones exist at present is on the south side between the Plains of Abraham and the South Fork Toutle River Canyon. The 1980 eruption obliterated them on the north slopes. Even though the south slopes were not drastically affected by the 1980 eruption, they have been affected by other volcanic events over the past few centuries. This has caused the timberline to be at a much lower elevation than you'd expect.

You leave the trailhead in the Canadian Zone, dominated by noble fir (*Abies procera*) and Pacific silver fir (*A. amabilis*) with some Douglas fir (*Pseudotsuga menziesii*). At about 4,600 feet elevation, near the junction with the Loowit Trail, the route enters the smaller and generally more scattered timber of the Hudsonian Zone.

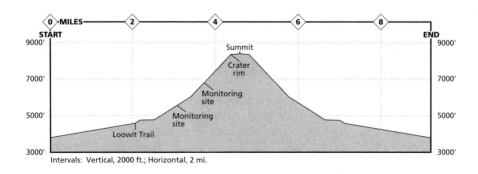

Intervals: Vertical, 2000 ft.; Horizontal, 2 mi.

Avalanche lilies

The Hudsonian Zone is very narrow on Mount St. Helens, because the relatively recent volcanic activity has not allowed enough time for these alpine trees to grow to the elevation that would be normal for this latitude and maritime climate. Subalpine fir (*Abies lasiocarpa*) grows in this narrow belt. On the corresponding south slope of close-by Mount Hood, this zone begins at about 5,500 feet elevation and reaches up to about 6,500 feet. On Mount Adams only about 30 miles to the east, lighter snowfall and plenty of time since the last eruption have allowed the small alpine timber to march up to nearly 8,000 feet elevation on some south-slope ridges. Given enough time without volcanic activity—perhaps a millennium or more—the timberline could reach 6,000 feet or slightly higher on Mount St. Helens.

Shortly you leave the trees behind and get into the harsher, sometimes almost desertlike environment that characterizes the Alpine-Arctic Zone.

The Ptarmigan Trail begins to climb gently to the north as it leaves the parking area at Climbers Bivouac. The route is marked with blue-diamond cross-country ski markers. The wide, well-maintained trail heads north through Canadian Zone forest. Avalanche lilies (*Erythronium montanum*), bunchberries (*Cornus canadensis*), and queencups dot the ground between the bushes and trees.

Growing from slender creeping rhizomes, the queencup (*Clintonia uniflora*) is a small plant, reaching only up to about 6 inches tall. Its white flowers with six petals and yellow stamens emerge from the top of a slender, leafless stalk.

A sign marks the boundary of Mount St. Helens National Volcanic Monument 0.3 mile from the trailhead. The first mile of the trail climbs at a gentle grade, but after that it becomes somewhat steeper. At 1.3 miles is the first good view of Mount St. Helens since you left the parking area. Now bear grass (*Xerophyllum tenax*) shares the openings with black huckleberry bushes (*Vaccinium membranaceum*). The tread gets close to a lava flow 0.3 mile farther along. As you climb, Mount Hood and Mount Adams come into view to the south and east.

To the left of the trail on the sandy ground between the boulders of the lava flow, pink mountain heather (*Phyllodoce empetriformis*), aka pink mountain heath, prospers. The pink mountain heather is a low mat-forming evergreen plant with needlelike leaves. Its small but showy flowers are bell shaped and usually nodding. The pink mountain heather is not a true heather, but resembles it enough to explain the name.

Two miles from the trailhead, the trail makes a switchback to the left. The junction with the Loowit Trail is reached 0.1 mile beyond, at 4,600 feet elevation. Cross the Loowit Trail; just after it, a short path to the right leads to a restroom.

The trail soon bears to the left and leaves the larger timber 0.2 mile from the Loowit Trail, at about 4,750 feet elevation. Then you hike on up through the Hudsonian Zone timber, which in this area isn't much different, species-wise, than the upper Canadian Zone timber below. The trees are just smaller and more scattered. Between the trees much of the volcanic soil—which is mostly sand and rocks—is not covered by vegetation. The trail heads west for a short distance through the small subalpine firs. This is where the trail ends and the climbing route begins.

After heading west for a few yards, the route climbs onto a lava flow. From here up to the pumice slopes near the summit, the route is marked with wood posts. Once you are on the lava flow, turn right and continue to climb to the north along a small ridge. At 5,200 feet elevation you may notice a now unused monitoring site a short distance west of the route. As you scramble up through the boulders, watch for golden-mantled ground squirrels and pikas.

Golden-mantled ground squirrels are common in many areas of Mount St. Helens National Volcanic Monument. Often mistaken for a chipmunk, the golden-mantled ground squirrel (*Spermophilus lateralis*) is an entirely different species. When you are trying to make the distinction between the two, first look at the color. The golden-mantled has a rich yellow-tan head, while the chipmunk's head is brown like the rest of the body. Then check the stripes along the back. If the stripes continue across the head and face, it's a chipmunk; there are no stripes on the golden-mantled's head. The golden-mantled is also larger.

Usually the first indication that there is a pika in the area is the sound of its call. The high-pitched, shrill *eeee* warns the rest of the colony that there is an intruder close by. The pika (*Ochotona princeps*), or coney as it is often called, appears at first glance to be some type of ground squirrel or tiny marmot, but is actually more closely related to rabbits and hares. A full-grown pika may be up to 8 inches long and weigh four ounces. Its coat is gray-brown, becoming lighter on its chest and belly. The pika's short rounded ears, compact body, thick fur, short legs, and lack of a tail help it conserve body heat. Added to its haying habits, these features make the pika very well suited to the harsh environment it inhabits.

Remaining active throughout the year, the pika cuts grasses and other plants and lays them on rocks to dry in the sun before storing them away deep in its burrow between the boulders. This allows the pika to go on about its business below ground, even if the snow above is many feet deep and the temperatures are far below freezing.

The view improves steadily as you gain elevation. Mount Adams is to the east; to the southeast is Mount Hood. If the atmosphere is really clear, you can also see Mount Jefferson slightly to the right of Mount Hood. Swift and Yale Reservoirs are far below to the south and southwest.

The line of posts follows the tiny ridgeline up to 5,400 feet elevation. There are paths on both sides of the small ridge, so you can take your choice of which one to use. Then the line of posts bears slightly left of the ridgeline, and the main path closely follows them. At 6,000 feet elevation the route regains the ridgeline, well above the peak marked 5,994 (elevation) on both the USGS and Green Trails maps. This is a good spot for a rest break.

Below peak 5,994 you may have noticed a strip of green timber reaching higher on the slope than the other timber in the area. It appears that these trees have been at least somewhat protected from volcanic action by the peak. This has allowed them to grow closer to what would be the natural timberline on Mount St. Helens if it weren't such an active young volcano.

The steepest part of the climb is between 6,000 and 7,000 feet elevation. You will scramble up and over several humps on the ridgeline. The route passes another monitoring site at 6,700 feet elevation and reaches the top of the dark lava rocks at 7,000 feet. Above the dark rock the route becomes better defined. The path continues up a light-colored ridge to the base of the pumice slopes at about 7,800 feet elevation.

Lava Dome and new glacier

Usually light tan or nearly white in color, pumice is a solidified form of highly gas-charged lava. Full of tiny bubbles, pumice is light enough to float on water. Most of the upper parts of Mount St. Helens are covered with a layer of pumice ejected by the 1980 eruption, but there was a lot of pumice already here from previous events.

As you climb the pumice slope, you may want to bear to the left where the path forks. The left fork is a shorter way to the summit. The route reaches the crater rim at 8,280 feet elevation. On the rim turn left and climb gently for 0.2 mile to the summit.

Try to allow yourself plenty of time to enjoy the view from the summit, 8,365 feet above sea level. Stay back from the edge of the crater—the loose rock may give away. If there is snow, the cornices that build up along the crater rim may be unstable; don't walk out on them. To the north across the Pumice Plain, look for Spirit Lake and the jagged, nearly naked ridges of the Mount Margaret Backcountry. In the distance Mount Rainier rises above the lesser peaks.

The crater walls show the layering of strata caused by the many volcanic events over the millennia. The black Lava Dome nearly covers the crater floor. Notice the new glacier that is forming behind this dome.

Return the way you came.

OPTIONS: From the summit an alternate descent route can be taken to the southwest. Descend to the junction of the Loowit and Butte Camp Trails, then follow the Butte Camp and Toutle Trails to Redrock Pass Trailhead. This route should only be used when it is completely or nearly completely snow covered to avoid damage to the fragile alpine environment. Descending via this route requires a car shuttle to Redrock Pass Trailhead.

HIGHLIGHTS: The Ape Canyon Trail provides one of the best possible places to observe and study the effects that a large lahar has on the landscape. This route climbs along the edge of the huge Muddy River Lahar, then treats you to a spectacular view down the sharply cut upper gorge of Ape Canyon—and the possibility of being entertained by the marmots that live close by.

START: Ape Canyon Trailhead.

DISTANCE: 9.6-mile out-and-back day hike.

DIFFICULTY: Moderate.

SEASON: Late June through September.

TOTAL CLIMBING: 1,340 feet.

TRAILHEAD ELEVATION: 2,850 feet.

PERMITS: Northwest Forest Pass.

MAPS: Mount St. Helens National Volcanic Monument, aka Brown Map. USGS Mount St. Helens and Smith Creek Butte quads cover the area, but this trail isn't shown.

SPECIAL CONSIDERATIONS: Water sources are very limited along this trail; take all you will need with you. There are a couple of places along this trail that are fairly exposed to falling. If you have children along, keep a close eye on them.

PARKING AND TRAILHEAD FACILITIES: There is parking for several cars but no other facilities at the trailhead. The Lava Canyon Trailhead, a short distance to the east at the end of Forest Road 83, has restrooms.

FINDING THE TRAILHEAD: From Seattle, drive south on Interstate 5 for approximately 150 miles to Woodland; from Portland take I–5 north to Woodland. Then take exit 21 off I–5 and drive east on Washington Route 503 (which becomes WA 503 Spur, then Forest Road 90) through Cougar. Turn left off FR 90, 34.8 miles east of I–5 (6.8 miles east of Cougar), onto FR 83. Follow FR 83 for 10.9 miles to the Lahar Viewpoint parking area, which is on the left (south) side of the road. If you have the time and inclination, take a few moments to stop at Lahar Viewpoint and walk the 0.2-mile-long trail that's located next to it.

The Lahar Viewpoint Trail 241 leaves the parking area heading northeast as a wide gravel path across the lahar debris. Soon the trail turns southeast as you stroll through the scattered small firs and willows that dot the desertlike area. At 0.2 mile from the trailhead, you will reach an interpretive sign at the

Ape Canyon (Trail 234)

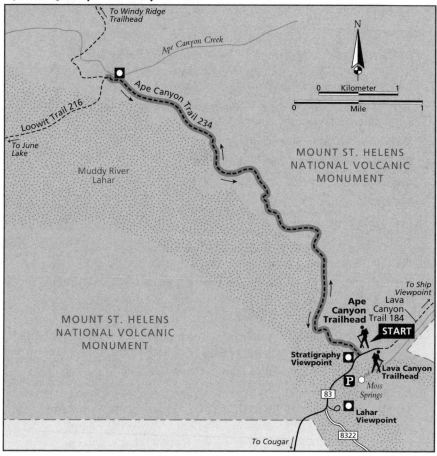

end of the trail. The sign, titled "What Happened Here," describes the events that took place here during the 1980 eruption of Mount St. Helens. As you read this sign, look up the mountain and imagine what it would have been like to be at this spot as the volcano blew.

To continue to Ape Canyon Trailhead, get back onto FR 83, heading east (right). In a short distance you will come to the Moss Springs turnoff. To the right is the Moss Springs parking area, overlooking Moss Springs, the principal source of the Muddy River. It's believed that the water that flows from Moss Springs is meltwater from the Shoestring Glacier, which flows underground from the glacier to this point.

Just past the Moss Springs parking area, on the left (north) side of FR 83, is the Stratigraphy Viewpoint. Here you can see several layers of older volcanic strata that were exposed by the 1980 Muddy River Lahar.

Shortly after passing the Stratigraphy Viewpoint, Ape Canyon Trailhead will be on your left. This trailhead is 11.5 miles from the junction with FR 90 (0.6 mile from Moss Springs).

KEY POINTS:

0.0 Ape Canyon Trailhead (GPS 46 09.917 N 122 05.536 W).

2.6 Cross ridgeline.

4.7 Viewpoint of Ape Canyon.

4.8 Junction with Loowit Trail.

9.6 Ape Canyon Trailhead (GPS 46 09.917 N 122 05.536 W).

THE HIKE: Leaving the trailhead, the Ape Canyon Trail climbs gently. After a short distance the path turns right along the bank of the Muddy River Lahar. The ground you are walking over is made up of the older lahar deposits that were in view from the Stratigraphy Viewpoint, which you may have stopped at just before reaching the trailhead.

Mount St. Helens began its May 18, 1980, eruption slightly more than thirty seconds after 8:32 A.M., removing the top of the beautifully symmetrical peak and the upper portions of the glaciers that clothed it. By 8:34 a pyroclastic surge, made up of volcanic gases, rocks, and ash, had burst over the eastern rim of the mountain's newly formed crater. This boiling, turbulent cloud swiftly descended the eastern and east-southeastern flanks of the mountain. Much of it was funneled down the shallow, narrow, steep valley that held the Shoestring Glacier. The heat of the pyroclastic surge almost instantaneously melted 25 to 30 feet of snow and glacial ice from the surface of the now decapitated Shoestring Glacier.

Within one and a half minutes, the surge descended 5,000 vertical feet, reached the base of the mountain, and spawned a massive lahar. The lahar, a mixture of heated meltwater, ash, sand, pumice, boulders, and (farther down on

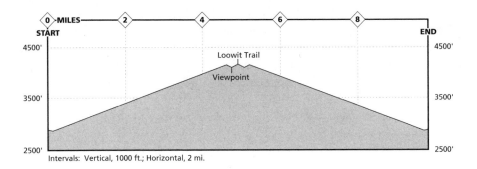

Intervals: Vertical, 1000 ft.; Horizontal, 2 mi.

Mount St. Helens' Shoestring Glacier

the slopes) the remains of the smashed forest it overwhelmed, split near the present site of Lahar Viewpoint. Part of the lahar raced down Pine Creek, while the rest rushed down the Muddy River Gorge (Lava Canyon).

At 0.4 mile from the trailhead, the trail follows an abandoned roadbed for a short distance. Soon the route leads up a small, open ridge with great views. The path then traverses off the left side of the ridge, through the alder (*Alnus* spp.) and vine maple bushes.

The vine maple (*Acer circinatum*) is a large deciduous shrub or small tree. It usually grows to about 20 feet tall but on occasion may reach 40. The foliage is often thinly dispersed, giving the shrub a scraggly appearance. Vine maple leaves have seven to nine pointed lobes and are 2 to 5 inches across. As with other maples (*Acer* spp.), its winged seeds normally grow in pairs.

The only shrub that can be easily confused with the vine maple is the Rocky Mountain maple (*Acer glabrum*). The Rocky Mountain maple has leaves with only three to five pointed lobes. It also grows in the western Cascades but is more common as you travel to the drier climates to the east.

Vine maple grows as an understory shrub in much of the Cascade's low- to midelevation forest, provided the canopy is thin enough to allow in at least some direct sunlight. It also quickly colonizes areas that have been logged or disturbed in some other way, allowing adequate sunlight to reach the ground. An interesting feature of vine maple is the color that its leaves turn in autumn. If they have grown in good sunlight, they turn a bright red, but in a mostly shaded spot they will be golden yellow.

The wood of the vine maple—though very limited in size—is hard and dense. It's quite flexible when first cut and was once bent and used in the construction of snowshoe frames. Some aboriginal peoples used the young shoots for weaving baskets and constructing fish traps. The branches of the vine maple burn so poorly when green that outdoorspeople often use them for pot hangers and campfire pokers. Chips, twigs, and sawdust from the vine maple are sometimes used for home smoking of fish.

You will continue to climb gently through the small forest until you are about 0.9 mile from the trailhead. Here the route enters larger timber with some large old-growth Douglas fir (*Pseudotsuga menziesii*), Pacific silver fir (*Abies amabilis*), and noble fir (*A. procera*).

The Douglas fir is not a true fir, but a separate and unique species. The Latin name *Pseudotsuga* (pronounced *soo-dough-soo-gah*) means "false hemlock." Douglas firs have been known to reach a height of 385 feet, making this one of the tallest—if not the tallest—trees to grow anywhere. The largest living specimen known at present is about 220 feet tall and more than 14 feet in diameter. The deeply furrowed dark red-brown bark can be as thick as 10 inches or more and provides the tree with substantial protection from low-intensity fire, although it offers only very limited protection from lahars. Many of the large, mature trees you'll encounter will have fire scars, indicating that they have survived one or more forest fires during their long lives—which on occasion may be as long as 1,000 years.

A mature Douglas fir, growing in an old-growth forest setting, often has no limbs in the first 40 or 50 feet above the ground, so it may be difficult to examine its needles. If you can see the foliage clearly, you will notice that the 1-inch-long needles are attached singly to the twigs in no particular pattern. Like true firs (*Abies* spp.), but unlike spruces (*Picea* spp.), the needles are nearly blunt at their tips. If you can slide your hand along the needles, you will find them to be relatively soft and supple.

The noble is the largest of the true firs. The midelevation country around Mount St. Helens provides nearly perfect growing conditions for this magnificent tree. Some outstanding specimens reach 250 feet or more in height, but 100 to 150 feet is closer to average. The 1- to 1.5-inch-long needles of the noble fir are roughly four sided and bluish green. The needles grow from all sides of the stem but turn upward and appear from a distance to all be on top. Pick off one of the needles and you will notice that it strongly resembles a hockey stick in shape. The cones of the noble fir are green until they mature and large (4 to 6 inches long) when compared to those of other true firs. As with all true firs, the cones stand straight up from the branches and come apart before falling to the ground, unless squirrels clip them off while they are still intact.

For the layperson it is easy to confuse the noble fir with its close relative the Pacific silver fir, which is similar in size, shape, and color. The cones of the silver fir are somewhat smaller than those of the noble and are purple. Still, the easiest way to tell them apart is by the noble's hockey-stick-shaped needles, which on the silver fir are more nearly straight.

Half a mile farther along, the trail makes the first of five switchbacks taking you up to a ridgeline. The path crosses the ridge 2.6 miles from the trailhead, then traverses a brushy area. Here Mount Rainier comes into view to the north, while Mount Adams is to the east.

Continuing to climb, the trail generally follows the ridge. The Blast Zone across Ape Canyon comes into view 3.5 miles from the trailhead. The path makes its way up the ridge for another 1.2 miles to the viewpoint of the gorge in upper Ape Canyon.

At about the same time the Muddy River Lahar rushed down the southeast flank of Mount St. Helens, another lahar raced down Ape Canyon. This smaller but still powerful mudflow scoured the vegetation off the walls of Ape Canyon and continued down Ape Canyon Creek and Smith Creek to join the Muddy River Lahar below Lava Canyon. The lahar became too deep in places to be contained within the walls of Ape Canyon and spilled over the rim, taking with it any timber that was in its path. Another lahar also descended Smith Creek at approximately the same time.

Take the time to walk the short distance to the right of the trail to a viewpoint overlooking the narrow slot in the rock that forms the upper part of Ape Canyon. If you have children with you, be very careful: The cliffs drop away below, and the ground is none too stable. From the viewpoint the route heads west-northwest for another 0.1 mile to its junction with the Loowit Trail, at 4,190 feet elevation. This is your turnaround point.

The junction with the Loowit Trail is very near the timberline, and flowers cover much of the open area in July. One of the more common flowers is dwarf mountain lupine (*Lupinus lyallii*), a tiny lupine with slightly hairy leaves. Dwarf mountain, like all lupines, is a nitrogen-fixing plant. Despite its size, it is adding nutrients to the mineral soil.

Phlox (*Phlox diffusa*) also makes its appearance in this subalpine setting. Phlox is a mat-forming perennial, usually less than 5 inches tall. Its small flowers vary

Whistle pig

from nearly lavender to white in color. The flowers may nearly cover the plant at the height of their bloom.

Watch for a colony of whistle pigs (hoary marmots) that inhabit the upper part of Ape Canyon above the gorge. If a lazy and relaxed look was a sought-after attribute, the whistle pig, aka hoary marmot (*Marmota caligata*), would win the prize. These chubby, gray-grizzled marmots—they can weigh as much as twenty pounds—spend as much time as possible lounging in the sun atop boulders. Along with its close cousin the Olympic marmot (*M. olympus*), which inhabits only the Olympic Mountains of western Washington, this is the largest marmot in North America.

French-Canadian trappers called this marmot *le siffeur*, which means "little whistler." Their very loud, shrill whistle, which is often used to show their annoyance at your approach, can be heard for up to a mile under the right atmospheric conditions. The Latin species name, *caligata*, refers to the hoary's black feet, which were thought to resemble the black boots of Roman soldiers.

Mount St. Helens is close to the southern limit of the whistle pig's range, which reaches far to the north into Alaska. Whistle pigs prefer sunny, south-facing slopes, with plenty of boulders to burrow under. In these well-insulated underground homes, they may hibernate as long as nine months of the year, living off stored fat and escaping the rigorous climate of their high-country environment. These habits, and the snow cover, allowed hoary marmots to survive in many places within the Blast Zone of the 1980 eruption.

Unique in marmot society, whistle pig males are very tolerant of other males living in close proximity. The young aren't mature until two years of age, but even then they are allowed to live close by.

OPTIONS: By turning right (north) onto the Loowit Trail you can hike across the Plains of Abraham to Windy Ridge Viewpoint and Trailhead, about 6 miles away. Hiking to Windy Ridge would require a long car shuttle, however.

A one-way hike requiring a much shorter car shuttle can be made via June Lake. If you turn left onto the Loowit Trail, you will be heading for the June Lake Trail, 4.9 miles away. Then turn left again onto the June Lake Trail and hike, mostly downhill, for 1.4 miles, passing June Lake and its waterfall, to June Lake Trailhead.

Another nearby option is the Lava Canyon Trail.

HIGHLIGHTS: There are two hike possibilities from the Lava Canyon Trailhead: a short loop past some of the best waterfalls at Mount St. Helens, and a difficult descent of the Muddy River Gorge, aka Lava Canyon. Whichever hike you choose, the first 0.3 mile is paved and barrier-free.

START: Lava Canyon Trailhead.

DISTANCE: 6-mile out-and-back day hike with shuttle option, or 1.4-mile loop day hike.

DIFFICULTY: Easy to moderate along the loop; strenuous beyond.

SEASON: June through October.

TOTAL CLIMBING: Shuttle 1,130 feet; loop 300 feet.

TRAILHEAD ELEVATION: 2,840 feet.

PERMITS: Northwest Forest Pass.

MAPS: Mount St. Helens National Volcanic Monument, aka Brown Map. Smith Creek Butte USGS quad covers the area, but the trail is not shown.

SPECIAL CONSIDERATIONS: A child drowned here in 2002. Since then new handrails and barriers have been installed, but nothing will make this area completely safe for people who choose to ignore the dangers. When hiking here, obey the posted signs, stay on the trails, and be sure any children you may have along are closely attended to.

The loop trail is rough and slippery in a few places. Beyond the loop the trail is very rough, narrow, exposed, and sometimes slippery. You must descend a ladder to continue down to the Ship and to Lower Smith Creek Trailhead, and this can be slippery if it's wet. The trail to The Ship Viewpoint is also difficult and exposed.

PARKING AND TRAILHEAD FACILITIES: You'll find adequate parking and restrooms at Lava Canyon Trailhead. At Lower Smith Creek Trailhead, there is parking for several cars.

FINDING THE TRAILHEAD: From Seattle, drive south on Interstate 5 for approximately 150 miles to Woodland; from Portland, take I–5 north to Woodland. Then take exit 21 off I–5 and drive east on Washington Route 503 (which becomes WA 503 Spur) through Cougar. WA 503 Spur becomes Forest Road 90 east of Cougar at the Skamania County line. Turn left off FR 90, 34.8 miles east of I–5 (6.8 miles east of Cougar), onto Forest Road 83. Follow FR 83 for 11.7 miles to its end at Lava Canyon Trailhead.

Lava Canyon (Trails 184, 184A, 184B)

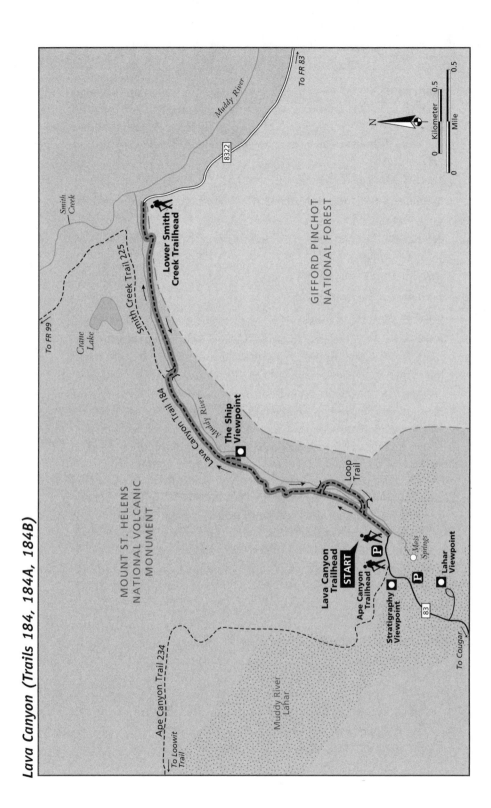

To leave a shuttle vehicle at Lower Smith Creek Trailhead, where the Lava Canyon Trail ends, drive back the way you came (southwest) on FR 83 for 0.8 mile to the Lahar Viewpoint parking area. Just past the parking area, turn left (southeast) onto Forest Road 8322. Follow this 4.8 miles to Lower Smith Creek Trailhead. FR 8322 is a rough, narrow, gravel road.

KEY POINTS:

0.0 Lava Canyon Trailhead (GPS 46 09.912 N 122 05.286 W).

0.3 Junction with Loop Trail, near end of barrier-free trail. Continue straight (northeast).

0.7 Junction with Loop Trail at suspension bridge. Continue straight (northeast).

1.4 Ladder.

1.7 Junction with trail to Ship Viewpoint. Continue straight (northeast).

2.0 Junction with Smith Creek Trail. Turn right to cross new bridge on Lava Canyon Trail.

3.0 Lower Smith Creek Trailhead (GPS 46 10.926 N 122 03.302 W).

6.0 Lava Canyon Trailhead (GPS 46 09.912 N 122 05.286 W).

THE HIKE: The May 18, 1980, eruption of Mount St. Helens blew the top off the once beautifully symmetrical mountain. Along with the rock the upper portions of the glaciers that clothed it were also blasted away. A couple of minutes after the eruption began, a pyroclastic surge—made up of ash, rocks, and volcanic gases—turbulently rolled over the eastern rim of the mountain's newly formed crater. This boiling cloud rushed down the southeastern and eastern slopes of the mountain. Much of it was funneled down the shallow, narrow, steep valley that held the Shoestring Glacier. Almost instantaneously 25 to 30 feet of snow and glacial ice were melted from the surface of Shoestring Glacier.

The surge took only one and a half minutes to descend the 5,000 vertical feet to the base of the mountain. The mixture of heated meltwater, ash, sand,

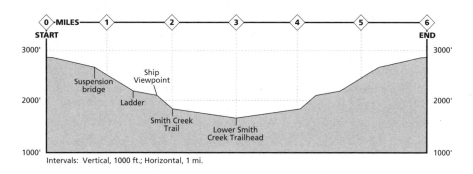

Intervals: Vertical, 1000 ft.; Horizontal, 1 mi.

pumice, boulders, and (farther down on the slopes) the remains of the smashed forest it overwhelmed produced a massive lahar. This lahar split near the present site of Lahar Viewpoint, with part of it racing down Pine Creek. The rest rushed down the Muddy River Gorge, aka Lava Canyon, removing all the vegetation as it went. Below the gorge the lahar continued down the Muddy River, smashing and carrying away almost everything in its path and depositing a large volume of logs into Swift Reservoir.

This is not the first time a lahar has scoured the timber from Lava Canyon. Geologic evidence shows that this has happened before and in all likelihood will happen again.

Begin your exploration of these volcanic remnants on a paved trail that leaves the south side of the parking area. Descend gently through the forest of red alder (*Alnus rubra*), Douglas fir (*Pseudotsuga menziesii*), noble fir (*Abies procera*), Pacific silver fir (*Abies amabilis*), and western hemlock (*Tsuga heterophylla*). Beneath the trees vine maple (*Acer circinatum*), huckleberry (*Vaccinium* spp.) bushes, and a few Pacific dogwoods (*Cornus nuttallii*) complete the understory. The dogwoods here are small and for some reason seem to bloom slightly later (early July) than others in the area. On the ground beneath the bushes are bunchberry (*Cornus canadensis*) and vanilla leaf (*Achlys triphylla*). Where the canopy thins enough to allow lots of direct sunlight, look for fireweed (*Epilobium angustifolium*), pearly everlasting (*Anaphalis margaritacea*), and an occasional pink wild rose (*Rosa* spp.).

The paved path makes a couple of switchbacks and passes some benches before reaching an interpretive viewpoint at a wooden platform with a handrail.

Lava from volcanoes erupting twenty-five million years ago covered the landscape around the site of present-day Mount St. Helens. This was long before Mount St. Helens pushed through the earth's crust and began to build its cone, which is thought to be only about 40,000 years old. This lava was folded and eroded through the millennia to form terrain much like what we see today. Glaciers carved the mountains, and streams eroded canyons into them.

Then, about 40,000 years ago, Mount St. Helens began building its towering cone. Not a lot is known about the earlier eruptions of the mountain because most of the material that was ejected is now buried beneath succeeding deposits. Most of the later and more visible history of the mountain shows that the eruptions were mostly explosive, producing pumice and cinders but little lava. However, for a period of time about 2,500 years ago, the composition of the eruptions changed for some reason.

Lava flowed down the peak's steep slopes in several streams at different times. One of the lava streams descended the already existing canyon of the Muddy River, now known as Lava Canyon. The twenty-five-million-year-old lava is now the tan and purple rock that underlies the dark gray-black lava that flowed into the canyon 2,500 years ago.

Oregon stonecrop

After the lava flow cooled, the Muddy River generally reclaimed its old course and began eroding the new lava. Further volcanic action caused lahars to periodically scour the canyon's bottom and sides, removing most of the vegetation that had grown and further eroding the lava that had once nearly filled the canyon. This erosion has continued to the present day. The beautiful pools you see in Lava Canyon are a result of this erosion.

Past the viewpoint the trail continues to descend gently to the upper junction with the Loop Trail. A short distance ahead is the end of the barrier-free trail, at another interpretive viewpoint. The rough Loop Trail turns to the right (east) and drops to cross a bridge over the Muddy River. This alternate route then descends, sometimes steeply, for 0.5 mile to rejoin the main trail at the suspension bridge. See the options below for more information about the Loop Trail 184A.

To continue on the Lava Canyon Trail, bear left (nearly straight ahead to the northeast) at the junction. The route now becomes steeper and rougher as it works its way down from the upper junction with the Loop Trail. In 0.4 mile you will reach the lower junction with the Loop Trail at the suspension bridge.

Between the junction and the bridge, look across the river at the standing cliffs of dark gray-black rock that are part of the 2,500-year-old lava flow. At the base of the cliffs, there is a distinct indented line where the rock changes. The lower rock and the riverbed at this point are the much older lava that made up the original canyon.

The bridge is suspended over a narrow gorge; it sways and bounces as you walk across it. If you want to return from here via the Loop Trail, cross the bridge and climb back up on the other side of the river. The suspension bridge is the turnaround point for the casual hiker. Beyond this point the trail is steep, very rough, and exposed in some places. To continue, descend north and northeast from the suspension bridge.

Broad-leaved penstemon (*Penstemon ovatus*) droops from the rock bank above the trail to the left. The penstemon's deep blue-purple flowers show up in early July. Soon you will cross a stream with the aid of a cable handrail; a little farther along, the trail crosses another small stream.

In the damp soil next to the crossing grows a patch of false bugbane (*Trautvetteria carolinensis*). The perennial false bugbane grows from rhizomes and can reach up to 3 feet in height. Its small, almost fluffy-looking white flowers form flat-topped clusters at the top of the stems and bloom in July. The leaves of the false bugbane are large and coarsely toothed. The false bugbane plant contains an irritant compound that may cause redness or even blistering if rubbed on the skin. Some aboriginal tribes used the smashed roots of this plant as a poultice to treat boils. There is the distinct possibility that this cure may have been worse than the original ailment.

The route makes several switchbacks in the 0.7 mile to the ladder, passing wonderful falls and beautiful pools along the way. These falls rush over the more erosion-resistant strata of twenty-five-million-year-old rock in which the canyon was originally carved.

Oregon stonecrop sprouts from the dry rocky ledges and slopes along this section of the route. Oregon stonecrop (*Sedum oreganum*) is a spreading perennial herb that grows only up to about 6 inches tall and produces small yellow flowers. Widely distributed in the Northwest but limited by its need for a dry environment, Oregon stonecrop lives only in the very specialized habitat of dry rocky slopes, ledges, talus slopes, and ridgelines up to middle elevations. The fleshy leaves are an adaptation for water conservation so that the plant can prosper under these rocky and often very dried-out conditions.

The 30-foot steel ladder, 1.4 miles into the hike, allows the trail to descend an overhanging cliff. This slippery-when-wet ladder must be descended to continue. As you climb down, notice the maidenhair ferns (*Asplenium viride*) growing from the cliff, in a couple of cases in an inverted position.

A bridge on Loop Trail

Once you have reached the bottom of the ladder, the rough path heads on down, crossing another stream to the junction with a side trail leading to the Ship Viewpoint. The side trail turns to the right (southeast) and climbs very steeply for 0.2 mile to the viewpoint. The Ship is a large rock outcropping that is part of the 2,500-year-old lava flow. The view from the top is well worth the effort it takes to get there, but the trail is very steep and exposed and includes another steel ladder. Don't send children up the trail to this viewpoint alone. Below the junction with the path to the Ship Viewpoint, the Lava Canyon Trail continues to descend, crossing a couple more exposed spots.

Two miles from Lava Canyon Trailhead is the junction with the Smith Creek Trail. The Lava Canyon Trail used to continue another 0.9 mile east to the banks of Smith Creek, where it met the Smith Creek Trail, but the bridge over the Muddy River near that junction washed out in the 1990s. Now that lower 0.9 mile of the former Lava Canyon Trail has become part of the Smith Creek Trail. If you bear left (almost straight ahead to the east) at this junction, it is a strenuous 9.9-mile hike to Upper Smith Creek Trailhead on Forest Road 99. See the options below for more information about the Smith Creek Trail.

To continue to Lower Smith Creek Trailhead, turn right and cross a bridge over the Muddy River. Then descend for 1 more mile, making a couple of switchbacks along the way, to Lower Smith Creek Trailhead at 1,700 feet elevation, 3 miles from Lava Canyon Trailhead. Unless you've arranged a shuttle, this is your turnaround point.

OPTIONS: The Loop Trail 184A, though it is steep in places and may be slippery if wet, is an excellent option for a family hike. Along the loop you will be able to see close up the difference between the twenty-five-million-year-old lava (the tan and purple rock) and the dark gray-black lava that flowed into the canyon 2,500 years ago. If you take the loop please, for your safety, stay on the trail.

For a long day hike—which unfortunately also involves a 62-mile car shuttle—begin your hike at Upper Smith Creek Trailhead on FR 99. Then make the mostly downhill 9.9-mile hike along the Smith Creek Trail 225 to the junction with the Lava Canyon Trail. Turn right onto the Lava Canyon Trail and climb for 2 miles to Lava Canyon Trailhead. To reach the Upper Smith Creek Trailhead from Lava Canyon Trailhead, first drive back the way you came (southwest) along FR 83 for 11.7 miles to the junction with FR 90. Bear left (straight ahead to the north) onto Forest Road 25 and drive 24.3 miles to the junction with Forest Road 99. Turn left (west) onto FR 99 and follow it for 14.4 miles to the Upper Smith Creek Trailhead (GPS 46 15.499 N 122 07.027 W). A sign marks the trailhead, which is on the left (east) side of the road.

Northeastern Region

Access from Forest Roads 25, 26, and 99

The eastern region of Mount St. Helens National Volcanic Monument is mostly within the Blast and Singe Zones of the May 18, 1980, eruption and resulting pyroclastic events. Much of this region is covered with flowers between the broken stumps, blown-down timber, and standing silvered snags. With the exception of Trail 23, Woods Creek Watchable Wildlife Loops—which lies along Forest Road 25 south of Randle—all the routes described here start from or very close to Forest Road 99. FR 99 is the road to Windy Ridge Viewpoint and Trailhead. Several good trails along and north of the Green River have been omitted because of timber company road closures and the temporary closure of Forest Road 26 north of Norway Pass Trailhead.

Heading west on FR 99 from FR 25, you first drive through old-growth forest to Bear Meadows Trailhead, the starting point for Trail 22, Boundary Trail. A short distance farther along, FR 99 enters the Blast Zone. Soon you will reach the junction with FR 26, which leads to Norway Pass Trailhead and Trails 18, 20, and 21. A few yards past the junction is the Miners Car Exhibit and the starting point for Hike 19, Meta Lake. Between here and Windy Ridge Viewpoint and Trailhead, you pass the Harmony Trailhead, the starting point for Trail 17, Harmony Trail. Trail 15, Plains of Abraham Loop, and Trail 16, Loowit Trail, leave from the Windy Ridge Trailhead.

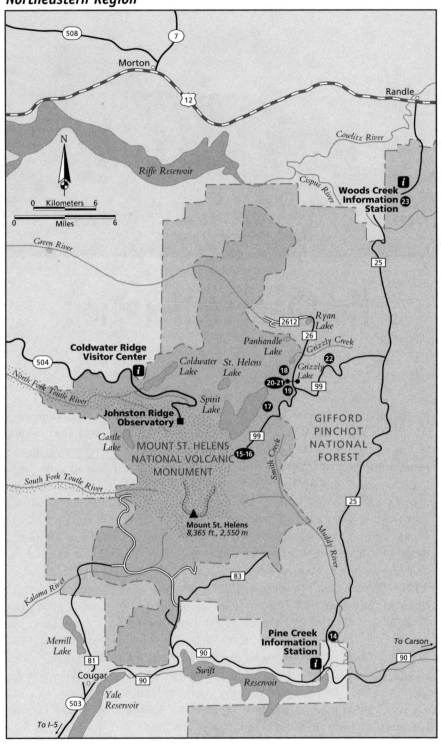

Morton

Randle

Riffe Reservoir

Cowlitz River

Cispus River

Woods Creek Information Station ℹ ➋➌

Green River

N

Kilometers 6

Miles 6

Ryan Lake

2612

Panhandle Lake

26

Grizzly Creek

Coldwater Ridge Visitor Center ℹ

504

Coldwater Lake

St. Helens Lake

18

Grizzly Lake ➋➋

20-21

North Fork Toutle River

99

19

Johnston Ridge Observatory ■

Spirit Lake

17

Castle Lake

MOUNT ST. HELENS NATIONAL VOLCANIC MONUMENT

99

15-16

Smith Creek

GIFFORD PINCHOT NATIONAL FOREST

25

South Fork Toutle River

▲ **Mount St. Helens** 8,365 ft., 2,550 m

25

Muddy River

83

Kalama River

Pine Creek Information Station ℹ ➊➍

To Carson →

Merrill Lake

81

Cougar

90

Swift Reservoir

90

Yale Reservoir

503

To I-5

HIGHLIGHTS: This short loop walk through magnificent old-growth forest is an excellent hike for small children, with adult supervision. Allow plenty of time to enjoy the huge trees, moss- and fern-covered ground and logs, and dense understory of this low-elevation, Temperate Zone rain forest.

START: Cedar Flats Trailhead.

DISTANCE: 0.9-mile loop day hike.

DIFFICULTY: Easy.

SEASON: April through October.

TOTAL CLIMBING: Minimal.

TRAILHEAD ELEVATION: 1,350 feet.

PERMITS: None.

MAPS: Cedar Flats USGS quad.

SPECIAL CONSIDERATIONS: Be sure that any small children you may have along are well supervised while you are close to the high riverbank. A couple of spots drop off very steeply, and a dangerous fall could occur.

PARKING AND TRAILHEAD FACILITIES: There is parking for several cars but no other facilities at the trailhead.

FINDING THE TRAILHEAD: Head north from Portland on Interstate 5 to exit 21 (21 miles north of the Columbia River Bridge) at Woodland. Then drive east for 27.5 miles on Washington Route 503 (which becomes WA 503 Spur) to Cougar. Continue east through Cougar on WA 503 Spur (which becomes Forest Road 90 at the Skamania County line) for another 18.6 miles to its junction with Forest Road 25. Bear left (nearly straight ahead) and head northeast on FR 25.

In 0.7 mile, just before crossing the bridge over Pine Creek, there will be a sign marking the Pine Creek Boulder parking area. Park and read the interpretive sign, then walk a few yards down the path to the south to the thirty-seven-ton Pine Creek Boulder. This huge chunk of rock was dropped here, 33 feet above the normal creek level, by the 1980 Pine Creek Lahar. After checking out the Pine Creek Boulder, get back on FR 25 and drive another 2.9 miles north to Cedar Flats Trailhead.

From Seattle, take I–5 south to exit 133 at Tacoma, and then follow Washington Route 7 for 55 miles to Morton. From Morton, drive east on U.S. Route 12 for 17 miles to Randle. Turn right and take Washington Route 131, then FR 25, south for 41 miles to the Cedar Flats Trailhead on the east side of the road.

Cedar Flats Nature Loop (Trail 32)

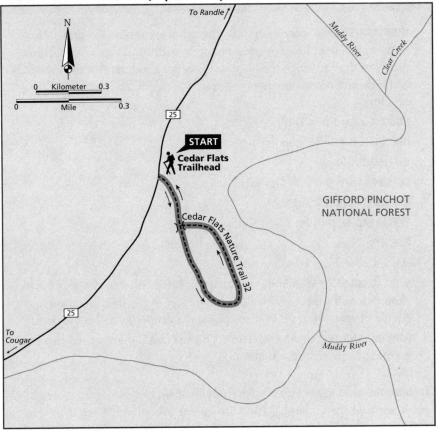

KEY POINTS:

- **0.0** Cedar Flats Trailhead (GPS 46 06.729 N 122 01.019 W).
- **0.1** Wooden bridge and fork in trail. Bear right.
- **0.6** Viewpoint overlooking Muddy River. Continue straight.
- **0.9** Cedar Flats Trailhead (GPS 46 06.729 N 122 01.019 W).

THE HIKE: Descending a few feet from the east side of the parking area, the Cedar Flats Nature Trail enters the old-growth forest. The broad trail passes an interpretive sign and reaches a wooden bridge 0.1 mile from the trailhead. In spring, when the new leaves are just out on the understory of vine maple (*Acer circinatum*), the pale green light that filters down through the canopy makes these deep woods especially beautiful. Just past the bridge the trail forks.

Bear right at the fork and continue along the well-maintained trail. Quickly you will come to some large western red cedar trees.

The western red cedar (*Thuja plicata*, pronounced *thoo-yah ply-cate-ah*) is the larger and more common of the two species of cedars that are native to the Mount St. Helens area. When mature these trees may reach a height of 200 feet or more. Their trunks are huge, often with a very pronounced and deeply fluted butt swell.

The thin bark of the western red cedar is a cinnamon color and appears stringy. This fibrous bark was often peeled from the trees by Native Americans and used to weave fabric for cloths. Because of its thin bark, the western red cedar is very susceptible to fire damage. Its small, scalelike leaves are shiny and a yellow-green color. The cones are only about 0.5 inch long and light brown in color. Each cone produces six seeds, which don't seem to be an important food source for small forest dwellers.

The heavy rainfall and mild, humid climate in the canyon bottoms around Mount St. Helens provide nearly perfect growing conditions for western red cedars. They are usually found along streambanks or around wetlands, where their feet (roots) can be wet most of the year. Because they live in these wet areas and have no need to reach deep into the ground for water, the roots of the western red cedar are shallow. These shallow roots make even large mature trees very susceptible to windthrow. When mature the highest parts of the western red cedar trees often die, leaving a naked, spiked top.

The western red cedar is an important timber tree with countless uses for its rot-resistant wood. Cutting the huge trees into bolts (short sections) then splitting them for shakes was once an important industry around Mount St. Helens; it continues in a limited way today outside the national monument.

A few yards farther along, past a small stand of moss-hung big-leaf maples (*Acer macrophyllum*), there will be two very large Douglas fir trees to the left of the trail. This seems to be a favorite picture-taking spot—there is a path to the base of the largest tree.

Douglas fir (*Pseudotsuga menziesii*) is not a true fir, but a separate and unique species. The Latin name *Pseudotsuga* (pronounced *soo-dough-soo-gah*) means "false hemlock." Formerly the Latin name was *P. taxifolia*, which means "false hemlock with yew leaves," but it has now been changed to *P. menziesii*.

The most common conifer in Mount St. Helens National Volcanic Monument, the Douglas fir can be a very large tree. Doug firs, or just Dougs, as they are commonly called, have been known to reach a height of 385 feet, making these among the tallest trees to grow anywhere—if not the tallest. The largest living specimen known at present is about 220 feet tall and more than 14 feet in diameter. The lower canyons around Mount St. Helens seem to

Stringy-barked western red cedar

have nearly the perfect growing conditions—heavy winter rainfall and mild humid summers—for these giants of the forest.

Usually the first characteristic the casual botanist will notice when approaching a mature Doug in the woods is its deeply furrowed dark red-brown bark. This bark can be 10 inches or more thick and provides the tree with substantial protection from low-intensity fire. In fact, many of the mature trees you'll encounter will have fire scars, indicating that they have survived one or more forest fires during their long lives—up to 1,000 years.

There will also be cones on the ground beneath the tree. Dougs have their own unique cone, which normally falls to the ground intact after opening and dispersing its winged seeds. The cones, which are normally 3 to 4 inches long and oval shaped, have rounded scales with three pronged bracts protruding between them.

Mature Douglas firs, growing in a climax or old-growth forest setting, often have no limbs in the first 40 or 50 feet above the ground, so it may be difficult to examine their needles. If you can see the foliage clearly, you will notice that the 1-inch-long needles are attached singly to the twigs in no particular pattern. Like true firs but unlike spruces, the needles are nearly blunt at their tips. If you can slide your hand along the needles, you will find them to be relatively soft and supple.

Because of its high value for wood products, much of the old-growth Douglas fir timber had been logged in the area around Mount St. Helens before it became a national monument. Thus most of the Dougs you see will be younger trees. The younger specimens don't have the deeply furrowed bark found on mature trees, but the foliage will be closer to the ground and easier to check out. In their youth Dougs have a sharply pyramidal overall shape topped by a central leader stem that often grows skyward more than 2 feet per year. In their first years of life, the trees often have branches nearly down to ground level. By the time they reach thirty years old, especially if they are growing in dense stands, the lower branches begin to die and eventually fall off. This leaves their trunks straight and virtually free of large knots, making them prized by the timber industry.

Squirrels and chipmunks prize the seeds of the Doug fir. Walking beneath a Doug during the time of the year when the cones have formed, but not yet opened, may be an invitation to be "bombed" by the squirrels. They aren't really trying to intimidate you, but rather clipping off the cones high in the tree and dropping them to the ground to make them easier to process into a winter food supply.

The trail reaches the high bank of the Muddy River 0.4 mile farther along, after passing many more large trees. A lahar flowed down the Muddy River during the 1980 eruption; evidence of the deluge is still present in the form of logs and stumps scattered along the river bottom. Cedar Flats itself is under-lain by lahars that descended from Mount St. Helens and followed the Muddy River drainage about 2,700 years ago.

The trail follows the riverbank for a couple of hundred yards to a viewpoint with a short rail fence. From the vista high above the riverbed, notice the stands of red alder (*Alnus rubra*) that are reclaiming the flats next to the rush-ing water. These trees are quickly covering much of the 1980 lahar deposits. Red alders, like all members of the alder family, are nitrogen-fixing plants, which means that they take nitrogen from the atmosphere and "fix" or deposit it in the soil. This process is tremendously important to the plants that follow the alders, which need the soil nitrogen to live and grow. The copious amounts of leaves shed by the alders each year add large amounts of humus to the basi-cally mineral soil of the lahar deposit, also aiding in the growth of future plants.

Leaving the viewpoint, the route turns away from the river and heads back through the woods and moss covered logs. In about 300 yards you will reach the fork in the trail next to the bridge. Turn right and walk the last 0.1 mile to the trailhead.

OPTIONS: The Woods Creek Watchable Wildlife Loops are 33 miles to the north along FR 25. The elevation and rainfall of the Cedar Flats Nature Loop and the Woods Creek Watchable Wildlife Loops are similar. But at Woods Creek the younger forest, growing on deep, moist organic soil, is mostly decid-uous, whereas here at Cedar Flats the older conifer woods grow from the min-eral soil of an ancient lahar deposit. Because of the two hikes' similarities—and even more because of their differences—I strongly suggest hiking both on the same trip. Along the way to Woods Creek, you could also stop and take the short walk to Iron Creek Falls.

15 Plains of Abraham Loop (Trails 207, 216D, 216, 216E)

HIGHLIGHTS: This route first heads south along Windy Ridge, with views of Mount Adams to the east, then climbs a flower-covered ridge to the Plains of Abraham. After climbing Windy Pass it returns across the Pumice Plain. The entire loop is within the Blast Zone of the May 18, 1980, eruption.

START: Windy Ridge Viewpoint and Trailhead.

DISTANCE: 8.7-mile loop day hike.

DIFFICULTY: Moderate.

SEASON: Mid-June through September.

TOTAL CLIMBING: 800 feet.

TRAILHEAD ELEVATION: 4,110 feet.

PERMITS: Northwest Forest Pass.

MAPS: Mount St. Helens National Volcanic Monument, aka Brown Map. Mount St. Helens USGS quad covers the area but does not show these trails.

SPECIAL CONSIDERATIONS: Some sections of this trail travel through loose pumice, so the use of gaiters is highly recommended. When it is very windy, there may be blowing dust in places.

PARKING AND TRAILHEAD FACILITIES: There are restrooms and adequate parking at the trailhead.

FINDING THE TRAILHEAD: Head north from Portland on Interstate 5 to exit 21 (21 miles north of the Columbia River Bridge) at Woodland. Then drive east for 27.5 miles on Washington Route 503 (which becomes WA 503 Spur) to Cougar. Continue east through Cougar on WA 503 Spur (which becomes Forest Road 90 at the Skamania County line) for another 18.6 miles to its junction

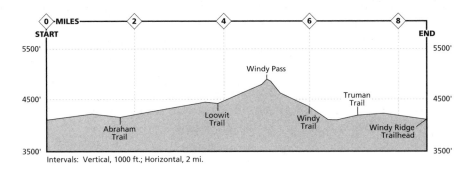

Intervals: Vertical, 1000 ft.; Horizontal, 2 mi.

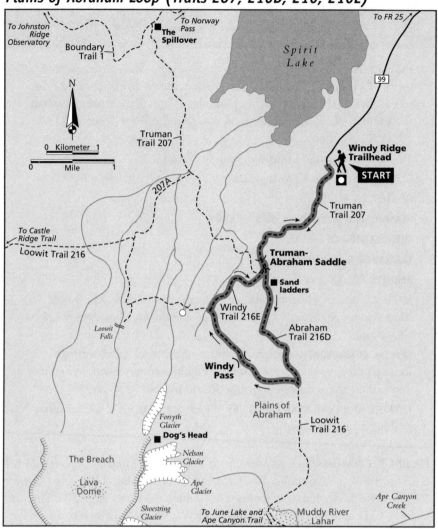

with Forest Road 25. Bear left (nearly straight ahead) and head northeast on FR 25 for 24.3 miles to its junction with Forest Road 99.

From Seattle, take I–5 south to exit 133, then follow Washington Route 7 south for 55 miles to Morton. From Morton, drive east 17 miles to Randle on U.S. Route 12. Turn right in Randle and take Washington Route 131, which soon becomes FR 25, south for 20 miles to the junction with FR 99.

From the junction of FR 25 and FR 99, head west and south on FR 99 for 15.8 miles to Windy Ridge Viewpoint and Trailhead.

KEY POINTS:

0.0 Windy Ridge Viewpoint and Trailhead (GPS 46 15.990 N 122 08.200 W).

1.7 Junction with Abraham Trail (GPS 46 14.018 N 122 09.017 W). Turn left (southeast).

3.9 Junction with Loowit Trail on Plains of Abraham. Turn right (west).

5.0 Windy Pass.

6.0 Junction with Windy Trail (GPS 46 13.636 N 122 09.646 W). Turn right (northeast).

6.8 Junction with Truman Trail (GPS 46 13.814 N 122 09.006 W). Turn right (north).

7.0 Junction with Abraham Trail in Truman-Abraham Saddle. Take Truman Trail northeast.

8.7 Windy Ridge Viewpoint and Trailhead (GPS 46 15.990 N 122 08.200 W).

THE HIKE: The loop begins on the Truman Trail 207. This trail—really a closed section of FR 99 at this point—was named for Harry Truman, the longtime owner of Spirit Lake Lodge who died in the 1980 eruption. The route heads south, then south-southwest from Windy Ridge Viewpoint and Trailhead. First you travel along the east side of Windy Ridge through severely blasted but slowly regenerating forest. Cardwell's penstemon (*Penstemon cardwellii*) and common red paintbrush (*Castilleja miniata*) color the slopes between the black huckleberry bushes (*Vaccinium membranaceum*) and low-growing mountain alders (*Alnus incana*).

Mountain alder is easily distinguished from the red alder (*Alnus rubra*), a tree that is also common around Mount St. Helens, by its size and erect shape; the mountain alder is a many-branched shrub. The leaves of the red alder are blunt toothed whereas the mountain alder's leaves are sharply saw-toothed.

The leaves of alders have a high nitrogen content. When they fall to the ground and decay, the nitrogen rich compost adds nutrients to the soil. Like all alders, the mountain alder is a nitrogen-fixing species, which means it has the ability to extract nitrogen from the atmosphere and "fix" or deposit what it doesn't use in the soil. This is accomplished with the help of bacteria on the alder's root, which combines oxygen from the air with the nitrogen before depositing it in the soil. Nitrogen in the soil is essential for the growth of most plants, so the alders are getting the soil ready for the diverse plant communities that will grow here in the future, if the mountain doesn't have other ideas.

Lewis monkey flower

As you stroll along, the bulky, ice-sheathed form of Mount Adams towers above the green hills to the east across Smith Creek Canyon. About 1.5 miles from the trailhead, a wet spot on the right side of the trail (roadbed) produces a patch of Lewis monkey flowers, aka pink monkey flowers (*Mimulus lewisii*).

The perennial Lewis monkey flower plant sprouts from rhizomes to produce a trumpet-shaped red to pink flower from 1.25 to 2.25 inches in length. It is common at medium to high elevations along streams and in other wet areas, especially if the water is very cold. Lewis monkey flowers were named for Captain Meriwether Lewis of the Corps of Discovery, aka the Lewis and Clark Expedition, in the first decade of the nineteenth century.

In another 0.2 mile you will reach the junction with the Abraham Trail in the Truman-Abraham Saddle, at 4,160 feet elevation. See the options below for more information about the Truman Trail.

To make the Plains of Abraham Loop, turn left at the junction and follow the Abraham Trail 216D heading southeast. The path climbs a narrow pumice covered ridge. This ridge—which was here long before Mount St. Helens—is not made of pumice, just covered with it following the mountain's explosive eruptions. Smith Creek Canyon is to your left, and Mount St. Helens lies ahead and to the right as you walk along the ridge. In late July the flowers along this ridge are unrivaled. Cardwell's (*Penstemon cardwellii*) and small flowered (*P. procerus*) penstemon, along with common red paintbrush (*Castilleja miniata*) and lupines (*Lupinus* spp.), nearly cover the slopes.

The route climbs its first "sand ladder" 0.3 mile from the junction. The purpose of a sand ladder—a series of wooden rungs held together with cables—is to allow easier climbing and descending over steep, loose pumice slopes. A little farther up you will climb another sand ladder and regain the ridgeline. The route then follows the ridge to the south and climbs to a high point. Here the path flattens out for a short distance. Leopard lilies and red columbines line the trail along the ridgeline.

The leopard lily, aka tiger lily and Columbia lily (*Lilium columbianum*), is one of the most colorful flowers growing in the Cascades. This beautiful perennial grows 3 feet or more tall from a bulb. The flowers, which are bright orange, have red to purple spots and petals that turn backward. The bulbs of the leopard lily were sometimes harvested by Native Americans for food.

The red columbine (*Aquilegia formosa*) is a perennial plant that may grow up to 3 feet tall. Its drooping flowers are red and yellow with five straight reddish spurs. Some groups of Native Americans used a milky pulp extracted from the roots as a healing lotion for cuts and sores. This plant also had several other medicinal uses for aboriginal peoples.

The route climbs a bit more, then bears left off the ridgeline, 0.9 mile from Truman Trail. You will cross six draws in the next 0.7 mile. A couple of these draws may have water through midsummer. All of them are flower gardens in late July. The wetter draws grow stands of both Lewis monkey flower and yellow monkey flowers (*Mimulus guttatus*). After you cross the sixth draw, the Plains of Abraham come into view ahead.

The tread descends, then crosses a wash as it nears the plains. You will make a switchback as you climb out of the wash onto the desertlike pumice-covered plains. The open plains, once known as Abraham Flat, rise gently to the west to the very base of the cone of Mount St. Helens. Not many plants can withstand the rigors of this pumice desert, but a few penstemons seem to prosper and bloom. The route crosses the plains heading south-southeast for 0.3 mile to the junction with the Loowit Trail 216. Straight ahead on the Loowit Trail, it's about 1.6 miles (across the plains to the south) to a junction with the Ape Canyon Trail 234.

To continue on this loop, turn right at the junction onto the Loowit Trail and hike west across the plains. The shrunken remains of Ape and Nelson Glaciers hang on the mountain slopes ahead and high above. These glaciers were once part of the more or less contiguous ice cap that covered the northeast slope

The Plains of Abraham

of pre-eruption Mount St. Helens. The upper parts of glaciers were nearly instantaneously removed when the top of the mountain slid away in the Debris Avalanche on the morning of May 18, 1980. The heat from the pyroclastic surge that quickly swept down the side of the mountain as the May 18 eruption began melted a considerable amount of the remaining ice. These glaciers are now little more than pathetic remnants of what they once were.

Just to the right of the glaciers, on the very rim of the crater, is the rock outcrop called the Dog's Head, a dacite lava dome that was built up on the northeast slope of Mount St. Helens by a volcanic event approximately 2,000 years ago. Before the 1980 eruption the route over the Dog's Head was one of the most popular ways to reach Mount St. Helens' summit. In fact, a relatively flat 600-foot-long bench on top of the Dog's Head often served as a campsite for climbers. This route to the summit is now in the Restricted Zone and unavailable to climbers.

As you get closer to the base of the mountain, the path bears slightly to the right and crosses a couple of washes. This section of the Loowit Trail is marked with large cairns. In the washes the trail is rough and vague in spots. You will leave the plains and begin to climb toward Windy Pass 0.7 mile from the junction. The route climbs the south-facing slope, making a couple of switchbacks before reaching the pass. This pumice slope is nearly covered with Cardwell's penstemon.

Cardwell's penstemon has been extremely successful in recolonizing many locations devastated by the 1980 eruption of Mount St. Helens. It is a small shrub, from 4 inches to a foot tall, with blue-violet to bright purple flowers. These striking perennials often form large patches, which grow from widely spreading root mats.

Being composed of nearly 100 percent pumice, the trail tends to slip away in spots here if it hasn't been recently maintained. Pumice is a solidified form of highly gas-charged lava. It's high in silica content, as is obsidian; in fact, it could be defined as gas-charged obsidian. Pumice is usually light in color and, being full of tiny bubbles, is light enough to float on water. Part of the spiritual aura of Spirit Lake came from the fact that the rocks (pumice) floated and some of the wood (wet western hemlock) sank. To people who didn't understand the basic reasons for these phenomena, it would be a very strange lake.

At 4,890 feet elevation Windy Pass is the highest point on this loop. The shining waters of Spirit Lake come into view to the north as you cross the pass. Beyond the lake are the rugged peaks and ridges of the Mount Margaret Backcountry. The trail makes four switchbacks as it descends northwesterly from the pass. It then descends a gully that may be snow filled through July. As you leave the gully, the route makes a traverse to the northwest. The tread works its way in and out of a couple more washes and passes a small waterfall before reaching a junction with the Windy Trail 216E; this junction is 1 mile from the pass and 6 miles into the hike. Turn right (northeast) onto the Windy Trail.

The junction of the Windy and Loowit Trails is very close to the pre-eruption site of Timberline Campground and parking area. Before the 1980 eruption the most popular climbing routes to the summit of Mount St. Helens started here. The road to the campground was paved in the early 1960s in the hope of putting in a ski area, but one was never developed. Nothing remains of the campground and parking area today.

On April 28, 1975, a climbing class from the University of Puget Sound left from this parking area. That night they were camped above and about 1.5 miles to the southwest on the Forsyth Glacier, near the Sugar Bowl Dome and below the Dog's Head. An avalanche swept down the glacier from above and buried the campsite, killing five people. Despite the poor weather members of Tacoma Mountain Rescue, assisted by helicopters from the National Guard base in Portland, dug out and removed the bodies over the next two days.

I was part of that body recovery and got my first taste of what it felt like to see death on a mountain. The images of the bodies being dug from the snow are forever stuck in my brain as a reminder to always be observant, knowledgeable about the conditions and risks, and above all very careful when in the mountains.

Continuing northeast on the Windy Trail, you will descend gently through mounds of pumice. The pumice on the surface of the ground here was deposited by one or more of the pyroclastic flows that swept down the northern slopes of Mount St. Helens during and shortly after the 1980 eruption, but pumice from previous eruptions was common here before that.

As you descend along the Windy Trail, slowly getting farther away from the crater, more vegetation begins to show up. Dwarf mountain lupine (*Lupinus lyallii*), a tiny lupine with slightly hairy leaves, makes its appearance pushing up through the chunks of pumice. Like all lupines, the dwarf mountain is a nitrogen-fixing plant. Even though it's very small, this pioneer plant is adding nutrients to the mineral soil, making it suitable for the plants that will follow.

The path descends into a large wash 0.6 mile after leaving the Loowit Trail. As you descend along the slope, which is partially protected from the direct sunlight, more moisture is available to the plants. The vegetative covering becomes much thicker and far more diverse. Kinnikinnik (*Arctostaphylos uva-ursi*) and pearly everlasting (*Anaphalis margaritacea*) nearly cover the once barren pumice. A few small and very widely scattered Douglas fir (*Pseudotsuga menziesii*), lodgepole pine (*Pinus contorta*), noble fir (*Abies procera*), and western hemlock (*Tsuga heterophylla*) trees have pushed above the flowers. As can be attested to by their slow growth rates, these are still very difficult conditions for these trees. But they are trying to reclaim the domain in which they were once monarchs. Given enough time before the mountain again blasts them from existence, they will reestablish the vibrant forest that stood on this landscape before 1980.

Another 0.2 mile of hiking across the bottom of the wash brings you to the junction with the Truman Trail. Turn right onto the Truman Trail and climb gently for 0.3 mile along this abandoned roadbed to the junction with the Abraham Trail in the Truman-Abraham Saddle to complete the loop. Then retrace your route, heading northeast for 1.7 miles along the Truman Trail to Windy Saddle Viewpoint and Trailhead.

OPTIONS: A one-way hike requiring a very long car shuttle can be made by following the Truman Trail and the Boundary Trail to Johnston Ridge Observatory. To make this trip turn right at the junction in the Truman-Abraham Saddle and cross the ridgeline. The route then makes a descending traverse, first south then west and northwest, to the flatter ground below, passing the junctions with the Windy Trail and Trail 207A and a brushy oasis on the Pumice Plain.

Past the brushy area cross the rest of the plain before climbing to the crest of Johnston Ridge and the junction with the Boundary Trail 1, at the Spillover. Before you start the climb of Johnston Ridge, the route passes over old Spirit Lake Highway near the site where the Mount St. Helens Lodge stood before the 1980 eruption; nothing remains of the lodge or the highway today. Nearly all of the Truman Trail is in full view of the crater of Mount St. Helens.

The 1980 eruption caused the mountain's upper 1,300 feet and much of its north side to slide away. This slide formed a Debris Avalanche, which rushed north. Part of the Debris Avalanche climbed over Johnston Ridge, then continued into the South Fork Coldwater Creek Canyon. The place where the Debris Avalanche crossed Johnston Ridge is now called the Spillover.

Another option is to make a loop hike by turning left (southwest) onto Trail 207A at the junction mentioned above. From this junction it's a short climb to the Loowit Trail. By turning left onto the Loowit Trail and following it for 2.1 miles to its junction with the Windy Trail, then turning left again and following the Windy Trail for 0.8 mile back to the Truman Trail, you will have completed the loop. As you are hiking along the Loowit, you will also pass a junction with the short side trail to the Loowit Falls Viewpoint. Back on the Truman Trail, retrace your steps to Windy Ridge Trailhead.

Hiking south from the junction of the Abraham and Loowit Trails, across the Plains of Abraham to the Ape Canyon Trail, then from there on along the Ape Canyon Trail to Ape Canyon Trailhead, makes a great day hike. The car shuttle to Ape Canyon Trailhead is quite long, however.

A series of steps from the north end of the Windy Ridge parking area climbs to a viewpoint high above. From the viewpoint the southern segment of the Independence Pass Trail 227 leads northeast for 1.4 miles to Donnybrook Trailhead on FR 99. The short but strenuous climb to the viewpoint is very worthwhile, and with a short car shuttle you can make the one-way trip to Donnybrook Trailhead.

The Truman and Windy Trails are one of the easiest ways to access the Loowit Trail for a multiday backpack trip around the mountain.

16 Loowit Trail (Trail 216)

HIGHLIGHTS: A 34-mile round-the-mountain trek that offers spectacular views of a landscape often devastated, but sometimes almost untouched, by the 1980 eruption.

START: Windy Ridge Viewpoint and Trailhead.

DISTANCE: 34-mile loop backpack.

DIFFICULTY: Strenuous, especially around the northern side of the mountain between the South Fork Toutle River and Windy Ridge Viewpoint and Trailhead.

SEASON: July through September.

TOTAL CLIMBING: Approximately 6,000 feet.

TRAILHEAD ELEVATION: 4,110 feet.

PERMITS: Northwest Forest Pass.

MAPS: Mount St. Helens National Volcanic Monument, aka Brown map, or Green Trails Mount St. Helens NW, Wash NO 364 S. Mount St. Helens and Goat Mountain USGS quads cover the area but don't show this trail.

SPECIAL CONSIDERATIONS: The weather near or above timberline is very changeable. It may be warm, clear, and sunny when you leave the trailhead, then quickly turn windy and cold; a dust storm is always a possibility on the north side of the mountain. Rain is common before late June and possible all summer. In sunny weather these slopes can be very warm and dry. The wind picks up the fine particles of pumice dust, so be sure to protect your camera. There is no camping allowed in the Restricted Zone, which reaches from near the South Fork Toutle River in the west to Windy Pass in the east.

PARKING AND TRAILHEAD FACILITIES: There are restrooms and adequate parking at the trailhead.

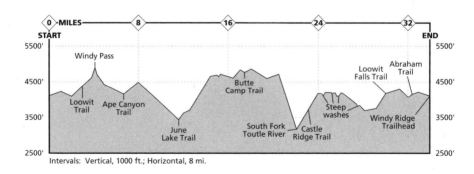

Intervals: Vertical, 1000 ft.; Horizontal, 8 mi.

Loowit Trail (Trail 216)

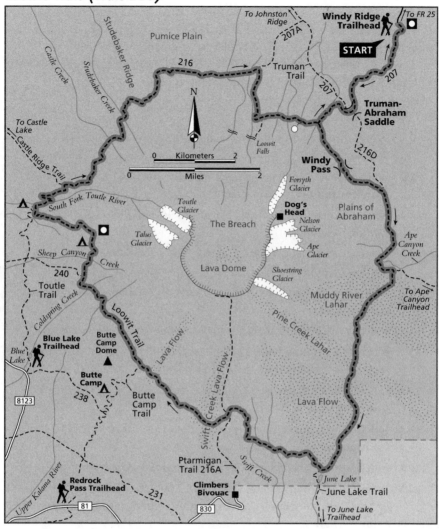

FINDING THE TRAILHEAD: Head north from Portland on Interstate 5 to exit 21 (21 miles north of the Columbia River Bridge) at Woodland. Then drive east for 27.5 miles on Washington Route 503 (which becomes WA 503 Spur) to Cougar. Continue east through Cougar on WA 503 Spur (which becomes Forest Road 90 at the Skamania County line) for another 18.6 miles to its junction with Forest Road 25. Bear left (nearly straight ahead) and head northeast on FR 25 for 24.3 miles to its junction with Forest Road 99.

From Seattle, take I–5 south to exit 133, then follow Washington Route 7 south for 55 miles to Morton. From Morton, drive east 17 miles to Randle on U.S. Route 12. Turn right in Randle and take Washington Route 131, which soon becomes FR 25, south for 20 miles to its junction with FR 99.

From the junction of FR 25 and FR 99, head west and south on FR 99 for 15.8 miles to Windy Ridge Viewpoint and Trailhead.

KEY POINTS:

0.0 Windy Ridge Viewpoint and Trailhead (GPS 46 15.990 N 122 08.200 W).

1.7 Junction with Abraham Trail 216D (GPS 46 14.018 N 122 09.017 W). Bear right on Truman Trail.

2.0 Junction with Windy Trail 216E (GPS 46 13.814 N 122 09.006 W). Turn left (southwest).

2.8 Junction with Loowit Trail 216 (GPS 46 13.636 N 122 09.646 W). Turn left (southeast).

4.9 Junction with Abraham Trail on Plains of Abraham. Turn right (south).

6.7 Junction with Ape Canyon Trail. Continue straight (southwest).

11.6 Junction with June Lake Trail and end of hike's first section. To begin second section, continue west of Loowit Trail.

14.9 Junction with Ptarmigan Trail (GPS 46 09.865 N 122 11.433 W). Continue straight (west).

17.4 Junction with Butte Camp Trail (GPS 46 10.527 N 122 13.023 W). Continue straight (northwest).

19.4 Junction with Sheep Canyon Trail. Continue straight (north).

22.0 Junction with Toutle Trail (GPS 46 12.607 N 122 15.179 W) and end of hike's second section. To begin third section, turn right (east) with Loowit Trail.

23.4 Junction with Castle Ridge Trail. Turn right (east) with Loowit Trail.

29.1 Junction with Trail 207A. Turn right (south) with Loowit Trail.

29.9 Junction with Loowit Falls Trail 216F. Continue straight (east).

31.2 Junction with Windy Trail (GPS 46 13.636 N 122 09.646 W). Turn left (northeast).

34.0 Windy Ridge Viewpoint and Trailhead (GPS 46 15.990 N 122 08.200 W).

THE HIKE: The Truman and Windy Trails offer one of the easier access routes to the Loowit Trail. On the northern side of the mountain, where this hike starts and ends, there is little vegetation along the Loowit Trail, but the view is breathtaking. As you work your way around to the southern slopes of Mount St. Helens, which were not as dramatically effected by the 1980 eruption, you see much of the terrain and vegetation in almost the same condition as it was before 1980. Most of the trail around the southern side of the mountain is in the narrow belt of the Hudsonian Zone.

Around the northern side of the mountain between the South Fork Toutle River and Windy Ridge Trailhead, the trail crosses terrain where the vegetation was nearly completely obliterated by the 1980 eruption. Plants are slowly reclaiming this area, but at times you may think you are hiking in a barren desert. This part of the hike is the best for seeing herds of Roosevelt elk (*Cervus elaphus roosevelti*), with the lack of trees and brush making the viewing easy. Remember that nearly this entire section of the route is within the Restricted Zone, so it must be crossed in one day.

This hike's first segment, from Windy Ridge Trailhead to the June Lake Trail (11.6 miles), begins on the Truman Trail 207. The Truman Trail, named for the longtime owner of Spirit Lake Lodge who died in the May 18, 1980, eruption, is really a closed section of FR 99 at this point. The tread leads south, then south-southwest from Windy Ridge Viewpoint and Trailhead. You first hike along the east side of Windy Ridge through severely blasted but slowly regenerating forest. Common red paintbrush (*Castilleja miniata*) and Cardwell's penstemon (*Penstemon cardwellii*) color the slopes between the low-growing mountain alders (*Alnus incana*) and black huckleberry (*Vaccinium membranaceum*) bushes. To the east Mount Adams towers above the green hills across Smith Creek Canyon.

There will be a wet spot that produces a patch of Lewis monkey flowers (*Mimulus lewisii*) on the right side of the trail (roadbed) 1.5 miles from the trailhead. Lewis monkey flowers were named for Captain Meriwether Lewis of the Corps of Discovery, aka the Lewis and Clark Expedition, in the first decade of the nineteenth century. Monkey flowers are perennial plants that sprout from rhizomes. The flowers are trumpet shaped, red to pink in color, and from 1.25 to 2.25 inches long. The Lewis monkey flower is common at medium to high elevations along streams and in other wet areas, especially if the water is very cold.

In another 0.2 mile you will reach the junction with the Abraham Trail 216D, in the Truman-Abraham Saddle, at 4,160 feet elevation. The Truman Trail crosses the ridgeline at the saddle. Bear right onto the Truman Trail and make a descending traverse to the flatter ground below. Once off the ridge the route turns to the northwest and reaches a junction with the Windy Trail 2 miles from the trailhead. Turn left (southwest) onto the Windy Trail. Climb gently across the pumice-covered terrain for 0.8 mile to a junction with the Loowit Trail and the beginning of your loop around Mount St. Helens. At the junction turn left (southeast) and begin a mile-long climb, along the Loowit Trail, to the summit of Windy Pass, then descend to another junction with the Abraham Trail on the Plains of Abraham. Turn right (south) at the junction and cross the light-colored, nearly barren plains to the junction with the Ape Canyon Trail 234. Here you may encounter a colony of whistle pigs (*Marmota caligata*), aka hoary marmots. The elevation at the junction is 4,190 feet. A large lahar swept down Ape Canyon on the morning of May 18, 1980. In places the lahar was too deep to be contained within the canyon walls and spilled over the rim, removing the timber.

Leaving the junction with the Ape Canyon Trail, the Loowit Trail heads southwest and crosses an area of scattered, stunted, alpine trees for 0.3 mile. Mount Hood can be seen ahead in the distance. Soon you will cross the Muddy River Lahar (aka Shoestring Lahar), which is 0.8 mile wide at this point. This large lahar was formed by the 1980 eruption, when much of the snow and ice of Shoestring Glacier melted and combined with rock, sand, and ash. This mixture flowed down the mountainside, wiping out nearly everything in its path. Part of this flow made a sharp left turn, about 3 miles downstream from the trail, and scoured out the timber lining Lava Canyon (aka Muddy River Gorge).

After crossing the lahar the Loowit Trail crosses an open slope that may be nearly covered with flowers in July. It then crosses the smaller Pine Creek Lahar, also an event that took place on May 18, 1980. Heading south and leaving the Pine Creek Lahar, the trail soon crosses a streambed that may or may not have water. The path then starts to work its way across a rough lava flow for about 1 mile.

The tread then descends off the lava, making a couple of switchbacks as it leaves. You'll soon cross a finger of mostly small timber, then follow the lower edge of the lava flow nearly to the junction with the June Lake Trail 216B. Shortly before the junction a spring flows from beneath the lava flow below the trail. The junction with the June Lake Trail is at 3,380 feet elevation, and is 4.9 miles from the junction with the Ape Canyon Trail. This completes the first section of your hike.

The hike's second section takes you 10.4 miles to the Toutle Trail. Begin by following the Loowit Trail as it climbs gently to the northwest past the junction with the June Lake Trail. The rough, rocky tread skirts the lower edge of a lava flow for a short distance, then (with cairns marking the route) climbs onto the flow. Shortly the rough tread crosses a boulder-strewn gully and a

Loowit Trail crossing a lava flow

creek. Once across the creek you climb back onto the lava. The trail is marked with cairns and posts as it crosses this rough flow.

The path enters a small pocket of green timber 1.1 miles from the junction with the June Lake Trail. There is a campsite next to the trail in this small timbered spot. As you leave the timber, a waterfall splashes into a canyon to the left of the trail. This waterfall is called Chocolate Falls because it often runs heavily silted and brown in color. The path crosses the East Fork Swift Creek above the falls. Climb out of the creekbed and turn right to follow the rim of the gully up for a short distance. The path soon turns away from the creekbed and continues to climb to the northwest. A line of posts marking a cross-country ski trail heads to the north as you turn away. Follow the trail, not this line of posts.

After you cross a small gully, the route enters large, well-spaced timber 0.3 mile beyond the line of posts. Here, 1.9 miles from the junction with the June Lake Trail, the route begins to climb more steeply. The path makes a switchback 0.2 mile farther along as it continues its steep climb. As you gain elevation, the view improves. Mount Adams stands alone to the east, across the lava flows. Part of this climb is on a slope that has avalanched in the past, knocking down the large timber. In the spaces between the downed logs, flowers cover the steep slope.

The route switches back to the left and soon leaves the avalanched area. After getting back into the forest, you'll pass what appears to be a weather station. The equipment is 50 yards to the left of the path. In the open spots in the woods, lupine (*Lupinus* spp.) and false hellebore add a bit of color.

False hellebore (*Veratrum californicum*) stands up to 6 feet tall, with wide, pointed, prominently veined leaves up to 10 inches long. The small white flowers form a pyramid-shaped cluster from the main stem and short lateral stems at the top of the stalk. Although aboriginal peoples had several medical uses for it, false hellebore is a poisonous plant. It usually grows at middle elevations in the area around Mount St. Helens.

Easily confused with false hellebore, Indian hellebore (*Veratrum viride*), aka green false hellebore, is a closely related plant that's also common in the Cascade Range. It's difficult to tell these two plants apart before they come into bloom. When in flower, however, they are easily distinguished by the Indian hellebore's green blossoms. Indian hellebore is even more poisonous than its cousin; it's one of the most poisonous plants in the Cascades. In southern Washington it usually lives at middle to subalpine elevations.

The route follows the upper edge of the timber, traversing steep green slopes, and soon flattens out at about 4,500 feet elevation. Phlox (*Phlox diffusa*), bear grass (*Xerophyllum tenax*), and subalpine spirea (*Spiraea densiflora*)—a shrub with beautiful pinkish red flower clusters—line the trail.

The route enters a patch of small fir trees 3.2 miles from the junction with the June Lake Trail. In another 0.1 mile you will come to the junction with the Ptarmigan Trail 216A, the access to the popular Monitor Ridge climbing route to the summit of Mount St. Helens. If you turned left onto the Ptarmigan Trail, it would be 2.1 miles down to the Climbers Bivouac Trailhead. To the right it's a steep climb (3,700-foot elevation gain) to the summit. Climbing permits are required above 4,800 feet elevation on Mount St. Helens. This hike continues west on the Loowit Trail.

At first you hike through subalpine forest with huckleberries growing between the trees. Soon the route traverses a sandy sidehill, where the path is marked with posts. Then the trail becomes very rough and a bit hard to follow as you enter the Swift Creek flow of *aa* lava. (*Aa* is a Hawaiian term describing a lava flow with a rough, broken surface.) As you cross the flow on the vague path, which is still marked with posts, Mount Hood is in view on the southern horizon. You will do a lot of boulder-hopping working your way across this flow. In spots between the rocks, pink mountain heather grows in abundance.

After crossing the aa lava for nearly a mile, the route descends a few feet and enters a lightly wooded area of small lodgepole pine and subalpine fir. Subalpine fir (*Abies lasiocarpa*) is the smallest of the true fir species that inhabit the country around Mount St. Helens. Its spire shape normally reaches 65 to 100 feet at maturity, but in some cases it can grow to 150 feet. The trees you see along the Loowit are generally much smaller, however. The bluish green needles are 1 to 1.75 inches long and flat in cross section. They are attached all around the twig and tend to turn upward. The deep purple cylindrical cones are 2 to 4 inches long, and as with all true firs, they disintegrate on the tree.

A couple of tiny streams that will dry up by midsummer cross the path in these woods. For the next 0.6 mile, the route is a little smoother and easier to follow. Then, 1.8 miles from the Ptarmigan Trail, you will cross a stream with a series of small waterfalls. Once across the stream the tread climbs onto another aa lava flow. Here the post-marked route becomes rough and vague again. This flow is much narrower than the one you crossed earlier. In about 0.3 mile the path leaves the flow, crosses an open boulder-strewn slope, and continues for another 0.3 mile to a junction with the Butte Camp Trail 238A. At 4,750 feet elevation this junction is 5.8 miles from the June Lake Trail. Here a climbing route up the southwest side of Mount St. Helens leaves the trail. The Loowit Trail goes straight ahead (northwest).

A few yards after leaving the junction, you will cross a tiny stream, which is usually dry by midsummer. This section of the Loowit Trail is just above timberline. In spots the sandy ground is covered with pink mountain heather, which blooms in July. The pink mountain heather (*Phyllodoce empetriformis*), aka pink mountain heath, is a low mat-forming plant with needlelike evergreen leaves. Its showy but small flowers are bell shaped and usually nodding. Pink mountain heather is not really true heather but resembles it enough to account for the name. Many other alpine flowers also dot the landscape. Mount St. Helens looms above to the right.

The trail crosses a lahar 0.8 mile from the junction. After crossing the mudflow you'll pass through an open stand of stunted lodgepole pines, then cross a small canyon 0.7 mile farther along. Cardwell's penstemon and common red paintbrush bloom here in profusion in July. The trail traverses out of the canyon, then descends through open fir, western white pine (*Pinus monticola*), and lodgepole pine (*P. contorta*) woods. These two species of pine are easy to tell apart. The western white pine is known as a five-needled pine, meaning that five needles emerge from the twigs at the same point. The lodgepole is a two-needled pine.

Soon the path makes a switchback to the right as it descends into another canyon. The remains of the Blue Lake Lahar can be seen far below in this canyon. The Loowit Trail climbs steeply out of the canyon and reenters the woods. In another 0.3 mile a junction with Sheep Canyon Trail 240 is reached. This junction, at 4,600 feet elevation, is 2 miles from the Butte Camp Trail. The Sheep Canyon Trail turns left (west) and descends to the Toutle Trail. The Loowit Trail goes straight ahead (north) at the junction.

The trail continues through the woods for a short distance, then descends slightly to cross the Sheep Canyon Lahar. Sheep Canyon Creek flows down this lahar deposit. As you leave the lahar, there will be a pond below the trail to the left. The relatively flat area just south of the pond makes a pretty fair campsite, one of the few along this section of the Loowit Trail. Camp carefully here, and don't trample any more flowers than necessary.

The trail passes the pond and skirts a small basin before making an ascending traverse to a flat-topped ridgeline. Once on the ridge the path heads north through snags and bear grass. Huckleberries and small firs are growing up between the snags. This area is part of the Singe Zone or Standing Dead Forest Zone created by the 1980 eruption. Soon the trail enters the Blast Zone—often called the Eruption Impact Zone. Here nearly all the trees were knocked down by the eruption. One mile from the junction with the Sheep Canyon Trail, look for a rocky outcropping on the right side of the trail. This outcropping on Crescent Ridge makes an excellent viewpoint overlooking the South Fork Toutle River Canyon. Coldwater Ridge Visitors Center can be seen to the north, across both forks of the Toutle River. Also in view to the north are Mount Margaret and even the ice-crowned summit of Mount Rainier, some 50 miles away to the northeast.

The May 18, 1980, eruption of Mount St. Helens melted huge amounts of snow and ice on the slopes of the mountain. The water quickly picked up the easily eroded volcanic debris that made up the slopes. The resulting lahar, which looked like thin, brown concrete, was the largest of eruption morning. At a rate of about 20 miles per hour, it rushed down the South Fork Canyon and on along the South Fork Toutle River to its confluence with the North Fork Toutle River and beyond. The South Fork Lahar preceded by several hours the much larger North Fork Toutle Lahar, whose deposits you will be crossing later in this hike.

Leaving the viewpoint, the Loowit Trail begins its 1,400-foot descent of Crescent Ridge. The trail winds and switchbacks its way down the ridge at the edge of the Blast Zone. Sometimes the trail is in large old-growth noble (*Abies procera*) and Pacific silver fir (*A. amabilis*) timber; at other times it's in the Blast Zone. After descending Crescent Ridge for 1.6 miles, you will come to the junction with the Toutle Trail 238. There is a campsite a couple of hundred yards west of the junction on the lahar deposit above the South Fork Toutle River. This is the last campsite before reaching Windy Ridge Trailhead, and it marks the end of this hike's second portion.

American dippers (*Cinclus mexicanus*) are often seen foraging along and in the South Fork Toutle River. These birds make an unusual bobbing motion while standing on streamside rocks. The dipper's plumage is a slate-gray color, often appearing black—especially when the bird is wet, which it is much of the time.

The hike's final section—from here to Windy Ridge—is roughly 12 miles and the trail has many slow and difficult places that must be negotiated. There is often no water available for the next 6 miles, so be sure you have enough with you. There is also no shade. The section of the Loowit Trail between here and Trail 207A should only be attempted by expert hikers in good condition. A good set of hiking poles would be an advantage when climbing into and out of the steep washes ahead. No camping is allowed in the Restricted Zone, so this section of the Loowit Trail must be done in one day.

At the junction, 3,180 feet in elevation and 2.6 miles from the Sheep Canyon Trail, the Loowit Trail turns to the right. The path descends a few more feet, crosses a stream, then heads upriver a short distance to a crossing. This crossing could be difficult at times of high water. Ford the river, then follow the vague cairn-marked trail on up the river bottom for 300 yards. Here the trail climbs steeply to the northeast for a short distance. It then makes a switchback to the left, and the grade moderates. The tread climbs through the vine maple (*Acer circinatum*) and silver snags, making three more switchbacks in the next 0.8 mile. In places the shrubs may have overgrown the trail if it hasn't been recently maintained.

Then the path traverses an open sandy slope for 0.3 mile. At present the trail is very narrow along this slope, and stepping off it on either the downhill or uphill side can be very tiring. Take your time here especially if you are carrying a heavy pack. The trail then makes a switchback to the left and continues to climb the sandy slope another 350 yards to a junction with the Castle Ridge Trail (signed FAIRVIEW TRAIL). At this junction, elevation 3,840 feet and 1.4 miles from the junction with the Toutle Trail, the Loowit Trail turns to the right.

The route now climbs gently for 0.5 mile along the rim of the South Fork Toutle River Canyon. Thick mats of pine-mat manzanita (*Arctostaphylos nevadensis*), a low-growing evergreen shrub, crowd the trail in spots along the rim. Pine-mat manzanita is easily confused with its close relative kinnikinnick (*A. uva-ursi*). To tell these plants apart, remember that pine-mat manzanita leaves are pointed while the kinnikinnick's are rounded at the end. The manzanita plants are doing a good job of stabilizing the loose volcanic soil here.

The Loowit Trail turns to the northeast to traverse an open, gentle slope. In about 0.4 mile you will cross the first of several washes that make this section difficult and time consuming. This is one of the easier washes so descend to the bottom and climb back out the other side. The route reaches another wash in 0.3 mile. Between the washes on the relatively flat benchland, black huckleberries and a few small noble fir and lodgepole pine trees are slowly but stubbornly growing, trying to reclaim the land that was theirs before the 1980 eruption. In a few spots foxglove (*Digitalis purpurea*) adds its bright blooms to the stark landscape.

Descending into this wash, the tread passes through a damper area where mountain alder forms a dense thicket, as it adds nitrogen to the humus-poor soil. Between the alders Indian hellebore sprouts next to the tread. The far side of the wash isn't very well vegetated, and the loose slope makes climbing out a chore.

After crossing another section of benchland, the route descends into a much broader wash that the map shows containing the two forks of Studebaker Creek. When I hiked this trail in late July, neither fork had water in it. Both sides of this wash were difficult to negotiate, and they will only get worse if they aren't maintained. On the south side of the wash as you descend, pearly everlasting (*Anaphalis margaritacea*) dots the trailside, and common red paintbrush's red flowers often attract hummingbirds.

Once across the broad wash, the route climbs to the top of Studebaker Ridge, crossing two more difficult washes along the way. On the ridge a few small noble firs sprout up between the widely scattered stumps and blown-down trees. Keep your eyes open for Roosevelt elk all along this section of the Loowit Trail. When I hiked it I saw nearly a hundred head. Past the ridgeline the route crosses two more washes. While the washes remain difficult and time consuming, they are not as bad as the ones you crossed before Studebaker Ridge.

The trail now crosses a bench that in spots is nearly covered with dwarf mountain lupine (*Lupinus lyallii*), with some grasses, sheep sorrel (*Rumex acetosella*), a few willows (*Salix* spp.), and kinnikinnick plants mixed in. Like all lupines, the dwarf mountain is a nitrogen-fixing plant. This tiny pioneer plant is slowly but steadily adding nutrients to the mineral soil, making it suitable for the plants that will follow.

A few small Douglas (*Pseudotsuga menziesii*) and noble firs are also trying to make their comeback here. Before long the route descends off the benchland to a stream crossing—the first water source since the South Fork Toutle River. To your right as you cross the stream is a bright yellow, volcanically altered clay formation, and farther upstream is a waterfall. After you cross the creek, the trail becomes very vague in the outwash fan below the Breach in the crater of Mount St. Helens.

The Breach is the space left when part of the crater rim (as well as the cone-shaped peak rising 1,300 feet above its present level) slid away in the Debris Avalanche at the beginning of the May 18, 1980, eruption. The crater now has a rim on only three sides, with the northern part missing. The Debris Avalanche was the largest landslide ever recorded.

Below the Breach

In the event of even minor volcanic activity, this section of trail could be very dangerous, with the possibility of flooding and/or lahars. This rock-strewn alluvial deposit is about 0.5 mile wide, and in most places there is no trail. Look well ahead as you hike and try to see the rock cairns that mark the route. The general route heads just a few degrees north of straight east here. As you near the other side of the alluvial deposit, the route crosses the stream that descends from the crater via Loowit Falls.

Shortly beyond the alluvial deposit, you will reach the junction with Trail 207A, 5.7 miles from the Castle Ridge Trail. Trail 207A is a short trail that connects with the Truman Trail, making a loop hike out onto these pumice flats possible from Windy Ridge Trailhead. The Loowit Trail makes a turn to the south and climbs a little more than 400 feet in the 0.8 mile to another junction.

Here the Loowit Falls Trail 216F turns to the right and climbs 300 feet in approximately 0.4 mile to a viewpoint close to Loowit Falls. The upper part of this trail is on top of some very unstable volcanic debris, so use the utmost caution. Don't send children up this trail alone. Loowit Falls is the larger of the two waterfalls that descend from the new crater area of Mount St. Helens. The

Loowit Falls

alternating strata over which the falls drop show, in a small way, the layered makeup of a strato-volcano.

Leave the junction by continuing east on the Loowit Trail. In 0.3 mile you come to a creek crossing. Above the trail to the right, the waters of the stream fall over layers of lava. Shortly you pass another waterfall, which is also to your right. Half a mile farther along, there is a beautiful set of springs to the right of the trail. The waters flow down to cross the trail, and the streamsides are choked with willows. Beside the trail and the stream grow bright pink stands of Lewis monkey flowers. From the spring on to the junction with the Windy Trail, 0.3 mile ahead, the route is marked with posts. You cross one more small stream before reaching the Windy Trail to complete the loop. Turn left onto the Windy Trail and retrace your steps to Windy Ridge Trailhead.

OPTIONS: The Loowit Trail need not be hiked all in one trip. Relatively easy access to the Loowit can be had via the June Lake Trail. The Ptarmigan Trail, Butte Camp Trail, and Sheep Canyon Loop are also possible access points.

HIGHLIGHTS: Hike from Harmony Viewpoint to the shore of Spirit Lake, all the way passing through landscape and plant communities that are rebuilding and reestablishing themselves after the catastrophic 1980 eruption.

START: Harmony Trailhead.

DISTANCE: 2.4-mile out-and-back day hike.

DIFFICULTY: Moderate.

SEASON: Early June through September.

TOTAL CLIMBING: 640 feet.

TRAILHEAD ELEVATION: 4,050 feet.

PERMITS: Northwest Forest Pass.

MAPS: Mount St. Helens National Volcanic Monument, aka Brown Map, or Spirit Lake East USGS quad.

SPECIAL CONSIDERATIONS: There may be three or four steeply sideways-sloping snowdrifts near the beginning of the trail early in the season. If this is the case, be sure you are wearing adequate boots. Ski poles or even an ice ax may be helpful here at times. This trail is within the Restricted Zone; you must stay on it even when you are at the shoreline of Spirit Lake. The Restricted Zone has been established to allow for comprehensive research of the recovery of the area; trampling vegetation, no matter how small, and/or inadvertently introducing plant species that are not presently found here will compromise this research. The lug soles of hiking boots often carry plant seeds. Camping is not allowed anywhere along the trail or on the shoreline.

PARKING AND TRAILHEAD FACILITIES: There is parking for several cars but no other facilities at the trailhead.

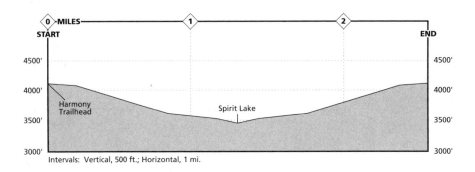

Harmony Trail (Trail 224)

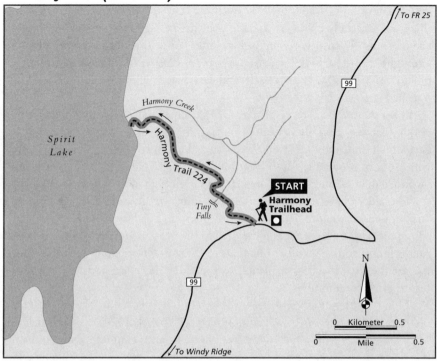

FINDING THE TRAIL: From Portland, drive north on Interstate 5 to exit 21 at Woodland, Washington. Then follow Washington Route 503 (which becomes WA 503 Spur) for 27.5 miles east to Cougar. From Cougar, drive east on WA 503 Spur (which becomes Forest Road 90) for 18.6 miles to its junction with Forest Road 25. At the junction FR 25 goes straight ahead (northeast). Follow FR 25 north for 24.3 miles to its junction with Forest Road 99.

From Seattle, take I–5 south to exit 133, and then follow Washington Route 7 for 55 miles to Morton. From Morton, drive east on U.S. Route 12 for 17 miles to Randle. Turn right and take Washington Route 131, then FR 25, south for 20 miles to its junction with FR 99.

Turn west onto FR 99 and drive 13.5 miles to the Harmony Trailhead.

KEY POINTS:

- **0.0** Harmony Trailhead (GPS 46 15.499 N 122 07.027 W).
- **0.4** Tiny waterfall.
- **1.2** Spirit Lake.
- **2.4** Harmony Trailhead (GPS 46 15.499 N 122 07.027 W).

THE HIKE: This trail is the only legal access to Spirit Lake, still partially covered with floating logs. Watch for Roosevelt elk (*Cervus elaphus roosevelti*) all along this trail, especially if you are making your hike early in the season and early in the morning. Even if you don't see the elk, you will probably see their tracks along the trail. Also look for outcroppings of volcanic rock that are many times older than Mount St. Helens itself, and view places where ancient glaciers have polished and scratched the rock.

From the trailhead the Harmony Trail immediately starts to descend into a cirque that was glacially excavated during the latter part of the last major ice age, which ended about 11,000 years ago. This north-facing slope is covered with western mountain ash (*Sorbus scopulina*), a few elderberry (*Sambucus* spp.) bushes, and an abundance of low-growing mountain alder (*Alnus incana*).

The alders have the ability to extract nitrogen from the atmosphere and "fix" or deposit what they don't use into the soil. The leaves of alders also have a high nitrogen content. When they fall to the ground and decay, the nitrogen-rich compost adds even more nutrients to the soil. Nitrogen in the soil is essential for the growth of most plants, so the alders here are paving the way for future plant communities.

Thinly scattered among the bushes and blown-down logs are a few small noble fir (*Abies procera*) trees. Salmonberry (*Rubus spectabilis*), western trillium (*Trillium ovatum*), fireweed (*Epilobium angustifolium*), common red paintbrush (*Castilleja miniata*), and pearly everlasting (*Anaphalis margaritacea*) plants complete the ground cover.

In a few yards the trail enters the Restricted Zone as it begins a descending traverse to the west. In this area hikers may not leave the trail or camp. After descending the traverse for 0.2 mile, make a switchback to the right, then turn left to continue your moderate descent. You will pass a tiny waterfall 300 yards farther along. Cross the tiny stream below the falls, then pass beneath an undercut rock face. On the far side of the face is another tiny falls and stream. These streams may dry up by midsummer.

Just past the tiny falls, an outcropping of bedrock above and to the left of the trail shows columnar jointing of old exposed lava. These columns formed as a result of contraction during the lava's cooling. This lava flow did not originate from Mount St. Helens, but rather from a much earlier volcanic event, long before Mount St. Helens existed.

The tread makes a switchback to the right 250 yards after passing the tiny waterfalls. Note the "trimline" to the north across the cirque. This is the scar left when a wall of water rushed up the hillsides as Spirit Lake was hit by the Debris Avalanche. The giant landslide that immediately preceded the 1980 Mount St. Helens eruption caused the Debris Avalanche. The wave funneled into the Harmony Creek basin, reaching heights of as much as 700 feet above

The shore of Spirit Lake strewn with logs

the old lake level. This huge amount of rushing water stripped nearly all the vegetation and much of the soil from the hillsides, washing it back into the lake.

Much of the bottom of the basin is now partly revegetated, mostly with mountain alder. In places a few black cottonwoods can be seen sticking above the other bushes. The black cottonwood (*Populus trichocarpa*) can reach heights of 150 feet or more on moist sites. Its large leaves, 3 to 5 inches long, are a dark, shiny green on top and silvery beneath. These leaves, which are broad and sharply pointed, have conspicuous veins and fine teeth on their margins and are suspended on a slender, round stem. Hairy catkins appear in early spring on the twigs, well before the leaves have emerged. Small, round, green capsules form on the catkins. Inside each capsule are the tiny, cottony seeds that give the tree its name. The terminal buds of the cottonwood are very sticky, with sweet-smelling resin. These cottonwoods are fast-growing trees; helped by the nitrogen-fixing abilities of the alders, they may quickly form a young deciduous forest.

The trail then descends a short distance and leaves the north-facing slope you have been on since the trailhead. For a short distance here, you will

Glacial scratches

descend along the top of a glacial moraine. The glacier melted more than 10,000 years ago, but evidence of its presence remains. The vegetation becomes sparser as you leave the slope. Making a turn to the left and heading west again toward the lake, you follow a line of posts across the pumice flats.

Scattered across the flats, many Cardwell's penstemons grow from the seemingly dry inhospitable pumice. Cardwell's penstemon (*Penstemon card-wellii*) is a small shrub, from 4 inches to a foot tall, with blue-violet to bright purple flowers. Spreading from root mats, which can be very large, these striking perennials often form large patches. Cardwell's penstemon has been extremely successful in recolonizing many locations devastated by the 1980 eruption of Mount St. Helens.

The trail starts to descend again 0.3 mile farther along. Soon you make a couple more switchbacks and reach Harmony Creek. There are several small waterfalls in this rushing stream, close to the trail. The once very beautiful and often-photographed, two-stage Harmony Falls dropped over layers of the same type of rock that you find along the trail close to the creek. The site of the falls is upstream from this point and not accessible because of the Restricted Zone.

Just before you reach the creek, look at the exposed bedrock on the right side of the trail. This purplish rock is thirty-million-year-old welded tuff. Embedded in the tuff, forming a conglomerate type of rock stratum, are bits and pieces of nearly white pumice. The tuff was laid down as hot volcanic material, then compressed by the weight of the layers above it. Notice that it, and the gray-green intrusive rock that forms a horizontal stripe through it, appear to have been smoothed and scratched.

Such smoothing and scratching are the result of glacial ice moving across the rock's surface. The ice that grooved these rocks also carved out the Harmony Creek basin. As the glacial ice receded, it left the small moraine mentioned earlier. Next to the trail, growing by itself from a crack in the tuff, is a small forlorn-looking western hemlock (*Tsuga heterophylla*) sapling. This tree, no matter how small, is a harbinger of what is to come, if the mountain stays quiet for a few hundred years.

At 1.2 miles the trail comes to an end near the log-strewn shore of Spirit Lake, at 3,410 feet elevation. You may notice that there are logs on the lakeshore up to about 20 feet above the present water level. These were placed here after the eruption but before the tunnel through Coldwater Ridge on the far side of the lake was completed. The level of the lake is now artificially stabilized by the drainage through the tunnel.

The end of the trail offers an excellent view of Mount St. Helens over the lake. Often the mountain reflects in the still water. Harmony Falls Lodge once sat next to the lakeshore, a short distance west of the end of the trail. The site of the old lodge is now well below the present lake level, which is about 200 feet higher than it was before the May 1980 eruption.

Return the way you came.

OPTIONS: For a short additional hike close by, climb the steps at Windy Ridge Viewpoint 2.3 miles south of Harmony Trailhead on FR 99.

18 Independence Loop (Trails 1, 227A, 227)

HIGHLIGHTS: The Independence Loop offers some of the best scenery to be found in Mount St. Helens National Volcanic Monument, including Spirit Lake, the gaping crater of Mount St. Helens, the huge volcanic cones of Mount Adams and Mount Rainier, and the jagged peaks and green ridges of the Mount Margaret Backcountry. All the while you are passing through terrain that nature is diligently working to revegetate.

START: Norway Pass Trailhead.

DISTANCE: 7.1-mile loop day hike.

DIFFICULTY: Moderate to strenuous.

SEASON: Mid-June through September.

TOTAL CLIMBING: 1,200 feet.

TRAILHEAD ELEVATION: 3,670 feet.

PERMITS: Northwest Forest Pass.

MAPS: Mount St. Helens National Volcanic Monument, aka Brown Map, or Spirit Lake East USGS quad.

SPECIAL CONSIDERATIONS: Water may not be available along this trail; take along all that you'll need.

PARKING AND TRAILHEAD FACILITIES: There are restrooms and adequate parking at the trailhead.

FINDING THE TRAILHEAD: Head north from Portland on Interstate 5 to exit 21 (21 miles north of the Columbia River Bridge) at Woodland. Then drive east for 27.5 miles on Washington Route 503 (which becomes WA 503 Spur) to Cougar. Continue east through Cougar on WA 503 Spur (which becomes Forest Road 90 at the Skamania County line) for another 18.6 miles to its junction with Forest Road 25. Bear left (nearly straight ahead) and head northeast on FR 25 for 24.3 miles to its junction with Forest Road 99.

From Seattle, take I–5 south to exit 133 at Tacoma, and then follow Washington Route 7 for 55 miles to Morton. From Morton, drive east for 17 miles to Randle. Turn right and take Washington Route 131, then FR 25, south for 20 miles to its junction with FR 99.

Turn west onto FR 99 and follow it for 8.8 miles to its junction with Forest Road 26. Turn right onto FR 26 and continue for 1 mile to Norway Pass Trailhead, on the left (west) side of the road.

Independence Loop (Trails 1, 227A, 227)

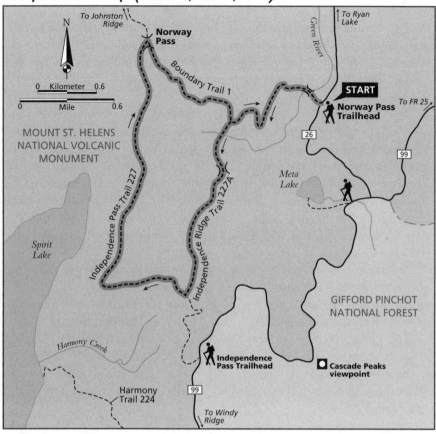

KEY POINTS:

0.0 Norway Pass Trailhead (GPS 46 18.330 N 122 04.948 W).

1.1 Junction with Independence Ridge Trail. Turn left (south).

1.6 Pass.

2.4 Junction with Independence Pass Trail (GPS 46 17.396 N 122 05.997 W). Turn right (northwest).

5.0 Norway Pass and the junction with Boundary Trail. (GPS 46 18.630 N 122 06.345 W). Turn right (southeast).

6.0 Junction with Independence Ridge Trail. Turn left (northeast).

7.1 Norway Pass Trailhead. (GPS 46 18.330 N 122 04.948 W).

THE HIKE: This loop begins on the Boundary Trail 1. Cross a wooden bridge over the Green River as you leave Norway Pass Trailhead; the river is just a small stream here. Climbing through blown-down timber and black huckleberry bushes (*Vaccinium membranaceum*), reach a small saddle 0.3 mile from the trailhead. Aptly named because it quickly establishes itself after a fire or other ground disturbance, fireweed's (*Epilobium angustifolium*) pink flowers brighten this stark landscape in August.

In the saddle grows a patch of foxglove. A large, usually biennial herb up to 6 feet tall, Foxglove (*Digitalis purpurea*) is an import from Europe that has been introduced into the Northwest. Its bell-shaped pink-purple or occasionally white flowers bloom in profusion, from the upper portion of the stalk, in July. The foxglove is a highly poisonous plant, affecting both muscle tissue and the circulatory system. The heart drug digitalis, a derivative of the foxglove plant, is widely used in treating heart disease. Common red paintbrush (*Castilleja miniata*), leopard lily, and false Solomon's seal add their cheery blooms to the trailside in early July.

The berries of the false Solomon's seal (*Smilacina racemosa*) are edible but not very tasty. Some Native American groups ate the berries, but they were mostly used for medicinal purposes. The roots were boiled to make a tea used to treat rheumatism or sometimes mashed to be used for healing cuts.

The leopard lily (*Lilium columbianum*), aka Columbia lily or tiger lily, is a beautiful perennial that grows to 3 feet or slightly taller from a bulb. Its eye-catching bright orange flowers have red to purple spots and petals that turn backward. The bulbs of the leopard lily were sometimes harvested by Native Americans for food.

Continuing to climb, the route makes a couple of switchbacks before reaching a junction with the Independence Ridge Trail 227A at 1.1 miles from the trailhead. Turn left here onto the Independence Ridge Trail and climb gradually to the south on the sometimes steep and rough trail that's fringed much of the way with Douglas aster (*Aster subspicatus*), Oregon sunshine (*Eriophyllum lanatum*), Menzies' larkspur (*Delphinium menziesii*), and three species of penstemon.

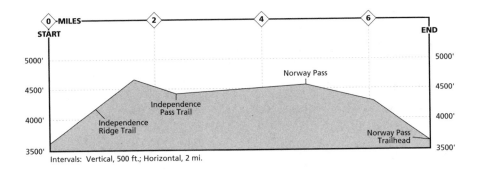

Intervals: Vertical, 500 ft.; Horizontal, 2 mi.

Oregon sunshine

With all these flowers growing here, hummingbirds are often busy. If you are wearing bright colors—especially red—they may also check you out. Meta Lake is below to the left (east) in a cirque carved by a glacier that melted 11,000 years ago. Mount Adams rises above the green hills in the distance.

Red columbines (*Aquilegia formosa*), lupines (*Lupinus* spp.), asters, tall blue-bells (*Mertensia paniculata*), and leopard lilies cover the more open slopes as you climb. The vegetation on this slope is as lush as any within the Blast Zone. Western mountain ash (*Sorbus scopulina*) and mountain alder (*Alnus incana*) form dense thickets. In other places small Pacific silver firs (*Abies amabilis*), noble firs (*Abies procera*), and Alaska cedars are trying to establish themselves and reclaim their lost territory.

Around Mount St. Helens the Alaska cedar, aka yellow cedar (*Chamaecyparis nootkatensis*), is neither as common nor large as the western red cedar (*Thuja plicata*). It can reach a height of 150 feet in some areas, but in this area it is usually much smaller. There are several ways to tell the Alaska cedar from its cousin the western red. First is its habitat: Alaska cedars generally grow at higher elevations in this region. Unlike the western red, the branches of the

Alaska cedar tend to hang down limply, and the central leader is usually drooped like a hemlock. Both the western red and Alaska cedar have scalelike leaves, but if you slide your hand along the foliage upstem (against the grain) you will notice that the Alaska has a prickly feel that the western red doesn't. The tiny cones of the Alaska cedar are at first a light green color and appear berrylike; when they mature they become brown. Alaska cedar is a very long-lived tree, sometimes reaching 1,500 years of age.

The route reaches a pass 0.5 mile from the junction. At the pass, 4,670 feet above sea level, the slope becomes drier and the vegetation less dense. Beyond the pass the path crosses a large gully then traverses a slope, crossing several small gullies in the 0.5 mile to another ridgeline. Paintbrush and penstemon color this slope. The tread follows the ridge for a short distance, then bears slightly to the right. You then descend through the short, broken-off, silvered snags of young firs and fireweed to the junction with the Independence Pass Trail, on the side of a little valley. This junction, which is shown incorrectly on the USGS map, is 1.3 miles from the junction with the Boundary Trail. See the options below for a possible alternate route to reach this point. From here to Norway Pass 2.6 miles ahead, the Independence Pass Trail is the boundary of the Restricted Zone, so off-trail travel and camping are prohibited.

At the junction turn right (northwest) onto the Independence Pass Trail and descend a few feet, crossing the tiny valley. Through midsummer there is usually a spring in the bottom of the valley a few yards below the trail to the south (left). Leaving the valley, the route climbs slightly to the west. Soon it descends and turns north along a steep slope above Spirit Lake. Here there is a great view to the southwest into the crater of Mount St. Helens. Far below to the south, the Harmony Trail can be seen descending to the shore of the lake.

At 0.9 mile after leaving the junction with the Independence Ridge Trail, the route passes beneath some cliffs. Look for pinnacles of rock below the trail as you pass the cliffs. These pinnacles are the remains of intrusive rock that pushed its way up through a crack or weak joint in the overlaying strata.

Intrusive rock is magma that has cooled and solidified below the earth's surface. A pluton is a large body of intrusive rock possibly several miles or more wide. Smaller intrusions may take place through cracks and weak spots in a pluton after it has solidified. The rock of these smaller (an inch to several yards wide) intrusions are often of a different chemical composition and in some cases are more resistant to erosion than the surrounding rock. When the less erosion-resistant rock wears away, it may leave these smaller intrusions standing above the general surface level.

The magma that was to form the Spirit Lake Pluton intruded, or pushed up, into older (by about three million years) volcanic rock approximately twenty million years ago. The ridge you are standing on is part of the Spirit

Spirit Lake from Independence Pass Trail

Lake Pluton uplift. Much of that older rock—which was itself raised by the pluton and left sitting atop it—has now eroded away, leaving the top of the pluton exposed in many places. The peaks and ridges of the Mount Margaret Backcountry to the northwest are mostly made up of the glacier-carved remnants of the Spirit Lake Pluton. The mineral deposits sought after by miners in this area were formed as a result of heat and thermal activity during and for several million years after the intrusion of the pluton.

The tread soon begins to climb, making a couple of switchbacks. Then it winds up through a saddle, at 4,580 feet elevation. Far below, above the northern shores of Spirit Lake, you may notice that there are no stumps or fallen trees for some distance above the water level. The level at which you begin to see the remains of the flattened forest is called the trimline. This trimline—or sloshline, as it is sometimes called—is the scar left when a wall of water rushed up the hillsides as Spirit Lake was hit by the Debris Avalanche, the giant landslide that immediately preceded the 1980 Mount St. Helens eruption. This huge amount of rushing water stripped nearly all the vegetation for several hundred feet up the hillsides and washed it back into the lake.

Past the saddle the path traverses the west-facing slope. Soon the broad, ice-sheathed bulk of Mount Rainier comes into view ahead. Mount Rainier, the highest peak in Washington and the fifth highest in the lower forty-eight, is an example of what Mount St. Helens could eventually look like. St. Helens, given enough time and the right types of eruptions, could build itself into a strato-volcano rivaling the size of its huge sister 45 miles to the northeast.

The building of Mount Rainier started about 1,000,000 years ago, so it had a better-than-950,000-year head start on St. Helens. Mount Rainier's eruptions have alternated between explosive events, like the one that happened in 1980 at St. Helens, and less violent episodes when liquid lava flowed from the crater. The molten flows covered the fragmental deposits from the explosive erup-tions, strengthening and stabilizing the cone. These processes continued inter-mittently for hundreds of thousands of years. At times the mountain blew large volumes of rock out of itself, shrinking the cone, as St. Helens did in 1980.

During the periods between eruptions, glaciers ground deeply into the mountain's flanks, but the volcanic events continued and the mountain always rebuilt itself. In places the canyons carved by the glaciers were filled by repeated lava flows. When this happened the erosion pattern was changed. The new lava was more resistant to erosion than the older material that formed the ridges between the original canyons. This older and weaker rock was eroded away, leaving the newer lava rock standing as ridges.

About 75,000 years ago—still 35,000 years before Mount St. Helens began to build—Mount Rainier reached its maximum size. At that time its altitude was approximately 16,000 feet, about 1,600 feet higher than its present eleva-tion. The eastern slope of Little Tahoma, the sharply pointed peak that stands more than 11,000 feet high on the east flank of Mount Rainier, represents the approximate surface of that flank at the time when Rainier was at its largest. Since that time the volcanic output of Rainier has not kept up with erosion. If you were to run an imaginary line up the east slope of Little Tahoma and con-tinue it to a point directly above the summit of Rainier, the line would roughly follow the slope that was there 75,000 years ago. As you can see, Mount Rainier was once much larger than it is today.

This present loss of volume doesn't mean that Rainier is in its declining stages or that it is extinct. It experienced minor eruptions well into the nine-teenth century. The last one was recorded in 1870, the same year that the mountain was first climbed. Mudflows probably caused by volcanic action have happened in the twentieth century. Today fumaroles release hot gases from near the summit. The 0.25-mile-wide crater is filled with ice, but fumaroles beneath it melt ice caves. Mount Rainier in all likelihood will have major erup-tions in the future, possibly regaining its former stature.

As you hike farther along the slope, a few avalanche lilies manage to survive in the shaded, damper spots. Usually found on moist north-facing slopes, the avalanche lily (*Erythronium montanum*), aka fawn lily, sprouts as soon as the snow melts. In fact, it will occasionally push up through the last thin remnants of snow to get a head start on the growing season. The stem pushes up from between the pale green leaves, reaching up to about a foot tall before blooming. The nodding flowers have six white petals surrounding their yellow centers.

There is a viewpoint to the right of the trail 2.5 miles from the junction with the Independence Pass Trail. Step over the few yards to it and view Mount Adams over the timbered hills 35 miles to the east. At 12,276 feet Adams is the second highest peak in Washington, exceeded only by Mount Rainier. It's a complicated structure of volcanic cones that appear to lean on each other, giving it its extremely bulky, humped form. Being a much older volcano than Mount St. Helens, Adams has been and continues to be deeply eroded by the glacial ice that covers much of its upper slopes.

After taking in the view of Mount Adams, descend the last 0.1 mile to Norway Pass and the junction with the Boundary Trail, at 4,520 feet elevation. As early as 1892 mining claims were staked on the slopes below Norway Pass. Fishermen and hunters had discovered sulfide materials, such as pyrite and galena, in the area. These minerals were in a porphyry copper deposit that is associated with the Spirit Lake Pluton.

About 1900 hundreds of new claims were staked in the Mount St. Helens Mining District, mostly north of Spirit Lake. All totaled, more than 11,000 feet of underground tunnels were dug, and there were thousands of prospect holes. The veins were hard to work, and only modest amounts of gold and silver were recovered from the rock. Most of the mines were abandoned by about 1929, but some activity continued until the May 18, 1980, eruption.

Turn right onto the Boundary Trail as you leave Norway Pass and traverse a northeast-facing slope through standing snags and blown-down timber. Huckleberry bushes and western mountain ash soon line the trail. In early summer the blooms of the western mountain ash, aka Cascade mountain ash, can be spotted well ahead as you stroll along a trail or drive a mountain road. The tiny but numerous white flowers form clusters up to 6 inches wide at the ends of the branches. The western mountain ash is a deciduous shrub or sometimes a small tree up to 15 feet tall. Generally growing at middle to upper elevations in the Mount St. Helens region, the ash prefers relatively open areas where it can get direct sunlight. Native Americans did not favor the red berries of the western mountain ash, but at least one group did consume them raw. At present a tart jelly is sometimes made from them. Another group of aboriginal people is said to have rubbed the berries on their scalps to combat head lice.

Several species of birds relish the berries, which at times ferment on the tree, making the birds drunk.

Between the bushes and downed logs are fireweed and a few avalanche lilies. Small noble and Pacific silver fir trees have shot up between the snags on their way to regrowing the forest that was here before the eruption. Soon the route crosses a gully with a tiny stream that may be dry by midsummer. You then cross a spur ridge where Meta Lake again comes into view. Then the route descends for 0.2 mile to the junction with the Independence Ridge Trail. From the junction continue along the Boundary Trail, retracing your steps to the Norway Pass Trailhead.

OPTIONS: A slightly shorter but nearly as interesting trip, requiring a car shuttle, can be made by starting your hike at Independence Pass Trailhead. To reach this trailhead continue southwest on FR 99 from its junction (near the Miners Car Exhibit) with FR 26. In 3.1 miles you will reach the trailhead, which is on the right side of the road.

Climb west from the trailhead on the Independence Pass Trail, which quickly reaches the ridgeline overlooking Spirit Lake. The route turns to the north along the ridge and reaches the junction with the Independence Pass Trail mentioned above, 0.9 mile from Independence Pass Trailhead. From the junction you can either continue on the Independence Pass Trail to Norway Pass and descend along the Boundary Trail to Norway Pass Trailhead, or follow the shorter Independence Ridge Trail above Meta Lake to a junction with the Boundary Trail.

HIGHLIGHTS: Take the short walk from Miners Car Exhibit through the blown-down forest of the Blast Zone as you stroll to Meta Lake, soaking in the proof of nature's tremendous survival and rejuvenating capabilities.

START: Miners Car Exhibit.

DISTANCE: 0.6-mile out-and-back day hike.

DIFFICULTY: Easy.

SEASON: Mid-June through September.

TOTAL CLIMBING: Minimal.

TRAILHEAD ELEVATION: 3,630 feet.

PERMITS: Northwest Forest Pass.

MAPS: Spirit Lake East USGS quad, but no map other than the one in this book is really needed for this short hike.

PARKING AND TRAILHEAD FACILITIES: There are restrooms and adequate parking at the trailhead. Drinking water is available 0.1 mile west at the Meta Lake parking area.

FINDING THE TRAILHEAD: Head north from Portland on Interstate 5 to exit 21 (21 miles north of the Columbia River Bridge) at Woodland. Then drive east for 27.5 miles on Washington Route 503 (which becomes WA 503 Spur) to Cougar. Continue east through Cougar on WA 503 Spur (which becomes Forest Road 90 at the Skamania County line) for another 18.6 miles to its junction with Forest Road 25. Bear left (nearly straight ahead) and head northeast on FR 25 for 24.3 miles to its junction with Forest Road 99.

From Seattle, take I–5 south to exit 133 at Tacoma, and then follow Washington Route 7 for 55 miles to Morton. From Morton, drive east for 17 miles to Randle. Turn right and take Washington Route 131, then FR 25, south for 20 miles to its junction with FR 99.

Turn west onto FR 99 and follow it for 4.5 miles to Bear Pass Viewpoint. On the morning of May 18, 1980, a small group of people was camped at Bear Meadows, near here. Among them was Gary Rosenquist, who took a spectacular series of quick-succession photographs of the eruption, which has been widely published, before the group made a harrowing drive to safety.

After spending a few minutes at the viewpoint, get back on FR 99 and drive another 4.3 miles (8.8 miles from FR 25) to the junction with FR 26, and the Miners Car Exhibit site.

Meta Lake (Trail 210)

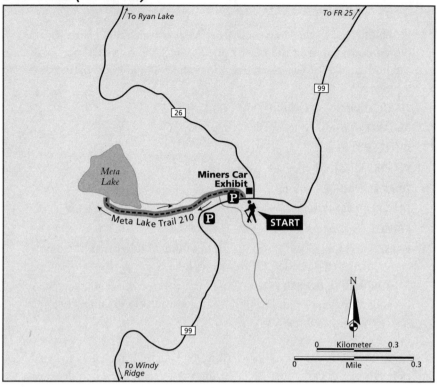

KEY POINTS:

0.0 Miners Car Exhibit (GPS 46 17.743 N 122 04.507 W).

0.1 Meta Lake parking area. Bear right (west).

0.3 Meta Lake.

0.6 Miners Car Exhibit (GPS 46 17.743 N 122 04.507 W).

THE HIKE: Next to the parking area is the fenced-in Miners Car Exhibit. A little more than one minute after the beginning of the May 18, 1980, eruption of Mount St. Helens, a hot, turbulent, stone-filled wind roared over the landscape where you are standing, 8.5 miles from the crater. Moving at an estimated 350 miles per hour here, this 400-degree blast cloud flattened the forest and tossed the Miners Car about like a toy. The car was rolled northward from the place where it was parked on the other side of FR 99. The car's owners were in a cabin at a nearby mine at the time and were instantly killed.

Even though the blast of the eruption was heard, in some cases, as far as 650 miles away, the people in the cabin by the mine may have heard almost nothing

Miners car

before the seething cloud reached them. People who survived in the outer edges of the Blast Zone reported hearing the sounds of trees being broken and tossed around but did not hear the eruption itself. This "zone of silence," as it was called, generally extended for about a 60-mile radius around the volcano. I was personally within the zone of silence, being approximately 35 miles from the mountain that morning, and heard nothing.

From the Miners Car Exhibit, the paved trail parallels FR 99 for a couple of hundred yards southwest to the Meta Lake parking area. Fireweed (*Epilobium angustifolium*) lines the trail, as you walk along a sluggish stream. Fireweed lives mostly in places that have been disturbed, such as road cuts, logged-over spots, and especially recently burned areas, hence its common name. The Blast and Singe Zones created by the 1980 eruption of Mount St. Helens have provided excellent habitat for this member of the primrose family. Under perfect conditions fireweed can attain a height of 9 feet, but it's usually 3 to 5 feet tall. The deep pink flowers grow from the upper part of the stem, forming a spire-shaped cluster. Fireweed blooms in late summer.

Leaving the Meta Lake parking area, the paved trail bears right (west) away from the road to wind its way through the small Pacific silver firs (*Abies amabilis*). These trees were very small and beneath a canopy of mostly old-growth Douglas fir before the mountain erupted. The larger trees were all blown down and killed, but the tiny trees beneath the snow cover survived. Under the excellent growing conditions in the Mount St. Helens region, these survivors can be expected to reach 150 to 180 feet in height when they mature.

The silver fir's needles are from 0.75 to 1.25 inches long, flat in cross section, and shiny green on their top sides. The lower side of each needle has two thin white bands, giving the tree its silvery appearance. The needles grow from all the way around the stem but turn upward and appear to be bunched on top. Pacific silver fir cones are dark purple in color and from 3.5 to 5 inches long. Like all true firs, they stand erect from the branch and disintegrate there before falling to the ground, unless the squirrels prematurely clip them off.

Across FR 99 from the Meta Lake Trailhead is a stand of young noble fir. The noble fir (*Abies procera*) is a tall conifer, with fairly short branches that stand straight out from its straight trunk. In the past the Latin name for the noble—as the noble fir is commonly called—was *Abies nobilis*, but it was found that another tree somewhere else in the world already had that name. Also in times past (and by some timber workers today), the noble was called larch, a real case of mistaken identity. Several hills around the Northwest were named Larch Mountain because of the noble firs that grew on their slopes.

The midelevation country around Mount St. Helens provides nearly the perfect growing conditions for the noble fir, with its heavy winter rain and snowfall, cool temperatures, and light summer precipitation. Under these conditions the noble normally grows to 100 to 150 feet in height at maturity. Some outstanding specimens reach 250 feet or more, making the noble the largest of the true firs (*Abies* spp.).

Noble fir needles are roughly four sided, bluish green, and 1 to 1.5 inches long. Although they grow from all sides of the stem, they turn upward and appear from a distance to all be on top. Pick off one of the needles and you'll notice that they strongly resemble a hockey stick in shape. The green (before maturing to a brown color) cones of the noble fir are large (4 to 6 inches long) when compared to other true firs. As with all true firs, the cones stand straight up from the branches and come apart before falling to the ground, unless squirrels clip them off while they are still intact. The long pointed bracts nearly cover the scales of the cone, giving it a shingled appearance.

Noble fir is a valuable timber tree. The wood is fairly hard and heavy, and works well. The lumber is often used for finish work. In the days when venetian blinds were made from wood, noble fir was used almost exclusively. Timber companies have planted large sections of land to noble fir in an effort to refor- est parts of the area devastated by the 1980 eruption.

For the layperson it is easy to confuse the noble fir with its close relative the Pacific silver fir; the trees are similar in size, shape, and color. The cones of the silver fir are smaller than those of the noble and lack the large pointed bracts. But the easiest way to tell them apart is by the noble's hockey-stick-shaped needles, which on silver fir are more nearly straight.

Willows (*Salix* spp.), western mountain ash (*Sorbus scopulina*), mountain alder (*Alnus incana*), salmonberries (*Rubus spectabilis*), and black huckleberry bushes (*Vaccinium membranaceum*) grow thickly among the surprisingly fast- growing firs and decomposing logs on the route to the lake. Along the way stop and read the interpretive sign about "survivors."

At 0.3 mile from the Miners Car parking area, the trail ends at a viewing plat- form (sometimes also used for fishing) on the shore of Meta Lake. An interpre- tive reader board here explains how the frogs, crawfish, and brook trout survived the blast and ash under a covering of snow and ice when the mountain erupted.

The brook trout (*Salvelinus fontinalis*)—aka brookie, speckled char, and eastern brook trout—isn't really a trout at all, but rather a char. Brookies are native to eastern North America and an introduced species to the western United States. In their preferred habitat of clear cold water, in lakes or inter- mittently slow streams, these transplanted fish have done very well. In the still or slow-moving waters they prefer, brook trout feed mostly on insects. This makes them a favorite target for fly anglers, but spin casting with a rooster tail also works very well.

Often brook trout are quite small, generally 5 to 12 inches long, but under good conditions they can reach a length of over 30 inches and weigh more than five pounds. The brookie's general color is olive green, darker on the back and lighter on the sides. On the sides of the fish are many small greenish spots, some with red centers and surrounded with a blue halo. The front edges of the lower fins have a white stripe, and the chest has a pink to orange tinge. The chests of the male fish are often a bright orange color.

Being quick to reproduce, and in many cases lacking significant predators, introduced brook trout populations often soar to the point that they deplete their food supply. When this happens their growth is stunted, and the small fish appear to have heads that are large and out of proportion to the size of the rest of their bodies. This doesn't seem to be the case in Meta Lake—these fish, though relatively small, look healthy and exhibit normal body proportions.

These fish, along with the other survivors at Meta Lake, probably had a very rough time during the first year after the eruption. The lake waters were clouded by ash, and the food supply was limited. But they made it, showing how nature can rebuild itself after almost any disastrous event.

Meta Lake

Look across the lake to the north and west slopes of the basin that holds it, and notice the swirled pattern of the blown-down trees. These patterns are the result of the rolling and swirling action of the blast density flow as it surged over the rough terrain.

In June scattered clumps of serviceberry (*Amelanchier alnifolia*) bloom on these slopes. Serviceberry, aka saskatoon, is a deciduous shrub or small tree up to 12 feet tall. Its leaves are round to oval and regularly fine toothed on the top margin. The white flowers, up to about 1-inch across, have five petals and bloom in late May and June around Meta Lake.

Later in summer the fruit, which is relished by birds, bears, chipmunks, and many other small animals, ripens, first with a dull red color but turning dark purple when completely mature. Native Americans and early settlers on the Great Plains and in the West made pemmican, an important storable food, by combining the berries with game meat.

As you stand on the platform enjoying the view, tree swallows (*Tachycineta bicolor*) often swoop and dive close by, foraging for insects, over the lake.

Red-winged blackbirds (*Agelaius phoeniceus*) are often seen, or at least their beautiful calls heard, from the willows along the lakeshore.

OPTIONS: Only 1 mile to the northwest on FR 26 is Norway Pass Trailhead. Along FR 26 on the way to the trailhead and along the Independence Loop Trail are bird's-eye views of Meta Lake. The area around Meta Lake and Norway Pass Trailhead is probably the best place in the Mount St. Helens National Volcanic Monument to observe a large, continuous area of blown-down old-growth forest. The whole area turns bright pinkish red with fireweed blooms in late summer.

HIGHLIGHTS: This hike climbs through the blown-down but slowly rejuvenating forest from Norway Pass Trailhead to Norway Pass, then follows the very spine of the Mount Margaret Backcountry to the summit of Mount Margaret. Mount Whittier is a short but challenging optional side trip.

START: Norway Pass Trailhead.

DISTANCE: 11.6-mile out-and-back backpack or long day hike.

DIFFICULTY: Moderate to strenuous.

SEASON: July through September.

TOTAL CLIMBING: Approximately 2,000 feet to either peak.

TRAILHEAD ELEVATION: 3,670 feet.

PERMITS: Northwest Forest Pass for parking at Norway Pass Trailhead. A Mount Margaret Backcountry permit is required for camping.

MAPS: Mount St. Helens National Volcanic Monument, aka Brown Map. Spirit Lake East and Spirit Lake West USGS quads. The Spirit Lake West quad does not show the trail, however.

SPECIAL CONSIDERATIONS: The weather near or above timberline is very changeable. It may be warm, clear, and sunny when you leave the trailhead, only to change to rain or possibly even a blizzard by the time you reach the summit. Rain and snow are common before late June and possible all summer. In sunny weather the south-facing slopes can be very hot and dry. Nearly the entire route is exposed to direct sunshine, with little or no shade available; take along your sunscreen and plenty of water.

PARKING AND TRAILHEAD FACILITIES: There are restrooms and adequate parking at the trailhead.

FINDING THE TRAILHEAD: Head north from Portland on Interstate 5 to exit 21 (21 miles north of the Columbia River Bridge) at Woodland. Then drive east for 27.5 miles on Washington Route 503 (which becomes WA 503 Spur) to Cougar. Continue east through Cougar on WA 503 Spur (which becomes Forest Road 90 at the Skamania County line) for another 18.6 miles to its junction with Forest Road 25. Bear left (nearly straight ahead) and head northeast on FR 25 for 24.3 miles to its junction with Forest Road 99.

From Seattle, take I–5 south to exit 133 at Tacoma, and then follow Washington Route 7 for 55 miles to Morton. From Morton, drive east for 17 miles

Mount Margaret (Trail 1)

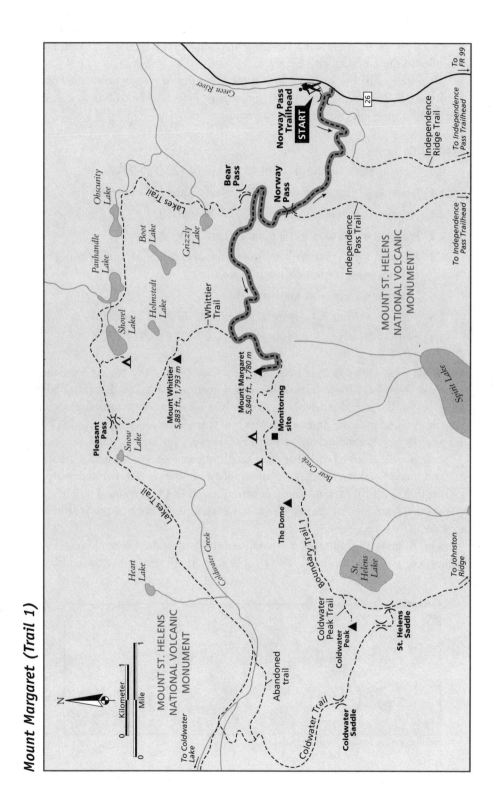

to Randle. Turn right and take Washington Route 131, then FR 25, south for 20 miles to the junction with FR 99.

Turn west onto FR 99 and follow it for 8.8 miles to its junction with Forest Road 26. Turn right onto FR 26 and follow it for 1 mile to Norway Pass Trailhead on the left (west) side of the road.

KEY POINTS:

0.0 Norway Pass Trailhead (GPS 46 18.330 N 122 04.948 W).

1.1 Junction with Independence Ridge Trail. Turn right (northwest).

2.1 Norway Pass (GPS 46 18.630 N 122 06.345 W).

2.8 Junction with Lakes Trail. Continue straight (west).

4.9 Junction with Whittier Trail and optional climb of Mount Whittier. For this hike, continue straight (southwest).

5.6 Junction with Mount Margaret Trail.

5.8 Summit of Mount Margaret (GPS 46 18.720 N 122 08.060 W).

11.6 Norway Pass Trailhead (GPS 46 18.330 N 122 04.948 W).

THE HIKE: This entire hike is over strata that are part of the twenty-million-year-old Spirit Lake Pluton. Intrusive rock is magma that has cooled and solidified below the earth's surface. A pluton is a large body of intrusive rock, possibly several miles or more wide. Much of this pluton was deeply eroded by ice age glaciers that melted only about 11,000 years ago. They formed the deep U-shaped valleys and bowl-shaped glacial cirques that are so evident here today. Of course, there are deposits of pumice and other recent volcanic material from Mount St. Helens thinly covering much of the terrain. The higher peaks have been mostly washed clean, however, and the rock of the pluton is exposed.

The Boundary Trail crosses a wooden bridge over the Green River as it leaves Norway Pass Trailhead. The river is just a small stream here. Climbing

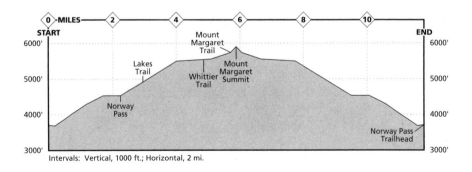

Intervals: Vertical, 1000 ft.; Horizontal, 2 mi.

through blown-down timber and huckleberry bushes, it reaches a small saddle 0.3 mile from the trailhead. Fireweed (*Epilobium angustifolium*) blooms in late summer much of the way to the saddle. The Blast and Singe Zones caused by the 1980 eruption of Mount St. Helens have provided excellent habitat for this member of the primrose family. Under perfect conditions fireweed can attain a height of 9 feet, but it's usually 3 to 5 feet tall. The deep pink flowers grow from the upper part of the stem, forming a spire-shaped cluster.

A patch of foxglove (*Digitalis purpurea*) grows in the saddle. An import from Europe, foxglove is a large, usually biennial herb up to 6 feet tall. Its pink-purple bell-shaped flowers bloom in profusion, from the upper portion of the stalk, in July. The heart drug digitalis is a derivative of foxglove, but if eaten the plant is highly poisonous.

Continuing to climb, the route makes a couple of switchbacks and reaches the junction with the Independence Ridge Trail 1.1 miles from the trailhead. The Boundary Trail turns right at this junction. Climbing to the northwest, the path soon crosses a ridgeline. It then cuts back into a gully and crosses a tiny stream, which may be dry by midsummer. After crossing the gully the tread traverses along the northeast-facing slope to Norway Pass, elevation 4,520 feet, and the junction with the Independence Pass Trail. Black huckleberries (*Vaccinium membranaceum*) and western mountain ash line the trail as it approaches the pass, 2.1 miles from the trailhead.

Generally growing at middle to upper elevations in the Mount St. Helens region, the western mountain ash (*Sorbus scopulina*) prefers relatively open areas where it can get direct sunlight. It's a deciduous shrub or sometimes a small tree up to 15 feet tall, blooming in early summer. The tiny but numerous white flowers form clusters up to 6 inches wide at the ends of the branches, then mature into the red berries that are relished by birds of many species.

At the pass Spirit Lake and Mount St. Helens come into view to the south. The Independence Pass Trail turns left (south) at the junction and leads to Independence Pass Trailhead on FR 99. From here to the junction with the Coldwater Peak Trail at the end of this hike description, the Boundary Trail is the border of the Restricted Zone. No camping or travel is allowed on the left (south) side of the trail.

Leaving the pass, the path climbs a ridge for a short way, then bears right to traverse around the head of a basin. Bleeding hearts (*Dicentra formosa*) grow in a few damp spots on the slopes. The route switches back to the left 0.5 mile from the pass. Another 0.2 mile and you reach the junction with the Lakes Trail, at 4,870 feet elevation. The junction, 2.8 miles from Norway Pass Trailhead, was not marked when I hiked this trail, but may be in the future. The Lakes Trail turns to the right and climbs to the northeast over Bear Pass. For this hike continue straight on the Boundary Trail.

Past the junction you climb another 0.4 mile to a saddle. This saddle, at 5,120 feet elevation, is a good place to stop, rest, and enjoy the view. To the northeast Grizzly Lake lies below, while Mount Rainier's icy summit rises above the hills 40 miles in the distance. Far to the northwest, from this high vantage point on very clear days the Olympic Mountains can be seen on the horizon 125 miles away.

Soon after leaving the saddle, the route begins a traverse along the south side of the ridge. Far in the distance, to the south-southeast, Mount Jefferson (120 miles away) breaks the horizon between Mount St. Helens and 70-mile-distant Mount Hood. Red columbines and cat's ear lilies dot the ground beside the tread.

The red columbine (*Aquilegia formosa*) is a perennial plant that may grow up to 3 feet tall. Its drooping flowers are red and yellow with five straight reddish spurs. Some groups of Native Americans used a milky pulp extracted from the roots as a healing lotion for cuts and sores. The plant also had several other medicinal uses for aboriginal peoples.

The cat's ear lily (*Calochortus subalpinus*), aka subalpine mariposa and mountain cat's ear, grows in open dry areas from middle elevations up to timberline. Its cream-colored flowers have three petals and are about 1 inch across. *Mariposa* means "butterfly" in Spanish.

After crossing several small gullies and ridges, the route reaches the ridgeline again in a small saddle, 1.9 miles from the junction with the Lakes Trail. Step a few feet to the right here for a view of Boot and Obscurity Lakes, far below to the northeast in cirques dug by ice age glaciers.

Another 0.2 mile will bring you to the unmarked junction with the Whittier Trail in another saddle at 5,560 feet elevation. Here the Whittier Trail turns to the right and leads 1.1 miles north to the summit of Mount Whittier, the highest peak in the Mount Margaret Backcountry.

Don't make the trip to Mount Whittier unless you are an agile and experienced hiker. Some mountaineering experience would be a great help here. If you decide that you're up to the climb, the Mount Whittier Trail traverses north from the junction with the Boundary Trail across a slope covered with small firs (*Abies* spp.) and mountain hemlocks (*Tsuga mertensiana*). Silver snags stick up between the small trees, and lupines (*Lupinus* spp.) cover the open spots in between. In 0.5 mile you will reach a ridgeline, where Obscurity and Boot Lakes come into view, far below to the northeast.

The path along the ridgeline quickly deteriorates. To follow the route you will need to watch very closely for any and all signs of it. You will descend and climb steps, scramble over steep sections of rock, and traverse very exposed slopes along this narrow path. Holmstedt Lake comes into view 0.4 mile after

Mount Whittier. PHOTO MIKE BARSTAD

reaching the ridge. After a little more rough scrambling, you reach the 5,883-foot summit of Mount Whittier.

From the summit the views in all directions are breathtaking. Panhandle Lake sits in a canyon below close by Holmstedt Lake. To the north Shovel Lake sparkles in the topmost cirque excavated by a long-gone glacier. Below and south is Coldwater Canyon. Far down the canyon is the upper end of Coldwater Lake, one of many formed by the 1980 eruption and resulting mudflow.

If you continue on the Whittier Trail for another 1.2 miles, you will come to the junction with the Lakes Trail, which can be used as an alternate return route to Norway Pass and Norway Pass Trailhead. As of late summer 2003, a small section of the Whittier Trail north of the summit of Mount Whittier had washed out, making passage difficult. The Forest Service notes that you use this trail at your own risk.

After you've climbed Mount Whittier—or chosen not to—the Boundary Trail traverses south around a high point on the ridge from the junction with

Mount Margaret

the Whittier Trail. Soon you reach another of the many saddles along this route. Then the path traverses an east-facing slope to a junction with the Mount Margaret Trail. This unmarked junction, at 5,700 feet elevation, is 0.7 mile from the Whittier Trail and 5.6 miles from Norway Pass Trailhead. Turn right at this junction and climb 0.2 mile west to the 5,840-foot-high summit of Mount Margaret. The view is spectacular in all directions.

Unless you are pursuing one of this area's many options (below), return the way you came.

OPTIONS: Options for loops and side trips abound along Boundary Trail. One of the most enticing, if you're a backpacker, is to continue southwest along the Boundary Trail from the Mount Margaret Trail junction.

The Boundary Trail descends southwest, then west, then crosses a spur ridge and makes a couple of switchbacks before reaching another saddle. When I hiked this trail in early August, there was a large herd of Roosevelt elk (*Cervus elaphus roosevelti*) below this saddle to the north. Roosevelt elk bulls may weigh 1,000 pounds and are the largest animals to inhabit the Cascades. Roosevelt elk are common in this area. The lower, semi-open slopes and valley bottoms of the Blast Zone are a prime winter range for the large animals. By June most of them have left for the higher country where you now are.

You reach another saddle 0.4 mile farther along, where a vague path turns to the left. This path, marked 1-F, climbs a small hill to a viewpoint and an abandoned volcano monitoring site. In a couple of hundred more yards on the Boundary Trail, a path turns right (north) to a campsite. There is a restroom and tent platforms at this designated camp. Water is available from a small stream just east of the camp.

Passing the campsite, the route traverses around the south side of a high point on the ridge to another saddle, with another campsite to your right. This camp also has a restroom and tent platforms; water is available.

Continuing along the ridge past the campsites, the route soon traverses around the south side of The Dome. Then you traverse the slopes above St. Helens Lake, passing a couple more small saddles to the junction with the Coldwater Peak Trail. This junction is 4.1 miles from the junction with the Mount Margaret Trail junction and 9.7 miles from Norway Pass Trailhead. Wild strawberries cover much of the ground amid the downed timber beside the trail near the junction. At the junction the route to Coldwater Peak turns to the right (west).

A hike requiring a long car shuttle can be made by continuing on the Boundary Trail to Johnston Ridge or taking the Coldwater Trail and Lakes Trail to Coldwater Lake Trailhead.

21 Lakes Trail (Trails 1 and 211)

HIGHLIGHTS: This route passes as least five lakes as it undulates through the Blast Zone and the glacially eroded remains of twenty-million-year-old Spirit Lake Pluton.

START: Norway Pass Trailhead.

DISTANCE: 24.8-mile out-and-back backpack, with loop and shuttle options.

DIFFICULTY: Strenuous.

SEASON: July through September.

TOTAL CLIMBING: 5,200 feet.

TRAILHEAD ELEVATION: 3,670 feet.

PERMITS: Northwest Forest Pass for parking at Norway Pass Trailhead. A backcountry permit is required for camping.

MAPS: Mount St. Helens National Monument, aka Brown Map. Spirit Lake East and Spirit Lake West USGS quads. The Spirit Lake West quad does not show the trail, however.

SPECIAL CONSIDERATIONS: Parts of this trail follow high and exposed ridgelines. Be sure you have adequate clothing for wet, windy conditions. Snow is possible at any time of year. In sunny weather these south-facing slopes can be very warm and dry. Nearly this entire route is exposed to direct sunshine, with little or no shade available; take along your sunscreen. If you plan to traverse the Mount Whittier Trail, be sure your mountaineering skills are up to it.

PARKING AND TRALHEAD FACILITIES: There are restrooms and adequate parking at the trailhead.

FINDING THE TRAILHEAD: Head north from Portland on Interstate 5 to exit 21 (21 miles north of the Columbia River Bridge) at Woodland. Then drive east for 27.5 miles on Washington Route 503 (which becomes WA 503 Spur) to Cougar. Continue east through Cougar on WA 503 Spur (which becomes Forest Road 90 at the Skamania County line) for another 18.6 miles to its junction with Forest Road 25. Bear left (nearly straight ahead) and head northeast on FR 25 for 24.3 miles to its junction with Forest Road 99.

From Seattle, take I–5 south to exit 133 at Tacoma, and then follow Washington Route 7 for 55 miles to Morton. From Morton, drive east for 17 miles to Randle. Turn right and take Washington Route 131, then FR 25, south for 20 miles to the junction with FR 99.

Lakes Trail (Trails 1 and 211)

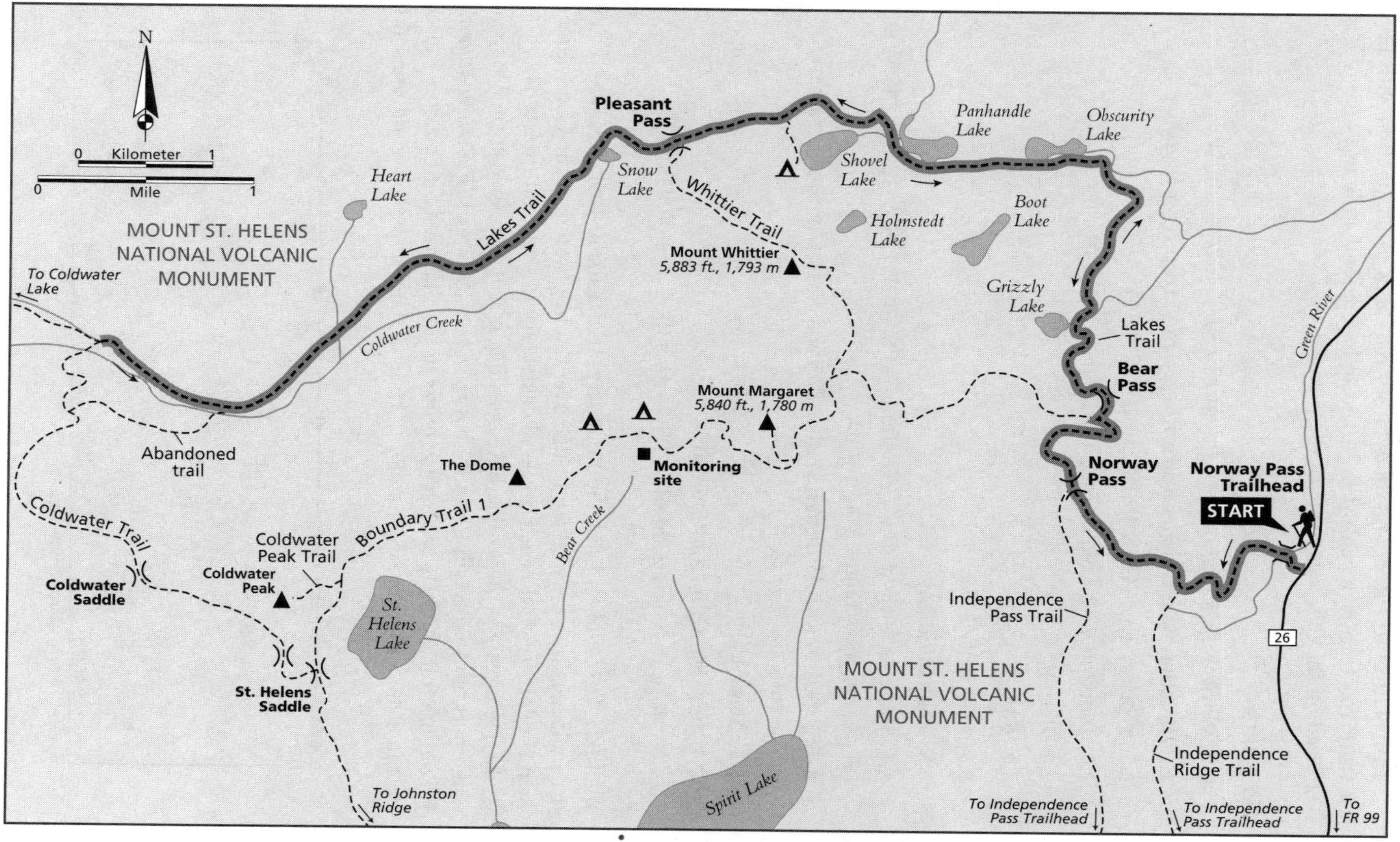

Turn west onto FR 99 and follow it for 8.8 miles to its junction with Forest Road 26. Turn right onto FR 26 and follow it for 1 mile to Norway Pass Trailhead on the left (west) side of the road.

KEY POINTS:

0.0 Norway Pass Trailhead (GPS 46 18.330 N 122 04.948 W).

1.1 Junction with Independence Ridge Trail. Turn right (northwest).

2.1 Norway Pass (GPS 46 18.630 N 122 06.345 W).

2.8 Junction with Lakes Trail. Turn right (northeast).

2.9 Bear Pass.

4.0 Grizzly Lake.

5.5 Obscurity Lake.

6.5 Panhandle Lake.

8.1 Junction with Shovel Lake Trail (GPS 46 20.134 N 122 08.245 W). Continue straight (southwest).

8.7 Junction with Whittier Trail at Pleasant Pass. Continue straight (southwest).

9.2 Snow Lake.

12.4 Junction with Coldwater Trail.

24.8 Norway Pass Trailhead (GPS 46 18.330 N 122 04.948 W).

THE HIKE: This route follows the Boundary Trail 1 for its first 2.8 miles. From the trailhead cross the wooden bridge over the headwaters of the Green River, then climb through downed timber, huckleberry bushes, and fireweed.

Living mostly in places that have been disturbed, such as road cuts, logged-over spots, and especially recently burned areas, fireweed (*Epilobium angustifolium*) has found nearly the perfect home in the Blast and Singe Zones caused by the 1980 eruption of Mount St. Helens. Under perfect conditions this

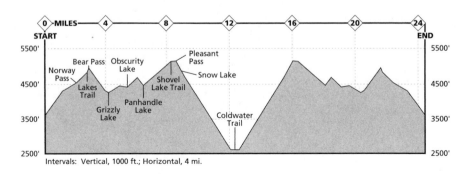

Intervals: Vertical, 1000 ft.; Horizontal, 4 mi.

member of the primrose family can grow as tall as 9 feet, but it usually reaches 3 to 5 feet. In August the deep pink flowers form a spire-shaped cluster along the upper part of the stem.

The route reaches a saddle 0.3 mile from the trailhead, where a patch of foxglove grows. A large, usually biennial herb up to 6 feet tall, foxglove (*Digitalis purpurea*) is an import from Europe. Its bell-shaped flowers add a splash of color in July. The drug digitalis, a derivative of the foxglove plant, is widely used in treating heart disease. The foxglove is a highly poisonous plant, however, affecting both the circulatory system and muscle tissue.

Next to the foxglove the perennial hairy cat's ear (*Hypochoeris radicata*) sprouts from the recently laid-down volcanic soil. Its yellow flowers contrast with the pink-purple or occasionally white blooms of the foxglove. Leopard lilies (*Lilium columbianum*) grow here, too, adding their orange color to the mix.

Continuing to climb, you will make a couple of switchbacks before reaching a junction with the Independence Ridge Trail 1.1 miles from the trailhead. Here the Boundary Trail turns to the right. The path climbs to the northwest and crosses a ridgeline, then cuts back into a gully and crosses a tiny stream, which is usually dry by midsummer. Beyond the gully the tread traverses along the northeast-facing slope to a junction with the Independence Pass Trail and Norway Pass, at 4,520 feet elevation, 2.1 miles from the trailhead. Western mountain ash (*Sorbus scopulina*) and black huckleberry bushes (*Vaccinium membranaceum*) line the trail as it approaches the pass.

The western mountain ash is a deciduous shrub or sometimes a small tree up to 15 feet tall that blooms in early summer. By July its white flowers have been replaced by clusters of green berries, which will turn bright red as they ripen. Several species of birds relish these berries, which at times ferment on the tree, making the birds drunk. Although the berries are not very palatable, at least one group of aboriginal people did consume them raw. Another group is said to have rubbed the berries on their scalps to combat head lice.

Spirit Lake and Mount St. Helens come into view to the south as you reach the pass. From Norway Pass to the junction with the Lakes Trail, the Boundary Trail is the border of the Restricted Zone. No travel is allowed on the left (south) side of the trail. Leaving the pass, the path climbs a ridge for a short distance, then bears right to traverse around the head of a basin.

Pacific bleeding hearts (*Dicentra formosa*) grow in a few damp spots on the slopes. Common in moist, usually shaded areas at low to middle elevations, the perennial Pacific bleeding heart grows up to 1.5 feet tall from rhizomes. Its light pinkish purple flowers, heart shaped at the base, bloom in late spring and early summer. The flowers droop in clusters from the tips of stems; the petals resemble drips, giving the plant its name.

Grizzly Lake

The route switches back to the left 0.5 mile from the pass. Another 0.2 mile and you reach the junction with the Lakes Trail, at 4,870 feet elevation. This junction, 2.8 miles from Norway Pass Trailhead, was not marked when I hiked this trail but may be in the future. Turn right onto the Lakes Trail and climb to the northeast. The sandy route makes its way through mountain ash and huckleberry bushes as it ascends for 0.1 mile to Bear Pass, elevation 4,940 feet.

Near the pass Douglas aster (*Aster subspicatus*) and pearly everlasting (*Anaphalis margaritacea*) grow from the pumice soil. Blooming in late summer and remaining until the first snow falls, pearly everlasting covers the ground in places. This species has adapted well to the open ash-covered slopes within the Blast Zone of Mount St. Helens. It is often the most common flower found in an area.

The route crosses Bear Pass and descends the north slope, covered with small noble (*Abies procera*) and silver fir (*A. amabilis*) trees. Grizzly Lake comes into view 0.4 mile after crossing the pass. The path descends on the left side of a small ridge, then crosses a small saddle before reaching Grizzly Lake, 1.2 miles from the Boundary Trail.

The sparkling waters of Grizzly Lake, at 4,300 feet elevation, are nestled in a glacial cirque and surrounded by standing silvered snags and blown-down timber. This route crosses the lake's outlet on stepping-stones.

Leaving the lake, the path crosses slopes covered with fireweed and pearly everlasting that blooms in August. It then crosses a small stream as it rounds the head of a basin 0.4 mile farther along. Monkey flowers (*Mimulus* spp.) grow next to the stream. A little farther along, the path follows a ledge for a short distance, then passes beneath a cliff. Pass Obscurity Lake, crossing a small stream as you go by. At the northeast end of the lake, a path leads a few yards to the left to a campsite and restroom. You are now 2.7 miles from Boundary Trail.

Leaving Obscurity Lake, the trail heads southwest along the inlet stream for a short distance, then crosses the stream on a single-log bridge. This stream is also the outlet from Boot Lake, which is about 0.5 mile to the southwest. The route now climbs, sometimes steeply, to the saddle between Obscurity and Panhandle Lakes, passing a waterfall. At the saddle Panhandle Lake comes into view. The path descends to a creek crossing, then traverses well above Panhandle Lake. Watch here for a trail to the right, which leads to a campsite with a restroom down on the lakeshore.

At either Obscurity or Panhandle Lake, you may encounter a great blue heron (*Ardea herodias*). Blue herons are the largest herons in North America, with a wingspan up to 82 inches and a length of more than 4 feet. Their plumage is generally blue-gray with a lighter, tan-colored neck. When it takes flight the heron arches its neck into a tight S position, dragging its long legs behind. Great blue herons feed primarily on aquatic life. When feeding is easy they have been known to gorge themselves to the point that they can't fly.

The Lakes Trail now descends gently and crosses the inlet stream at the west end of Panhandle Lake, 3.8 miles from the Boundary Trail, at 4,490 feet elevation. This is also the outlet stream from Shovel Lake. Between the groves of western mountain ash, monkey flowers and cow parsnips sprout in clusters along the stream.

The cow parsnip is usually found in moist areas that get at least some direct sunlight during the day. It grows at all elevations from near sea level to sub-alpine regions. Cow parsnip (*Heracleum lanatum*), aka Indian celery, is a large perennial that grows from a stout taproot or cluster of roots. It may grow as tall as 9 feet under perfect conditions but is usually 3 to 4 feet. The large leaves (up to a foot wide) are coarsely toothed and hairy. The white flowers of the cow parsnip are small but numerous, growing in a large umbrella-shaped cluster at the top of the main stem and in smaller similarly shaped clusters at the ends of side stalks. The plant contains a chemical that can cause skin irritation.

It is easy to confuse the cow parsnip with hogweed (*Heracleum mantegazzianum*), a non-native but fairly common plant in the Northwest. Hogweed

Cow parsnip

contains an even more powerful skin irritant. The irritation from both the cow parsnip and hogweed is compounded by exposure to sunlight.

Water hemlock (*Cicuta douglasii*) and poison hemlock (*Conium maculatum*) are similar to cow parsnip and can be confused with it. Both of these plants are very poisonous and often deadly. Poison hemlock, which is another European import, lives at low elevations; water hemlock grows at low to middle elevations.

Even though the cow parsnip has some very nasty relatives, it was used by Native Americans as a green vegetable. The young stalks were peeled, removing the skin irritant, then eaten raw or cooked. Still, unless you are 100 percent sure of the species of any plant in the carrot-parsley family, as all of these are, don't eat it or even allow it to rub against your skin.

Now the route really begins to climb, first heading up a ridgeline, then turning west to ascend the ridge. Climb along the right side of the ridge for a short distance, then make a switchback and climb to the crest. As you look ahead along the nearly vertical left side of the ridge, Shovel Lake comes into view. Continue up the ridge, making a couple more switchbacks. One mile above the stream crossing, at the west end of Panhandle Lake, the trail bears right off the ridgeline and the grade moderates. The tread now traverses the north slope of the ridge through standing dead snags and small fir trees. Lupines bloom along this slope in August.

Reach the junction with the trail to Shovel Lake 0.5 mile after leaving the ridgeline. This junction is in a saddle, at 5,160 feet elevation, on the same ridge you have been climbing since leaving Panhandle Lake. Shovel Lake is in view far below to the left. The poor path to Shovel Lake turns to the left (southeast) at the junction sign. The sign at the junction says SHOVEL LAKE 0.5 MILE, but this is a conservative estimate; it's actually about 0.8 mile.

If you choose to make the side trip to the lake, the Shovel Lake Trail descends south from the Lakes Trail. The pumice covered path soon becomes very vague. Shovel Lake is in view to the southeast and far below as you descend through the snags and blown-down timber. Western mountain ash, pearly everlasting, and bear grass grow among the logs, adding some color to the gray landscape.

When not in flower bear grass (*Xerophyllum tenax*) bears a strong resemblance to a large bunchgrass plant. This evergreen member of the lily family is, however, not a grass at all. Where the trees shade them, individual bear grass plants may only bloom every five to seven years, but in the open they bloom more frequently, often covering the slopes with a dazzling display. The small, creamy white flowers, which form an elongated oval, club-shaped cluster at the top of the up-to-4-foot high central stem, show up from June to August, depending on the elevation.

Elk and deer relish the succulent flowers, usually biting off the entire flower cluster and the upper part of the stem. Mountain goats—which lived in the area before the eruption but have not been seen since—were especially fond of bear grass flowers. Native Americans used the tough leaves of bear grass plants to weave hats, baskets, and sometimes capes.

The route to Shovel Lake switchbacks down the slope, but it's hard to follow it exactly. Watch ahead for logs that have been cut to make way for the trail. If you lose the trail, at least you can see your destination ahead. Shortly before reaching the campsite, the path flattens. Head south across the pumice flats to the campsite at the southwest end of Shovel Lake. Shovel Lake occupies a cirque that was formed or at least reshaped by glaciers during the last ice age about 11,000 years ago.

Continuing on from the junction with the Shovel Lake Trail, the Lakes Trail traverses a south-facing slope for 0.6 mile to Pleasant Pass and the junction with the Mount Whittier Trail. The Mount Whittier Trail turns off to the south and follows a rough ridge to the Boundary Trail. The junction is in the saddle between Shovel and Snow Lakes at 5,190 feet elevation. Below and south is Coldwater Canyon. Far down the canyon is the upper end of Coldwater Lake, one of the lakes formed by the Debris Avalanche preceding the May 18, 1980, eruption of Mount St. Helens.

If you would like to make the side trip to the summit of Mount Whittier, turn left at the junction. Don't use this route unless you are an agile and experienced hiker. Some mountaineering experience would be a great help here. The first 1.2 miles to the summit of Mount Whittier is a moderate climb, except for a short section of washed-out trail. The Forest Service warns that you use this section of trail at your own risk. The 1.1 miles from there on to the Boundary Trail is difficult and potentially very dangerous. If you are not 100 percent sure of your mountaineering ability or that of any member of your party, forgo this side trip.

From the 5,883-foot-high summit of Mount Whittier—the highest in the Mount Margaret Backcountry—the views in all directions are breathtaking. Panhandle Lake sits in a canyon below Holmstedt Lake. Shovel Lake sparkles in is cirque beneath cliffs to the north.

Leaving Pleasant Pass, the Lakes Trail begins its long descent into Coldwater Canyon through blown-down timber, crossing green slopes for 0.5 mile to Snow Lake. Below Snow Lake the descent continues at a fairly even grade. Here small firs grow between the downed logs and snags. The route skirts the base of a cliff, then crosses several slide areas. As you near the bottom of the canyon, alders appear next to the trail. The path crosses the outlet stream from Heart Lake 1.8 miles after passing Snow Lake. In another 0.8 mile is a junction with the old Coldwater Trail. This section of Coldwater Trail has recently been abandoned in favor of a new route farther west. Hike another 0.6 mile to the junction with the Coldwater Trail.

From the junction the Lakes Trail continues on to the Lakes Trailhead at the foot of Coldwater Lake. The Coldwater Trail turns left and climbs out of the canyon to the south. For this hike you've reached your turnaround point.

OPTIONS: There are several options for side trips and loop hikes off the Lakes Trail. The shortest loop involves turning south at Pleasant Pass onto the Whittier Trail and following this difficult, potentially dangerous route over Mount Whittier to the Boundary Trail. You then turn left (east) onto the Boundary Trail and take it back to its junction with the Lakes Trail to complete the loop. From there follow the Boundary Trail back to Norway Pass Trailhead.

To make a longer but safer loop, turn left (south) onto the Coldwater Trail and follow it to the Boundary Trail. Parts of the Coldwater Trail can be badly overgrown with brush; good route-finding skills may be necessary. Then turn left onto the Boundary Trail and return to Norway Pass Trailhead.

HIGHLIGHTS: Climb gently through old-growth forest, passing rushing streams, then enter the Blast Zone of the 1980 Mount St. Helens eruption. After hiking through another sheltered patch of large timber, and topping a ridge, you'll descend through the blasted forest to the trailhead.

START: Bear Meadows Viewpoint and Trailhead.

DISTANCE: 5.0-mile shuttle day hike or backpack.

DIFFICULTY: Moderate.

SEASON: Late June through September.

TOTAL CLIMBING: 410 feet.

TRAILHEAD ELEVATION: 4,120 feet.

PERMITS: Northwest Forest Pass.

MAPS: Mount St. Helens National Volcanic Monument, aka Brown Map, or Spirit Lake East USGS quad.

PARKING AND TRAILHEAD FACILITIES: There are restrooms and adequate parking at both trailheads.

FINDING THE TRAILHEAD: Head north from Portland on Interstate 5 to exit 21 (21 miles north of the Columbia River Bridge) at Woodland. Then drive east for 27.5 miles on Washington Route 503 (which becomes WA 503 Spur) to Cougar. Continue east through Cougar on WA 503 Spur (which becomes Forest Road 90 at the Skamania County line) for another 18.6 miles to its junction with Forest Road 25. Bear left (nearly straight ahead) and head northeast on FR 25 for 24.3 miles to its junction with Forest Road 99.

From Seattle, take I–5 south to exit 133 at Tacoma, and then follow Washington Route 7 for 55 miles to Morton. From Morton, drive east 17 miles to Randle. Turn right and take Washington Route 131, then FR 25, south for 20 miles to the junction with FR 99.

Turn west onto FR 99 and follow it for 4.5 miles to Bear Pass Trailhead. The trail leaves from the right side of the road across from the parking area.

To leave a shuttle vehicle at Norway Pass Trailhead, continue on FR 99 for another 4.3 miles, then turn right onto Forest Road 26. Follow FR 26 for 1 mile to the trailhead. The parking area and restrooms are on the left (west) side of the road; the Boundary Trail crosses FR 26 at the trailhead.

Boundary Trail—Bear Meadows to Norway Pass Trailhead (Trail 1)

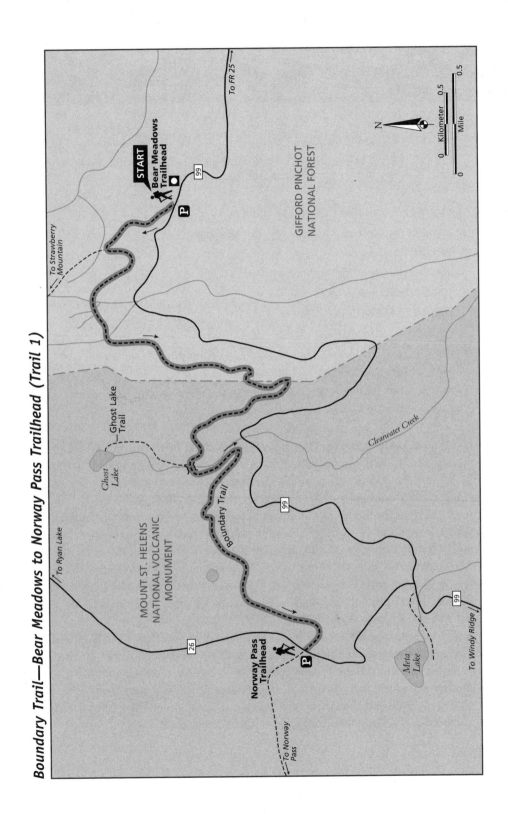

KEY POINTS:

0.0 Bear Meadows Trailhead (GPS 46 18.799 N 122 02.167 W).

0.6 Junction with Strawberry Mountain Trail. Bear left (south) on Boundary Trail.

3.3 Junction with Ghost Lake Trail. Continue straight (southwest).

5.0 Norway Pass Trailhead (GPS 46 18.330 N 122 04.948 W).

THE HIKE: A small group of people was camped at Bear Meadows—near the trailhead where this hike begins—on the morning of May 18, 1980. Gary Rosenquist was among them, and he snapped a spectacular series of quick-succession photographs of the eruption that has been widely published. Then he and his companions made a harrowing drive to escape.

This trailhead, by the way, isn't the beginning of the Boundary Trail, which actually starts far to the east near Mount Adams. For more information about the eastern section of the Boundary Trail, pick up a copy of *Hiking Washington's Goat Rocks Country*, another FalconGuide.

As you leave Bear Meadows Trailhead, the pumice-covered path climbs through small timber intermingled with common red paintbrush (*Castilleja miniata*), Cardwell's penstemon (*Penstemon cardwellii*), and small-flowered penstemon (*P. procerus*). The small-flowered is one of several species of penstemons that grow in abundance in Mount St. Helens National Volcanic Monument. It's an erect plant that can reach 18 inches tall, but it's usually shorter. The blue-purple flowers, which form dense clusters at the top of the stalks in July, are much smaller than those of the other penstemons in the area. Like most penstemons, the small-flowered prefers dry, open locations where it can get plenty of direct sunlight.

Three hundred yards from the trailhead, you will enter an old-growth forest of Douglas fir (*Pseudotsuga menziesii*), western hemlock (*Tsuga heterophylla*), Pacific silver fir (*Abies amabilis*), and noble fir (*A. procera*).

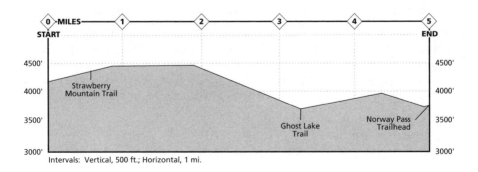

Intervals: Vertical, 500 ft.; Horizontal, 1 mi.

The noble fir and its close relative the Pacific silver fir are similar in size, shape, and color, so for the layperson the trees are easy to confuse. The cones of the silver fir are smaller than those of the noble, however, and purple in color, while noble fir cones are green. The cones are generally evident standing erect from a tree's upper branches by about July 1; by late July the noble's cones may have turned brown. Still, the easiest way to tell the species apart is by the noble's hockey-stick-shaped needles, which on silver fir are more nearly straight.

The path climbs gently but steadily for 0.6 mile to a junction with the Strawberry Mountain Trail, at 4,360 feet elevation. This trail turns to the right (northwest) to ascend Strawberry Mountain; see the options below for a description. To continue this hike bear left at the junction and continue through the large timber.

Avalanche lilies (*Erythronium montanum*), aka fawn lilies, dot the forest floor as you traverse the slope heading to the south. Usually found on moist slopes, sprouting as soon as the snow melts, the avalanche lily's stem pushes up from between the pale green leaves, reaching up to about a foot tall before blooming. The nodding flowers have six white petals surrounding their yellow centers.

The route rounds the end of a ridge, where you can spot FR 99 below. Mount St. Helens looms to the southwest through the trees. The tread crosses a small stream 1 mile from the trailhead, then crosses a larger stream at the base of a stepped waterfall. Continue the traverse of this steep sidehill, crossing a couple more small streams. In an opening on the slope, Menzies' larkspur (*Delphinium menziesii*), common red paintbrush, and shooting stars (*Dodecatheon* spp.) grow in profusion. As you hike along, watch to your left for a view of Mount Adams, which is only about 28 miles away to the southeast.

The trail enters the Blast Zone 2 miles from Bear Meadows. The standing dead snags attest to the heat and power of the 1980 eruption. Black huckleberries (*Vaccinium membranaceum*) are plentiful here; they ripen in August. You will make five switchbacks as you descend to a broken wooden bridge over a usually dry stream. A short distance past the bridge is an unmarked junction with the Ghost Lake Trail. At this junction, 3.3 miles from Bear Meadows, Ghost Lake is 0.7 mile to the right (north). See the options below for the details on Ghost Lake.

Just past the junction the trail crosses another broken-down wooden bridge, this one over Clearwater Creek. Cross the bridge, enter a stand of large trees that the eruption spared, and climb gently through snags and young firs. The path makes a switchback 0.3 mile past the junction, passes through another stand of old trees, then continues to climb, winding and switchbacking to pass a meadow.

Blown-down timber

A very poor and hard-to-find path 0.9 mile past the Ghost Lake junction leads a short distance up a gully to a small unnamed lake. There are no fish in this lake, but there are some possible campsites at its east end. The shallow lake warms up quite nicely for swimming in late summer.

Shortly after passing the path to the unnamed lake, the Boundary Trail crosses a pass at 3,950 feet elevation. Then it begins to descend toward Norway Pass Trailhead. From the pass Mount Adams can be seen to the east. As you cross the pass, you enter an area where the timber was completely blown down by the 1980 eruption. Fireweed (*Epilobium angustifolium*), paintbrush, and a few small Pacific silver and noble fir trees grow amid the downed logs.

In late summer pearly everlasting covers the ground in spots. Growing from low elevations all the way up into subalpine country, this species has adapted well to the open ash-covered slopes within the Blast Zone. It is often the most common flower found in an area.

The pearly everlasting (*Anaphalis margaritacea*) is a perennial herb that grows from 1 to 2 feet tall from an extensive rhizome system. The leaves are narrow and covered with white hairs, as are the usually unbranched stems, giving the pearly everlasting a dusty, gray-white appearance. The blossoms are small and white, with yellow centers, and appear in clusters at the top of the stem. Pearly everlasting is a late bloomers—the flowers don't appear until mid- to late summer, but they remain on the plant until the snow starts to fall. The flowers dry nearly intact and make great dried flower arrangements.

The route crosses another wooden bridge over a tiny stream 4.8 miles from Bear Meadows. It then turns to the right and descends between two small knobs to FR 26.

As you descend through the blasted-down timber, mountain alder (*Alnus incana*) lines the route in the damper spots. The mountain alder is a nitrogen-fixing species, which means it has the ability to extract nitrogen from the atmosphere and "fix" or deposit what it doesn't use in the soil. Thus the alder is fertilizing the soil for the plants that will follow it on these once devastated slopes. Next to the path arrow-leafed groundsel (*Senecio triangularis*) brightens the scene with its yellow flowers, and thimbleberry (*Rubus parviflorus*) grows to add the possibility of late-summer fruit.

After you cross the road, you may see golden-mantled ground squirrels scurrying among the bushes and along the trail. Many people mistake the golden-mantled ground squirrel (*Spermophilus lateralis*) for a chipmunk. It's an easy mistake to make, but the golden-mantled is an entirely different species. To make the distinction first look at the color: The golden-mantled has a rich yellow-tan head, while the chipmunk's head is brown like the rest of the body. Then check the stripes along the back. If these stripes continue across the head and face it's a chipmunk; there are no stripes on the golden-mantled's head. The golden-mantled is also the larger species.

Golden-mantled ground squirrels are common in many areas of Mount St. Helens National Volcanic Monument. Contrary to popular belief, they are omnivores, eating both animal and vegetable foods. Their diet includes seeds, berries, small eggs if they can find them, and insects. In many cases they will readily take handouts from people, but please don't feed them. Like chipmunks and other squirrels, the golden-mantled can carry a large amount of foodstuffs in its cheek pouches.

After crossing FR 26 it's only about another 100 yards to Norway Pass Trailhead and the parking area where your shuttle vehicle awaits.

OPTIONS: The side trip to Ghost Lake and back will add only 1.2 miles to your hike. From the unmarked junction with the Boundary Trail, the Ghost Lake Trail leads north. The path is right on the edge between the green forest on the left and silver snags to the right. The green timber is a pocket of trees that were shielded by a hill and survived the 1980 eruption. As the route heads up the east

Elk track

side of Clearwater Creek, it passes a small meadow. Soon you leave the large green trees behind and travel through dead snags and fallen timber. This forest is regenerating itself; young trees are growing up between the snags. Huckleberries cover the ground between the trees. The tread enters an area of pumice landslide debris 0.5 mile from Boundary Trail and nearly disappears.

Pumice is a highly gas-charged solidified form of lava. Its formation is somewhat like the foam that appears on top of a soda when you shake it. Like obsidian, it's high in silica; in fact, it could be defined as gas-charged obsidian. Pumice, being full of tiny bubbles, is light enough to float on water.

The blast of the 1980 eruption stripped away much of the vegetation that once covered and stabilized these slopes. The eruption also added a layer of pumice and ash to the area, further destabilizing the slopes. Heavy rains soaked the already unstable ground, and it slid. Gradually these slopes are being revegetated; eventually they will become stable again if the volcanic activity allows enough time.

Turn left (west) on the pumice and you will shortly reach the lakeshore. As you approach the lake, several flat spots on the pumice make acceptable campsites. Mosquitoes can be bad at Ghost Lake, so come prepared. Trout—some of them fairly good size—are plentiful in the lake.

Another option is to bear right (north) at the junction with the Strawberry Mountain Trail 0.6 mile from the Bear Meadows Trailhead; from here it's only 1.8 miles to the summit of Strawberry Mountain. First you follow the Strawberry Mountain Trail for 1.6 miles, gaining about 900 feet of elevation, to the southeast ridge of Strawberry Mountain. On the ridgeline look for a rough unsigned path to the left (west). Take this path, climbing 165 feet in the final 0.2 mile to the 5,465-foot-high summit.

Strawberry Mountain is made up of mostly dacite deposits. Studies of these deposits indicate that the volcanism that formed the mountain happened well over twenty million years ago. Like most of the lower mountains and hills surrounding Mount St. Helens, Strawberry was here long before the volcano first came to life—only about 40,000 years ago.

From the top the view is marvelous in all directions. To the west are Ryan Lake and the glacier-carved Green River Valley, flanked by Goat Mountain and the ridges and peaks of the Mount Margaret Backcountry. To the north Mount Rainier looms above the green hills. Looking east, Mount Adams is in full view, and to the south is the gapping crater of Mount St. Helens. Roosevelt elk (*Cervus elaphus roosevelti*) seem to like this summit for a bedding spot; you may see them, or at least their tracks in the dust.

23 Woods Creek Watchable Wildlife Loops (Trails 247, 247A)

HIGHLIGHTS: Woods Creek and Old Growth Loops make a figure-eight hike through a diverse lowland forest. For seeing the largely nocturnal wildlife, very early-morning hikes are best. This is an excellent hike for small children and open to hikers only.

START: Woods Creek Trailhead.

DISTANCE: 2.4-mile loop day hike.

DIFFICULTY: Easy.

SEASON: March through October.

TOTAL CLIMBING: Minimal.

TRAILHEAD ELEVATION: 1,140 feet.

PERMITS: None.

MAPS: The map in this book or in the trailhead pamphlet is all you'll need.

PARKING AND TRAILHEAD FACILITIES: There are restrooms, a picnic area, adequate parking, and an information sign at the trailhead.

FINDING THE TRAILHEAD: Head north from Portland on Interstate 5 to exit 21 (21 miles north of the Columbia River Bridge) at Woodland. Then drive east for 27.5 miles on Washington Route 503 (which becomes WA 503 Spur) to Cougar. Continue east through Cougar on WA 503 Spur (which becomes Forest Road 90 at the Skamania County line) for another 18.6 miles to its junction with Forest Road 25. Bear left (nearly straight ahead) and head northeast on FR 25 for 36.6 miles to the Woods Creek Information Station.

From Seattle, take I–5 south to exit 133 at Tacoma, and then follow Washington Route 7 for 55 miles south to Morton. From Morton, drive east 17 miles to Randle. Turn right and take Washington Route 131, then FR 25, south for 5.7 miles to the Woods Creek Information Station.

The trailhead is on the east side of FR 25, across from the information station.

KEY POINTS:

0.0 Woods Creek Trailhead (GPS 46 27.668 N 121 57.574 W).

0.3 Junction with Woods Creek Loop. Turn left (north).

0.8 Junction with Old Growth Loop. Turn left, then quickly right to walk loop counterclockwise.

Woods Creek Watchable Wildlife Loops (Trails 247, 247A)

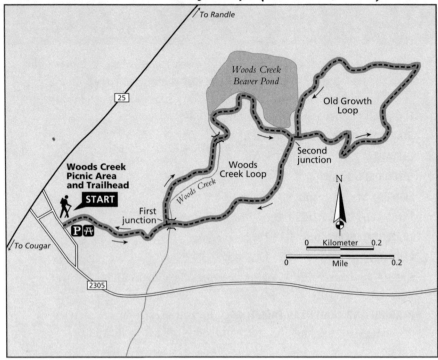

To Randle

Woods Creek
Beaver Pond

25

Old Growth
Loop

Woods Creek
Picnic Area
and Trailhead

START

Woods
Creek Loop

Second
junction

Woods Creek

First
junction

N

P A

To Cougar

0   Kilometer   0.2

0   Mile   0.2

2305

2.1 Junction with Woods Creek Loop. Turn right, then quickly left.

2.4 Woods Creek Trailhead (GPS 46 27.668 N 121 57.574 W).

THE HIKE: The Woods Creek Loops' elevation and rainfall are similar to those of the nearby Cedar Flats Nature Loop, but here the younger forest, growing on deep, moist organic soil, is mostly deciduous, while at Cedar Flats the older conifer woods grow from the mineral soil of an ancient lahar deposit. If time allows, it's a real learning experience to walk both the Woods Creek Watchable Wildlife Loops and the Cedar Flats Nature Loop on the same trip.

Flowers including three-leafed anemone (*Anemone deltoidea*) and western buttercup (*Ranunculus occidentalis*) grow in many places along the trail, but they are by no means the only ones. Take along a good plant and flower identification book to study the wide diversity of plants in the area. As you leave the parking area, also pick up one of the pamphlets covering the Woods Creek Watchable Wildlife Interpretive Trail. A dispenser for the pamphlets (and a donation box) is located on the signboard next to the trailhead.

The 4-foot-wide gravel tread heads east from the parking area through dense second-growth forest. Red alder (*Alnus rubra*), Douglas fir (*Pseudotsuga menziesii*), western red cedar (*Thuja plicata*), and big-leaf maple trees furnish the canopy.

The very large leaves, with three pointed lobes, identify the big-leaf maple (*Acer macrophyllum*). The only large-leaf maple found naturally in the western United States, the bigleaf is easily distinguished from the vine maple (*Acer circinatum*), which is the other common native maple in the Mount St. Helens area. The vine maple is more of a shrub than a tree and has leaves with seven or nine pointed lobes. The bigleaf, on the other hand, can grow up to 80 feet tall.

The trunk and larger branches of the big-leaf maple are often thickly covered with moss. In some instances the moss becomes so thick that it forms and/or collects enough humus soil to allow other plants or trees to sprout, take root, and grow from its limbs.

In spring, just as the new leaves begin to grow, the maple's yellow flowers emerge from the twigs. These flowers mature into fuzzy, yellow-brown, winged seeds. The 1.75-inch-long seeds detach from the twigs at maturity and twirl to the ground like helicopters, dispersing widely in the wind.

Mice, chipmunks, squirrels, and some birds relish the seeds of the bigleaf. Black-tailed deer (*Odocoileus hemionus columbianus*) often browse on any leaves that are close enough to the ground and eat the young tender shouts.

Native Americans used parts of the big-leaf maple in widely diverse ways. The huge leaves were used as we would use paper towels, to ensure a clean surface on which to prepare food. The wood was carved into implements and used for canoe paddles. In fact, in the languages of several tribes the name for the big-leaf maple means "paddle tree." At least one tribe ate the sprouted seeds.

The bigleaf is now the most important commercially harvested hardwood in the western United States, with wood that is moderately strong, uniform in texture, and close grained. It takes an excellent finish and is often used for flooring and in the construction of furniture. The sap of the big-leaf maple can be made into maple syrup, but it is not nearly as well suited to this purpose as is the eastern sugar maple.

Beneath the big moss-hung trees grows an understory of vine maple. Sword ferns (*Polystichum* spp.) and moss cover the ground. Soon after leaving the trailhead, you will want to stop and read the first interpretive sign about deer tracks, which you may have already seen along the trail.

If you walk quietly along the trail early in the morning, you may even see a black-tailed deer making the tracks. Blacktails are the most common large animals in the Mount St. Helens region and are a slightly smaller and darker subspecies of mule deer (*Odocoileus hemionus hemionus*) inhabiting the damp western slopes of the Cascades as well as the Coast Range. Typical of a forest-loving animal, the antlers of the blacktail are much smaller than those of the mule deer. The deer's eponymous tail is wider than that of a mule deer and completely black on its upper side. When alarmed, a blacktail will generally run with its tail carried horizontally, but they occasionally flag (hold their tail straight up).

After hiking 0.3 mile you will reach a trail junction; there is a clearing and marsh next to the trail, as well as a bench and sign about the tracks of the Roosevelt elk (*Cervus elaphus roosevelti*), the largest animal in the Mount St. Helens area.

Turn left at the junction and hike north along the sluggish Woods Creek. Foxglove (*Digitalis purpurea*)—a highly poisonous plant affecting both muscle tissue and the circulatory system—and blackberries (*Rubus discolor*) line the creek, as do stinging nettles.

Stinging nettles (*Urtica dioica*) range from 2 to 8 feet tall and often grow in fairly dense patches. The lance-shaped leaves are coarsely saw-toothed and covered with tiny hollow hairs that stick into the skin and release formic acid, causing the well-known stinging sensation and rash. When young the leaves can be cooked and eaten. The fibers from the nettle plant were used by Native Americans to make a strong twine for fishnets and other articles.

The route soon comes to another bench and sign about snowshoe hare tracks. The snowshoe hare (*Lepus americanus*), aka snowshoe rabbit and varying hare, is the smallest North American hare, weighing only about three pounds. The hare changes its brown summer coat each fall to a white winter one for the sake of camouflage. One problem with this arrangement comes if there is a stretch of warmer weather in the winter and the snow melts—then the white hare really stands out against brown forest floor.

Soon you cross a wooden bridge over Woods Creek. Beside the trail here you may notice the straight trunks of Oregon ash (*Fraxinus latifolia*) trees mixed in with the big-leaf maples. The ash trees are similar in size to the maples but tend to have much less moss clinging to their often branch-free lower trunks. Not to be confused with the western mountain ash (*Sorbus scopulina*), which grows at generally higher elevations around Mount St. Helens, the Oregon ash has relatively large, dark, olive-green compound leaves. The deep moist soil in the bottomland near Woods Creek is ideal habitat for the Oregon ash, which doesn't grow well on drier sites.

As they did with the big-leaf maple, Native Americans used the wood of the Oregon ash for making canoe paddles. Although not widely harvested for commercial purposes, ash is still considered one of the best for making tool handles.

At 0.1 mile farther along is a lookout porch to the left of the trail. Constructed in memory of Joe Frinche, this porch serves as a viewpoint over Woods Creek Beaver Pond. Just past the porch are another bench and a sign describing raccoon (*Procyon lotor*) tracks.

Stinging nettles

Great blue herons (*Ardea herodias*) frequent the pond, searching for a meal of tadpoles or other aquatic life. If the seeds of the cattails (*Typha latifolia*) are ripe, there may be red-winged (*Agelaius phoeniceus*) or Brewer's (*Euphagus cyanocephalus*) blackbirds feeding on them.

Soon you'll reach the junction with Old Growth Loop Trail. Turn left then quickly turn right at another junction a few yards away. The Old Growth Loop climbs gently, making a couple of switchbacks as it enters the larger trees of the old-growth forest. The largest of these trees are Douglas fir (*Pseudotsuga menziesii*). Look closely for bird life in this climax forest; you may see a varied thrush (*Ixoreus naevius*). The varied thrush is slightly smaller than a robin, with an orange throat and breast divided with a dark gray neck stripe.

At 0.4 mile into the Old Growth Loop, you will find another bench and a sign about marten tracks. Martens are relatively rare animals so your chances of seeing one here aren't very good. Still, this old-growth forest does provide nearly ideal habitat for the marten (*Martes americana*), also called pine marten and American sable. About as large as a house cat, martens are wandering animals, sometimes covering a home range of 10 square miles or more in their never-ending search for food. Prey species for this swift and cunning predator include squirrels, mice, chipmunks, and insects, as well as rabbits and hares. Although the marten is mainly carnivorous, its diet also includes bird eggs and huckleberries. The marten's very intense curiosity made it an easy animal to trap, and its beautiful fur was a prized catch. This along with habitat destruction led to a decline in the marten population. Several states now offer marten reintroduction programs in the hope that the numbers and range of these beautiful animals can be increased.

Another inhabitant of this old-growth forest is the spotted owl. Mostly nocturnal and not often seen by humans, the spotted owl (*Strix occidentalis*) inhabits the old-growth forests of the Cascade and Coast Ranges. It's a medium-size owl with a wingspan of about 42 inches. The plumage of the spotted owl is dark brown liberally spotted in white. The bird has no ear tufts, making it easy to distinguish from the more common and larger great horned owl. Spotted owls, which may on occasion hybridize with their close relative the barred owl where their ranges meet, feed mostly on small mammals and large insects, but will occasionally take a small bird.

The spotted owl is a federally protected endangered species, and it requires old-growth forest to prosper. These two facts are at the heart of one of the fiercest disputes over logging national forestlands in history. Much of the old-growth forest that is still standing in the Cascades owes its survival to the spotted owl and its listing as an endangered species.

This is, however, a two-edged sword for both the owl and the old-growth forest it needs. Given modern fire protection techniques, these magnificent forests are building up a huge dead fuel load. Before human intervention low-intensity fires on or close to the forest floor would have burned much of this fuel load. The huge old-growth trees, especially the Douglas fir with its thick bark, were resistant to this type of fire. You may have noticed that in many places the largest trees show the scars of such low-intensity fires, but survived. With the fuel buildup we now have, however, any fire that does manage to get going will have a tendency to be much hotter and may well kill even the largest trees. With the use of prescribed burns and other management techniques, the Forest Service is doing its best to lessen these loads, but in the Northwest's huge expanses of rugged and inaccessible territory, this is an unbelievably large task.

Unlike those of most of the rest of the western United States, the forests on the western slopes of the Cascades are moist much of the time, limiting the danger of catastrophic fire. But when the conditions are right, huge conflagrations can erupt. When they do we can expect to see some of this wonderful old-growth forest completely burned.

This bench is at the highest point of the hike. From here the trail descends, making another switchback, back to the junction with Woods Creek Loop. At this junction, first turn right, then left.

Once back on the Woods Creek Loop, the path heads east, then south, passing yet another bench and a sign discussing coyote (*Canis latrans*) tracks. Coyotes are common in the Mount St. Helens region, as well as over the entire western United States. The near elimination of the wolf—the main competitor of the coyote—worked in the coyote's favor. The species has greatly increased in numbers and expanded its range, despite human efforts to control it. Coyotes have a beautiful coat when it's dry, but the ones you see in this rain forest are often wet and their coats are matted down. This makes the coyote look skinny and impoverished—it isn't. Coyotes are opportunists when it comes to their feeding habits. They will eat a wide variety of foods from carrion to berries. Coyotes do have some effect on the deer population; they often find fawns to kill and eat, and at least in one instance, I saw a coyote hot on the trail of an adult deer, nearly running me over in the process.

Not long after crossing a wooden bridge you will reach another junction—the first one you came to when you began this hike. Turn left at the junction and hike the remaining 0.3 mile back to the trailhead.

OPTIONS: For a shorter hike don't take the Old Growth Loop; limit your walk to the Woods Creek Loop. There is a picnic area at the trailhead. Be sure to stop in at Woods Creek Information Station, preferably before you go on this hike, and get as much information about the area as possible.

Another short (only 0.2-mile round-trip) hike option is Iron Creek Falls Trail, 13.8 miles south of Woods Creek Trailhead on FR 25. A few yards from

Iron Creek Falls

the trailhead on the Iron Creek Falls Trail, you will start to descend the first of fifty-eight wooden steps that take you to a switchback. Western hemlock and Douglas fir line the path along the moss-covered slope. At the switchback turn right and walk 30 yards to a viewpoint looking at Iron Creek Falls. Past the switchback there are sixteen more wooden steps, then a long step down to the creekbed. You can walk up the creekbed 40 yards to get close to the falls for pictures if you like. Iron Creek Falls drops over an undercut, dark lava cliff to splash with a roar into a beautiful pool at its base.

As I noted, combining this hike with the Cedar Flats Nature Trail makes a fascinating day of nature study. Iron Creek Falls is about halfway between the two.

For More Information

USDA Forest Service

Mount St. Helens National Volcanic
Monument (Headquarters)
42218 NE Yale Bridge Road
Amboy (Chelatchie), WA 98601
(360) 247–3900
(360) 247–3961 (climbing hotline)
Fax (360) 247–3901

Mount St. Helens Visitor Center
3029 Spirit Lake Highway   (MP 5)
Castle Rock, WA 98611
(360) 274–2100

Coldwater Ridge Visitor Center
3029 Spirit Lake Highway   (MP 43)
Castle Rock, WA 98611
(360) 274–2131

Johnston Ridge Observatory
3029 Spirit Lake Highway (MP 51)
Castle Rock, WA 98611
(360) 274–2140

Cowlitz Valley Ranger Station
Randle Ranger District
P.O. Box 670
Randle, WA 98377

Other Information Sources

Jack's Restaurant
Junction of WA 503 and WA 503
Spur, 23 miles east of Woodland, WA

Weyerhaeuser Company
P.O. Box 1645
Tacoma, WA 98401-9970
(800) 458–0274

Emergency Phone Numbers

Cowlitz County Sheriff's Department
(360) 577–3092

Lewis County Sheriff's Department
(360) 748–8887

Skamania County Sheriff's
Department
(509) 427–9490

Glossary

Aa—A Hawaiian term for a lava flow with a rough, broken surface.

Andesite—Fine-grained lava with a silica content of 54 to 62 percent.

Avalanche—A snow and/or ice slide. An avalanche may also include large amounts of other material such as rock and forest debris.

Basalt—Fine-grained lava with a silica content of 45 percent to 54 percent.

Blast density flow—A dense flow of pyroclastic material produced by a large volcanic eruption.

Blast Zone—In this book, the area of blown-down and or singed vegetation caused by the lateral blast of Mount St. Helens.

Bracts—A modified leaf associated with a cone.

Central leader—The new growth at the very top of a tree's main stem or trunk. Usually used when describing conifers.

Cirque—A bowl-shaped area where a glacier has eaten its way into a mountain slope, then melted. A cirque is formed at the head of a glacier.

Climax forest—The oldest and most mature of old-growth forests. Attaining a climax forest usually takes several hundred years without major disturbance—in some cases 1,000 years or more.

Cornice—A wind-deposited snowdrift on the lee side of a ridgeline. Cornices are often overhanging and can be very unstable. They should be avoided—both above and below—when hiking and especially when skiing.

Dacite—Extrusive igneous rock with a silica content of about 62 to 69 percent.

Debris Avalanche—For the purposes of this book, the huge landslide that swept down the northern slope of Mount St. Helens at the start of the May 18, 1980, eruption.

Dike—A band of intrusive rock. The rock of a dike may be more erosion resistant than the surrounding rocks and after time may protrude from their surface.

Eruption Impact Zone—Same as Blast Zone.

Extrusive rock—Igneous rock that has solidified on or above the surface.

FR—Forest Road.

Fumarole—A vent where steam and or volcanic gases escape. A fumarole often releases hydrogen sulfide gas, which smells much like rotten eggs.

Gabbro—Coarse-grained intrusive igneous rock with about the same chemical content as basalt. Gabbro often forms dikes.

Granite—Intrusive igneous rock, coarse grained, with a silica content of 69 percent or higher.

Granodiorite—Intrusive igneous rock, coarse grained, with a silica content of 62 to 69 percent.

Harmonic tremor—Small but nearly continuous earthquakes happening beneath a mountain, indicating that magma is moving.

Igneous rock—Rock formed by the cooling of magma.

Intrusive rock—Magma that has cooled without reaching the surface.

Intrusive dike—Same as dike.

Lahar—A volcanic mudflow. Lahars are a mixture of rock, sand, and soil that flows swiftly off a mountain as a result of volcanic activity.

Lahar deposit—The solidified remains of a lahar.

Lateral blast—A volcanic blast that is directed more or less parallel to the surface of the ground, rather than upward.

Lava flow—A stream of molten rock flowing from a volcano, or a stream of rock after it has cooled and hardened.

Lava tube—An opening beneath or in a lava flow where a stream of molten rock has continued to flow after the outer crust has cooled and hardened, leaving a tube.

Lava tube cave—A lava tube large enough for a person to enter. Ape Cave on Mount St. Helens is the longest lava tube cave in North America.

Magnetic declination—The earth's poles and the earth's magnetic poles are not in the same place. A magnetic compass—the kind most of us use—points to the earth's magnetic North Pole. *Magnetic declination* refers to the difference in angle, stated in degrees, between true north (a straight line toward the North Pole) and magnetic north (a straight line toward the earth's magnetic North Pole). Magnetic declination is stated on all USGS quad maps and most other maps.

Magma—Molten rock.

Magma chamber—A chamber deep underground that holds the magma to feed a volcano.

Metamorphic rock—Igneous, sedimentary, or other rock that has been changed beneath the earth's surface by pressure, heat, or a combination of the two. Metamorphic rock is normally very old.

Obsidian—Volcanic glass. Obsidian is a form of high-silica-content rhyolite without bubbles in it.

Pahoehoe—Pahoehoe (pronounced *pah-hoey-hoey*) is a Hawaiian term for a lava flow with a rather smooth but sometimes ropy surface. Cave basalt is pahoehoe lava.

Pioneer trees—The first trees to grow in an area after a major disturbance of the soil. Alders are often pioneer trees along streambeds that have been scoured by lahars.

Pioneer plants—The first plants to grow in an area after the soil has been radically disturbed or burned in a fire hot enough to destroy nearly all the vegetation, including the roots. Lupine, which extracts its own nitrogen from the air rather than getting it from the soil, is often a pioneer plant.

Plug dome—A mound of lava that pushes up from a volcanic vent. The lava is too stiff to flow away, so it heaps up, around and over the vent.

Pluton—A large body of intrusive rock, possibly several miles across.

Prospect hole—A test hole dug into a vein of mineralized strata for the purpose of checking the mineral content for possible mining.

Pumice—The solidified froth of volcanic rock. Pumice is a high-silica-content, pale-colored rock that is light enough to float.

Pyroclastic—A term referring to heated rock material blown from a volcano. The material may vary in size from ash and sand to boulders.

Pyroclastic flow—A mass of hot volcanic debris and gases that moves swiftly along the surface of the ground.

Pyroclastic surge—Pyroclastic material flowing or being pushed at very high speed above the ground's surface.

Red Zone—A 10-mile-wide circle (5-mile radius from the old summit) around Mount St. Helens in 1980 prior to the eruption.

Restricted Zone—The area of Mount St. Helens National Volcanic Monument in which the public is not allowed to travel off established roads or trails. The Restricted Zone was created for both environmental and safety reasons.

Richter scale—A scale used for measuring the energy of earthquakes.

Sand ladder—A device that makes it easier to ascend and descend loose slopes. A sand ladder is series of wood steps (round or square) that are tied together with cables and laid on the slope to provide better footing.

Scoria—Igneous rock with many cavities or bubbles.

Second-growth forest—Forest that was logged many years ago and has regrown to medium-sized timber.

Shield volcano—A gently sloping volcanic cone formed by many consecutive lava flows.

Singe Zone—The area where the timber is still standing but dead as a result of Mount St. Helens' volcanic eruption. The Singe Zone is at the outside edge of the Blast Zone.

Stone wind—A swiftly moving gas cloud containing chunks of rock as well as ash and other volcanic debris.

Strato-volcano—A steep-sided or cone-shaped volcanic cone formed by alternating lava flows and eruptions of solid material. The major volcanic peaks in the Cascade Mountains, including Mount St. Helens, are strato-volcanoes.

True fir—Genus *Abies*. For the purposes of this book, grand fir, noble fir, subalpine fir, and Pacific silver fir are true firs; the Douglas fir is a completely different species.

Understory—Shrubs and small trees growing, usually shaded, beneath the forest canopy.

WA—Washington State highway or route.

Wash—A creekbed that is dry most of the time, usually with steep, unstable banks.

Welded tuff—Relatively fine volcanically ejected rock that was hot enough when put into place to weld itself together.

Windthrow—Trees that are blown down by wind. If a tree is susceptible to windthrow, it is fairly easily blown over.

Winter range—The area where migrating animals spend the winter.

Further Reading

Alpine Wildflowers, Dr. Dee Strickler, The Flower Press, 1990.

Ape Cave, William R. Halliday, MD, ABC Printing and Publishing.

The Big Game Animals of North America, Jack O'Connor, E. F. Dutton and Co., 1961.

Birds of North America, Chandler S. Robbins, Bertel Bruun, and Herbert S. Zim, Golden Press, 1966.

Birds of North America Western Region, Fred J. Alsop III, DK Publishing, 2001.

Cascade Alpine Guide: Columbia River to Stevens Pass, Fred Beckey, The Mountaineers, 1973.

Fire and Ice: The Cascades Volcanoes, Stephen Harris, The Mountaineers, 1980.

Forest Wildflowers, Dr. Dee Strickler, The Flower Press, 1988.

For the Greatest Good: Early History of Gifford Pinchot National Forest, Rick McClure and Cheryl Mack, Northwest Interpretive Association, 1999.

The Fresh-Water Fishes of British Columbia, G. C. Carl, W. A. Clemens, and C. C. Lindsey, British Columbia Department of Recreation and Conservation, 1967.

Islands and Rapids: The Geologic Story of Hells Canyon, Tracy Vallier, Confluence Press, 1998.

The Legend of Harry Truman, C. F. Boone Publishers, 1981.

Mount St. Helens: The Eruption and Recovery of a Volcano, Rob Carson, Sasquatch Books, 2000.

Mount St. Helens: The Story Behind the Scenery, Thom Corcoran, KC Publications, 1985.

Plants of the Pacific Northwest Coast, Jim Pajar and Andy MacKinnon, Lone Pine Publishing, 1994.

Plants of Yellowstone and Grand Teton National Parks, Richard J. Shaw, Wheelwright Press, 1981.

Prairie Wildflowers, Dr. Dee Strickler, The Flower Press, 1986.

Roadside Geology of Mount St. Helens National Volcanic Monument and Vicinity, Patrick T. Pringle, Washington Department of Natural Resources, 1993.

Volcano: The Eruption and Healing of Mount St. Helens, Patricia Lauber, Bradbury Press, 1986.

Western Forest Trees, James Berthold Berry, Dover Publications, 1966.

Western Trees, Maggi Stucky and George Palmer, Falcon Publishing, 1998.

Wild Animals of North America, National Geographic Society, 1979.

About the Author

While growing up in Oregon's Willamette Valley, Fred Barstad developed a keen interest in the Cascade Mountains at an early age. He hiked and fished extensively with his parents in the range, mostly between Mount Hood and Mount Jefferson in Oregon. The high volcanic peaks of the Cascades quickly became of special interest to him.

This interest had become an addiction for the high and remote country by the time he was a teenager in the 1960s. Fred has climbed most of the Cascade volcanoes in Washington and Oregon, including sixty-four climbs of Mount Hood and several of both Mount Rainier and Mount Adams using various routes. He climbed Mount St. Helens eleven times before the 1980 eruption and a couple of times since. Further from home, Fred has ascended Mount McKinley (Denali) in Alaska, Aconcagua in Argentina, and Popocatepetl, Citlaltepetl (Pico de Orizaba), and Iztaccihaatl in Mexico.

Now living in Enterprise, Oregon, at the base of the Wallowa Mountains, Fred devotes as much of his time as possible to hiking, climbing, and snowshoeing when he isn't working on a book.